Revolution and Romanticism, 1789-1834

A series of facsimile reprints chosen and introduced by
Jonathan Wordsworth

Volney
The Ruins 1811

Constantin François Volney

The Ruins: or
A Survey of the
Revolutions of Empires
1811

translated by James Marshall

Woodstock Books
Otley · Washington D.C.
2000

This edition first published 2000 by
Woodstock Books
Otley, West Yorkshire
England LS21 3JP
and
Books International
PO Box 605, Herndon
VA 20172, U.S.A.

ISBN 1 85477 246 5
Introduction copyright © 2000 Jonathan Wordsworth

British Library Cataloguing-in-Publication Data
A catalogue record for this book is
available from the British Library

Library of Congress Cataloging-in-Publication Data
applied for

Printed and bound in England by
Smith Settle
Otley LS21 3JP

Introduction

'The book from which Felix instructed Safie', we are
told by Victor Frankenstein's nameless Creature, 'was
Volney's *Ruins of Empire*'. 'It gave me', he continues,

an insight into the manners, governments and religions of the
different nations of the earth. I heard of the slothful Asiatics;
of the stupendous genius and mental activity of the Grecians;
of the wars and wonderful virtue of the early Romans – of
their subsequent degenerating – of the decline of that mighty
empire; of chivalry, Christianity and kings. I heard of the
discovery of the American hemisphere, and wept with Safie
over the hapless fate of its original inhabitants.

Presently the Creature will discover in the woods, near
the hovel from which he so assiduously watches Felix
and his family, 'a leathern portmanteau' containing
Paradise Lost, a volume (unspecified) of Plutarch's *Lives*,
and *The Sorrows of Werter* – each peculiarly calculated to
advance his education. But *The Ruins* comes first. It is
the book selected by Felix to instruct the 'beautiful
arabian', Safie (who so surprisingly turns up at their
cottage-door in remotest Switzerland), and it is the
book chosen by Mary Godwin to instruct the listening
Creature, who knows still less than Safie, but learns, we
are told, more rapidly. What part, one wonders had *The
Ruins* played in the eighteen year-old Mary's own
education by her future husband? What part had it
played in the education of Shelley himself?
Significantly Volney's translator was James Marshall,
lifelong friend of William Godwin.

Published in Paris in 1791, and in London a year
later, Volney's book was a best-seller throughout the
revolutionary period. In 1792 it was augmented by the
question-and-answer treatise *The Law of Nature*, then
subtitled *A Catechism of the French Citizen*. Volney

himself was a nobleman, a philosopher, a traveller, and a member of the Third Estate in the National Assembly. A scheme to grow crops from the New World in Corsica led to his buying land close to Napoleon's birthplace, Ajaccio, and to friendship with the future Emperor that lasted until Volney's radical thinking came to seem unwelcome. In Paris, where he studied history and languages, Volney knew Holbach, and was introduced by him to Franklin. Deciding to travel in the Near East, he prepared himself by a year's physical training that seems to us less surprising than it would have done to his contemporaries: sleeping rough, climbing walls, running, starving for days on end, leaping onto bare-back horses. He then spent eight months in a Coptic monastery learning arabic. Returned after almost four years away, he published *Travels in Egypt and Syria*, 1787, concerned more with accuracy than atmosphere, and famous for being used as a guide-book by Napoleon's troops in Egypt.

Meanwhile, *The Ruins* had been planned. At once the difference in tone and purpose is there for all to see:

SOLITARY Ruins, sacred Tombs, ye mouldering and silent Walls, all hail! To you I address my INVOCATION ... Pregnant, I may truly call you, with useful lessons, with pathetic and irresistible advice, to the man who knows how to consult you ... Mixing the dust of the proudest kings with that of the meanest slaves, you call upon us to contemplate this example of EQUALITY. From your caverns, whither the musing and anxious love of LIBERTY led me, I saw escape its venerable shade, and with unexpected felicity direct its flight, and marshal my steps the way to renovated France. (p.vii)

Effectively Ruins in this context are death – Death the Leveller:

It is you that bring home the rod of justice to the powerful oppressor; it is you that wrest the ill-gotten gold from the merciless extortioner, and avenge the cause of him that has none to help; you compensate the narrow enjoyments of the poor, by dashing [mingling] with care the goblet of the rich; to the unfortunate you offer a last and inviolate asylum.

'In fine', Volney concludes, taking us by surprise with the grandeur of his claim, 'you give to the soul that just equilibrium of strength and tenderness, which constitutes the wisdom of the sage and the science of life' (p.viii).

'A King', as we know from Hamlet, 'may go a progress through the guts of a beggar' – 'Imperial Caesar, dead and turned to clay, / Might stop a hole to keep the wind away' (Jonson). But Volney goes beyond the *memento mori*, beyond the traditional *ubi sunt* ('Where are those ramparts of Nineveh, those walls of Babylon, those palaces of Persepolis?' p.5), attributing to the ruins of past civilizations the gift of sanity, mental and emotional equilibrium:

We ascend the eminence you afford us, and, viewing with one glance the limits of nations and the succession of ages, are incapable of any affections [emotions] but such as are sublime, and entertain no ideas but those of virtue and glory. (p.viii)

Usefulness to our fellow-men will decide whether this 'virtue and glory' have indeed been achieved: 'Alas! when this uncertain dream of life shall be over, what then will avail all our busy passions, unless they have left behind them the footsteps of utility' (*ibid*)? The metaphor is incongruous. Volney as traveller through deserts, on foot and by camel, has left a million sandy footsteps. 'I looked for those ancient people and their works', he writes in one version of the image, 'and all I could find was a faint trace, like to what the foot of passenger leaves on the sand' (p.5). The last thing surely that an impression in the sands of time can offer is utility. Yet Volney, for all the gloomy reflections that ruins of empire bring out in him, is a political optimist. Led by a personal and present love of Liberty to visit the caverns of the past, he finds a spirit of Equality that conducts him back to France and contemporary revolutions.

Volney in the Near East was writing two books at once, keeping them separate because each had its separate validity. *Travels in Egypt and Syria* took precedence, and was published soon after his return to France in 1787. But the great philosophical work that should serve present achievement of liberty and equality by tracing utility in the footsteps of the past, was also planned, experienced, among the ruins. How much was written in Paris after publication of the *Travels* is unclear; 'the performance', we are told, 'was in some forwardness when the events of 1788 in France interrupted it' (p.v). Volney predicted change, and when it came was ready at once to play a part in it. *The Ruins* was finished in 1791 when the transfer of power seemed to have been completed, and a book placing recent changes in a longer view could be seen to have utility. Only the context of the past could show the Revolution to be new, different, potentially lasting:

who, said I to myself, can assure me that [the desolation of Egypt and Syria] will not one day be the lot of our own country? Who knows but that hereafter some traveller like myself will sit down upon the banks of the Seine, the Thames, the Zuyder See ... who knows but he will sit down solitary, amid silent ruins, and weep a people inurned, and their greatness changed into an empty name? (pp.7-8)

The question had to be answered.

Above all the thought that nags Volney is unfairness – the sense, not so much of 'man's inhumanity to man', as of man's irrelevance to God:

When these countries enjoyed what constitutes the glory and felicity of mankind, they were an *unbelieving* people who inhabited them. It was the Phoenician, offering human sacrifices to Moloch, who brought together within his walls riches of every climate; it was the Chaldean, prostrating himself before a serpent, who subjugated opulent cities ... it was the Persian, the worshipper of fire, who collected the tribute of a hundred nations ... Now that a *believing* and a *holy* people occupy the countries, nothing is to be seen but solitude and sterility. (p.6)

Amid the ruins of once powerful Palmyra – temple after temple, street after street, house after house, mouldering, silent, inhabited by a few poor arabian peasants – Volney gives himself up to despair: 'Unhappy man, a blind fatality plays with thy destiny! A fatal necessity rules by chance the lot of mortals ... A mysterious God has ... doubtless pronounced a secret malediction against the earth!'

These will be the thoughts that *The Ruins* examines. Despair it is that provokes the arrival of Volney's Dantesque guide, the 'pale apparition enveloped in an immense drapery' who will sternly conduct him in his tour of the stars, of history and comparative religion:

if these places are desolate, if powerful cities are reduced to solitude, is it [God] that has occasioned the ruin? ... Is it God who has introduced the sword into the city, and set fire to the country, murdered the people? ... Is it his pride that creates murderous wars? ... The caprice of which man complains, is not the caprice of destiny; the darkness that misleads his reason, is not the darkness of God; the source of his calamities is not in the distant heavens, but near to him upon earth – it is not concealed in the bosom of the Divinity, it resides in himself: man bears it in his heart. (pp.10-11)

Volney's God is the deist God with whom we are familiar through the Shelley of *Queen Mab* – the impersonal God of 'causes and effects, of principles and consequences, which, under an appearance of chance, govern the universe' (p.20). It could easily be Shelley speaking when Volney, looking down upon Earth with his attendant Apparition, puts the universe of his own experience into perspective:

Sovereign and mysterious Power of the Universe! secret Mover of Nature! Universal Soul of every thing that lives! infinite and incomprehensible Being, whom, under so many forms, mortals have ignorantly worshipped! God who in the immensity of the heavens dost guide revolving worlds, and people the abyss of space with millions of suns; say, what appearance do those human insects, which I can with difficulty distinguish upon earth, make in thy eyes? When thou directest the stars in their orbits, what to thee are the worms that crawl in the dust? Of what importance to thy infinite greatness are their distinctions of sects and parties? And how art thou concerned with the subtleties engendered by their folly? (p.49)

There can be no single definition of late eighteenth-century deism. It is a way of thinking that lies between the atheism of Voltaire and Holbach and the platonism/pantheism of Schelling, Coleridge, and so many others in this period. In Volney, as in the Shelley of *Mont Blanc* and *Adonais*, deism is (at some level) accompanied by a wish to believe, and merges into platonism. Implied in Volney's reference to the 'Universal Soul of every thing that lives' is a universe animated by the Coleridgean 'one life within us and abroad'. Volney, though, does not merely offer us insights into his own thinking, he summons in the second half of *The Ruins* the first (and largest) world congress on religion, with delegates of every faith and persuasion volubly putting forth their claims to be supporters of the one true God. Entire populations are in attendance. Delegates of France (referred to quaintly as 'this free and powerful nation', 'this free nation', 'this free people', never by name) make their plea for unity, carrying the people with them, but not the priesthood – 'You are in error', say the priests, pointing to each other, 'we alone are in possession of reason and truth' (p.86).

Volney's satire has a Swiftian elegance, as Christians, Jews, Muslims, convict themselves in turn: 'We are not ignorant', replied the Rabbin, 'that such are your pretensions, but they are perfectly supposititious and false … You have imagined a spiritual Messiah, where our prophets speak only of a political king' (p.108). Fascination with world religions allows him to personate an extraordinary number of different faiths, tying them into each other with claims, and counter claims, to have possessed an original truth. Implied on every page are the impossibility that all claims should be true, the certainty that man in his wishfulness and terror would create himself the God of human need, the usefulness to priests and rulers of his doing so. Implied too, from many different points of view, is the impossibility of accepting the Christian faith of modern Europe. A doctor of divinity rises to his feet, the Old Testament in one hand, the New in the other, and tells the assembled delegates that:

God (after having passed an eternity without doing anything) conceived at length the design (without apparent motive) of forming the world out of nothing; that having in six days created the whole universe, he found himself tired on the seventh; that having placed the first pair of human beings in a delightful garden to make them completely happy, he nevertheless forbade them to taste of the fruit of one tree which he planted within their reach; that, these first parents having yielded to temptation, all their race (as yet unborn) were condemned to suffer the penalty of a fault which they had no share in committing; that after permitting the human species to damn themselves for four or five thousand years, this God of compassion ordered his well-beloved son, engendered without a mother, and of the same age as himself, to descend upon the earth in order to be put to death ... for the salvation of mankind, the majority of whom have nevertheless continued in the road to sin and damnation; that to remedy this inconvenience, this God, the son of a woman who was at once a mother and a virgin, after having died and risen again, commences a new existence every day, and under the form of a morsel of dough is multiplied a thousand-fold at the pleasure of the basest of mankind.   (pp.105-6)

The would-be atheist Shelley of *Queen Mab* comes inevitably to mind:

A book is put into our hands when children, the purport of whose history is briefly this: that God made the earth in six days, and there planted a delightful garden, in which he placed the first pair of human beings; [that] in the midst of the garden he planted a tree, whose fruit, although within their reach, they were forbidden to touch; that the Devil, in the shape of a snake, persuaded them to eat of this fruit, in consequence of which God condemned both them and their posterity, yet unborn, to satisfy his justice by their eternal misery; that four thousand years after these events (the human race in the mean while having gone unredeemed to perdition), God engendered with the betrothed wife of a carpenter in Judea (whose virginity was nevertheless uninjured), and begat a son, whose name was Jesus Christ, and who was crucified and died in order that no more men might be devoted to hell-fire, he bearing the burthen of his father's displeasure by proxy.   (*Queen Mab*, 1813, pp. 190-1)

In attitude, tone, use of narrative and satirical aside, the two passages are remarkably alike. At times they seem even to have verbal connections. Yet where Shelley quotes ten pages of Holbach in the notes to *Queen Mab*, he nowhere mentions Volney, and may not have read him in 1813. They were like-spirits, each attracted to Holbach, and each basing his thinking on the cause-and-effect necessitarianism defined by Volney in *The Law of Nature*:

Q. *What is the Law of Nature?*

A. It is the regular and constant order of events, according to which God rules the Universe; the order which his wisdom presents to the senses and reason of mankind, to serve them as an equal and general rule of action, and to conduct them, without distinction of country or sect, towards happiness and perfection. (p.3)

Happiness, (somewhat inconsistently) is 'an accidental circumstance', a 'luxury superadded to the necessary and fundamental object of self-preservation':

Q. *In what manner does nature command self-preservation?*

A. By two powerful and involuntary sensations which she has attached as two guides or guardian genii to all our actions: one: the sensation of pain, by which she informs us of, and turns us from, what ever tends to our destruction. The other, the sensation of pleasure, by which she attracts and leads us towards everything that tends to our preservation, and the unfolding of our faculties:

Q. *Is pleasure the principal object of our existence, as some philosophers have asserted?*

A. No, no more than pain is: by pleasure, nature encourages us to live; by pain, it makes us shrink from death. (pp.11-12)

In all this we are to bear in mind that this is a Catechism for the French Citizen in Year Three of the Revolution. Clearly the question to be asked is '*How does the law of nature ordain justice?*' Volney's answer is for a moment surprising:

A. By means of three physical attributes which are inherent in the organization of man.

Q. *What are these attributes?*

A. Equality, liberty, property. (p.38)

We expect liberty, equality, fraternity, and get property, of all things, in lieu of fraternity. Added to which we are unlikely to think of any of the three qualities listed in terms of physicality. For Volney, equality is physical because, 'having equally eyes, hands, mouth, ears, and being alike under the necessity of making use of them for life's sake, [men] are by this very fact entitled to life'. Volney is aware that some people have better sight than others, but insists that, though we perceive equality to be relative, the physical nature of man shows all to be 'equal before God' (*ibid*). Liberty follows from the fact that all are possessed of 'senses fitted and sufficient for their preservation', made 'naturally independent and free'. Which leaves still the more difficult question:

Q. *How is property a physical attribute of man?*

A. Since every man is formed equal and similar to his fellows, and consequently free and independent, everyone is the absolute master, the entire proprietor of his body, and the products of his labour.

How then is justice to be derived from these three attributes? Answer, 'men, being equal, free, and owing nothing to each other, have no right to demand anything of their fellows, but in proportion as they return for it something equivalent' (p.39).

It is a pity not to have more detailed comments on Volney from Frankenstein's Creature. 'Once I falsely hoped', he tells Walton in the final moments of the novel,

to meet with beings who, pardoning my outward form, would love me for the excellent qualities which I was capable of unfolding. I was nourished with high thoughts of honour and devotion. But now vice has degraded me beneath the meanest animal. No crime, no mischief, no malignity, no misery, can be found comparable to mine. (*Frankenstein*, 1823, ii, p. 274)

If *The Ruins* inspired those 'thoughts of honour and devotion', it ought to have warned the unfortunate Creature too that upon earth there could be no pardon for his outward form, symbolic as it is of his unnatural (correctly 'monstrous') making. Felix, however rational, was bound to attack, Safie was bound to flee. Justice does not exist for one beyond the law of nature, not 'formed equal and similar to his fellows'.

J.W.

RUINS OF EMPIRES.

Thornton d.   Rhodes sculp.

Published Jan.ry 1.1819. by Thomas Tegg, N.o 111. Cheapside.

The

RUINS,

or

A Survey of the Revolutions

OF

EMPIRES,

by M. Volney.

The Fifth Edition.

London

Printed for THOMAS TEGG.
No. III,
Cheapside.
1811.

PREFACE.

———

THE plan of this publication was formed nearly ten years ago; and allusions to it may be seen in the Preface to Travels in Syria and Egypt, as well as at the end of that work, published in 1787. The performance was in some forwardness when the events of 1788 in France interrupted it. Persuaded that a developement of the theory of political truth could not sufficiently acquit a citizen of his debt to society, the author wished to add practice; and that particularly at a time when a single arm was of consequence in the defence of the general cause. The same desire of public benefit which induced him to suspend his work, has since engaged him to resume it; and though it may not possess the same merit as if it had appeared under the circumstances that gave rise to it,

b

yet he imagines that at a time when new passions are
bursting forth, passions that must communicate their
activity to the religious opinions of men, it is of importance to disseminate such moral truths as are calculated to operate as a sort of curb and restraint.
It is with this view he has endeavoured to give to
these truths, hitherto treated as abstract, a form likely to gain them a reception. It was found impossible
not to shock the violent prejudices of some readers;
but the work, so far from being the fruit of a disor-
derly and perturbed spirit, has been dictated by a
sincere love of order and humanity.

After reading this performance it will be asked,
how it was possible, in 1784, to have had an idea of
what did not take place till the year 1790? The solution is simple; in the original plan, the legislator
was a fictitious and hypothetical being: in the present, the author has substituted an existing legislator; and the reality has only made the subject ad-
ditionally interesting.

INVOCATION.

SOLITARY Ruins, sacred Tombs, ye mouldering and silent Walls, all hail! To you I address my INVOCATION. While the vulgar shrink from your aspect with secret terror, my heart finds in the contemplation a thousand delicious sentiments, a thousand admirable recollections. Pregnant, I may truly call you, with useful lessons, with pathetic and irresistible advice, to the man who knows how to consult you. A while ago the whole world bowed the neck in silence before the tyrants that oppressed it; and yet in that hopeless moment you already proclaimed the truths that tyrants hold in abhorence: mixing the dust of the proudest kings with that of the meanest slaves, you called upon us to contemplate this example of EQUALITY. From your caverns, whether the musing and anxious love of LIBERTY led me, I saw escape its venerable shade, and with unexpected felicity direct its flight, and marshal my steps the way to renovated France.

Tombs, what virtues and potency do you exhibit! Tyrants tremble at your aspect, you poison with secret alarm their impious pleasures; they turn from you with impatience, and, coward like, endeavour to

b 2

forget you amid the sumptuousness of their palaces.
It is you that bring home the rod of justice to the
powerful oppressor; it is you that wrest the ill-gotten gold from the merciless extortioner, and avenge
the cause of him that has none to help; you compensate the narrow enjoyments of the poor, by dashing with care the goblet of the rich; to the unfortunate you offer a last and inviolable asylum; in fine,
you give to the soul that just equilibrium of strength
and tenderness, which constitutes the wisdom of the
sage and the science of life.   The wise man looks towards you, and scorns to amass vain grandeur and
useless riches with which he must soon part: you
check his lawless flights without disarming his ad-
venture and his courage; he feels the necessity of
passing through the period assigned him, and he
gives employment to his hours, and makes use of the
goods that fortune has assigned him.   Thus do you
rein in the wild sallies of cupidity, calm the fever of
tumultuous enjoyment, free the mind from the anarchy of the passions, and raise it above those little interests which torment the mass of mankind.   We ascend the eminence you afford us, and, viewing with
one glance the limits of nations and the succession of
ages, are incapable of any affections but such as are
sublime, and entertain no ideas but those of virtue
and glory.   Alas! when this uncertain dream of life
shall be over, what then will avail all our busy passions, unless they have left behind them the footsteps
of utility!

   Ye Ruins, I will return once more to attend your
lessons! I will resume my place in the midst of your
wide spreading solitude.   I will leave the tragic
scene of the passions, will love my species rather
from recollection than actual survey, will employ my
activity in promoting their happiness, and compose
my own happiness of the pleasing remembrance that
I have hastened theirs.

CONTENTS.

CHAP. XXII.

THE

RUINS;

OR,

A SURVEY

OF THE

REVOLUTIONS OF EMPIRES.

———————

CHAP. I.

THE TOUR.

IN the eleventh year of the reign of Abd-ul Hamid, son of Ahmed, emperor of the Turks; when the No- gaian Tartars were driven from the Crimea, and a Mussulman prince, of the blood of Gengis Khan, be- came the vassal and *guard* of a woman, a Christian, and a queen*, I journeyed in the empire of the Otto- mans, and traversed the provinces which formerly were kingdoms of Egypt and of Syria.

* That is to say, in the year 1784. The reader is requested not to lose sight of this epocha. See the notes at the end of the volume.

B

Directing all my attention to what concerns the happiness of mankind in a state of society, I entered cities, and studied the manners of their inhabitants; I gained admission into palaces, and observed the conduct of those who govern; I wandered over the country, and examined the condition of the peasants: and no where perceiving aught but robbery and devastation, tyranny and wretchedness, my heart was oppressed with sorrow and indignation.

Every day I found in my route fields abandoned by the plough, villages deserted, and cities in ruins.— Frequently I met with antique monuments; wrecks of temples, palaces, and fortifications; pillars, aqueducts, sepulchres. By these objects, my thoughts were directed to past ages, and my mind absorbed in serious and profound meditation.

Arrived at Hamsa, on the borders of the Orontes, and being at no great distance from the city of Palmyra, situated in the desert, I resolved to examine for myself its boasted monuments. After three days' travel in barren solitude, and having passed through a valley filled with grottoes and tombs, my eyes were suddenly struck, on leaving this valley and entering a plain, with a most astonishing scene of ruins. It consisted of a countless multitude of superb columns standing erect; and which, like the avenues of our parks, extended in regular files farther than the eye could reach. Among these columns magnificent edifices were observable; some entire, others in a state half demolished. The ground was covered on all sides with fragments of similar buildings, cornices, capitals, shafts, entablatures, and pilasters, all constructed of a marble of admirable whiteness and exquisite workmanship. After a walk of three quarters of an hour along these ruins, I entered the inclosure of a vast edifice which had formerly been a temple dedicated to the sun; and I accepted the hospitality of some poor Arabian peasants, who had established their huts in the very area of the temple. Here I resolved for some days to remain, that I might contemplate, at leisure, the beauty of so many stupendous works.

Every day I visited some of the monuments which covered the plain; and one evening that, my mind lost in reflection, I had advanced as far as the *Valley of Sepulchres*, I ascended the heights that bound it, and from which the eye commands at once the whole of the ruins and the immensity of the desert. The sun had just sunk below the horizon; a streak of red still marked the place of his descent, behind the distant mountains of Syria; the full moon, appearing with brightness upon a ground of deep blue, rose in the east from the smooth bank of the Euphrates; the sky was unclouded; the air calm and serene; the expiring light of day served to soften the horror of approaching darkness; the refreshing breeze of the night gratefully relieved the intolerable sultriness of the day that had preceded it; the shepherds had led the camels to their stalls; the grey firmament bounded the silent landscape; through the whole desert every thing was marked with stillness, undisturbed but by the mournful cries of the bird of night, and of some *chacals**. The dusk increased, and already I could distinguish nothing more than the pale phantoms of walls and columns. The solitariness of the situation, the serenity of evening, and the grandeur of the scene, impressed my mind with religious thoughtfulness. The view of an illustrious city deserted, the remembrance of past times, their comparison with the present state of things, all combined to raise my heart to a strain of sublime meditations. I sat down on the base of a column; and there, my elbow on my knee,

* An animal considerably like the fox, but less cunning, and of a frightful aspect. It lives upon dead bodies; and rocks and ruins are the places of its habitation.

and my head resting on my hand, sometimes turning
my eyes towards the desert, and sometimes fixing
them on the ruins, I fell into a profound reverie.

===

CHAP. II.

MEDITATIONS.

HERE, said I to myself, an opulent city once flourished; this was the seat of a powerful empire. Yes,
these places, now so desert, a living multitude formerly animated, and an active crowd circulated in the
streets which at present are so solitary. Within those
walls, where a mournful silence reigns, the noise of
the arts, and the shouts of joy and festivity, continually resounded. These heaps of marble formed regular palaces, these prostrate pillars were the majestic
ornaments of temples, these ruinous galleries present
the outlines of public places. There a numerous
people assembled for the respectable duties of its
worship, or the anxious care of its subsistence; there
industry, the fruitful inventor of sources of enjoyment,
collected together the riches of every climate, and the
purple of Tyre was exchanged for the precious thread
of Serica; the soft tissues of cassimere for the sump-
tuous carpets of Lydia; the amber of the Baltic for
the pearls and perfumes of Arabia; the gold of Ophir
for the pewter of Thule (n).—

And now a mournful skeleton is all that subsists of
this opulent city, and nothing remains of its powerful
government but a vain and obscure remembrance! To
the tumultuous throng which crowded under these
porticos, the solitude of death has succeeded. The
silence of the tomb is substituted for the hum of pub-

lic places. The opulence of a commercial city is changed into hideous poverty. The palaces of kings are become the receptacle of deer, and unclean reptiles inhabit the sanctuary of the gods.—What glory is here eclipsed, and how many labours are annihilated!—Thus perish the works of men, and thus do nations and empires vanish away.

The history of past times strongly presented itself to my thoughts. I called to mind those distant ages when twenty celebrated nations inhabited the country around me. I pictured to myself the Assyrian on the banks of the Tygris, the Chaldæan on those of the Euphrates, the Persian, whose power extended from the Indus to the Mediterranean. I enumerated the kingdoms of Damascus and Idumea; of Jerusalem and Samaria; and the warlike states of the Philistines; and the commercial republics of Phenicia— This Syria, said I to myself, now almost depopulated, then contained a hundred flourishing cities, and abounded with towns, villages, and hamlets (b).— Every where one might have seen cultivated fields, frequented roads, and crowded habitations. Ah! what are become of those ages of abundance and of life? What are become of so many productions of the hand of man? Where are those ramparts of Nineveh, those walls of Babylon, those palaces of Persepolis, those temples of Balbec and of Jerusalem? Where are those fleets of Tyre, those dock-yards of Arad, those work-shops of Sidon, and that multitude of mariners, pilots, merchants, and soldiers? Where those husbandmen, those harvests, that picture of animated nature of which the earth seemed proud? Alas! I have traversed this desolate country, I have visited the places that were the theatre of so much splendour, and I have nothing beheld but solitude and desertion! I looked for those ancient people and their works, and all I could find was a faint trace, like to what the foot of a passenger leaves on the sand.

The temples are thrown down, the palaces demolished, the ports filled up, the towns destroyed, and the earth, stript of inhabitants, seems a dreary burying-place.—Great God! from whence proceed such melancholy revolutions? For what cause is the fortune of these countries so strikingly changed? Why are so many cities destroyed? Why is not that ancient population reproduced and perpetuated?

Thus absorbed in contemplation, new ideas continually presented themselves to my thoughts. Every thing, continued I, misleads my judgment, and fills my heart with trouble and uncertainty. When these countries enjoyed what constitutes the glory and felicity of mankind, they were an *unbelieving* people who inhabited them. It was the Phenician, offering human sacrifices to Moloch, who brought together within his walls the riches of every climate; it was the Chaldean, prostrating himself before a serpent*, who subjugated opulent cities, and laid waste the palaces of kings and the temples of the Gods; it was the Persian, the worshipper of fire, who collected the tributes of a hundred nations; they were the inhabitants of this very city, adorers of the sun and stars, who erected so many monuments of affluence and luxury. Numerous flocks, fertile fields, abundant harvests, every thing that should have been the reward of *piety*, was in the hand of *idolaters*; and now that a *believing* and *holy* people occupy the countries, nothing is to be seen but solitude and sterility. The earth under these *blessed* hands produces only briars and wormwood. Man sows in anguish, and reaps vexation and cares; war, famine, and pestilence, assault him in turn. Yet, are not these the children of the prophets? This Christian, this Mussulman, this Jew, are they not the elect of Heaven, loaded with gifts and miracles? Why then is this race, beloved of the Di-

* The dragon Bel.

vinity, deprived of the favours which were formerly showered upon the Heathen? Why do these lands, consecrated by the blood of the martyrs, no longer boast their former temperature and fertility? Why have those favours been banished, as it were, and transferred for so many ages to other nations and different climes?

And here, pursuing the course of vicissitudes, which have, in turn, transmitted the sceptre of the world to people so various in manners and religion, from those of ancient Asia down to the more recent ones of Europe, my native country, designated by this name, was awakened in my mind, and turning my eyes towards it, all my thoughts fixed upon the situation in which I had left it*.

I recollected its fields, so richly cultivated; its roads, so admirably executed; its towns, inhabited by an immense multitude; its ships scattered over every ocean; its ports filled with the produce of either India; and comparing the activity of its commerce, the extent of its navigation, the magnificence of its buildings, the arts and industry of its inhabitants, with all that Egypt and Syria could formerly boast of a similar nature, I pleased myself with the idea that I had found in modern Europe the past splendour of Asia: but the charm of my reverie was presently dissolved by the last step of the comparison. Reflecting that if the places before me had once exhibited this animated picture: who, said I to myself, can assure me, that their present desolation will not one day be the lot of our own country? who knows but that hereafter, some traveller like myself will sit down upon the banks of the Seine, the Thames, or the Zuyder sea, where now, in the tumult of enjoyment, the heart and the eyes are too slow to take in the multitude of sensations; who knows but he will sit down solitary,

* In the year 1782, at the close of the American war.

amid silent ruins, and weep a people inurned, and their greatness changed into an empty name?

The idea brought tears into my eyes; and covering my head with the flap of my garment, I gave myself up to the most gloomy meditations on human affairs. Unhappy man! said I in my grief, a blind fatality plays with thy destiny (c)! a fatal necessity rules by chance the lot of mortals! But, no: they are the decrees of celestial justice that are accomplishing! A mysterious God exercises his incomprehensible judgments! He has doubtless pronounced a secret malediction against the earth; he has struck with a curse the present race of men, in revenge of past generations. Oh! who shall dare to fathom the depths of the Divinity?

And I remained immoveable, plunged in profound melancholy.

CHAP. III.

THE APPARITION.

IN the mean time a noise struck my ear like to the agitation of a flowing robe, and the slow steps of a foot, upon the dry and rustling grass. Alarmed, I drew my mantle from my head, and casting round me a timid glance, suddenly, by the obscure light of the moon, through the pillars and ruins of a temple, I thought I saw, at my left, a pale apparition, enveloped in an immense drapery, similar to what spectres are painted when issuing out of the tombs. I shuddered; and while, in this troubled state, I was hesitating whether to fly, or ascertain the reality of the vision, a hollow voice, in grave and solemn accents, thus addressed me:

How long will man importune the heavens with unjust complaint? how long, with vain clamours, will
he accuse Fate as the author of his calamities? Will
he then never open his eyes to the light, and his
heart to the insinuations of truth and reason? This
truth every where presents itself in radiant brightness,
and he does not see it! The voice of reason strikes
his ear, and he does not hear it! Unjust man! if
you can for a moment suspend the delusion which
fascinates your senses, if your heart be capable of
comprehending the language of argumentation, interrogate these ruins! read the lessons which they present to you!——And you, sacred temples! venerable
tombs! walls once glorious! the witnesses of twenty
different ages, appear in the cause of nature herself!
come to the tribunal of sound understanding, to bear
testimony against an unjust accusation, to confound
the declamation of false wisdom or hypocritical piety,
and avenge the heavens and the earth of man, who
calumniates them!

What is this blind fatality, that, without order or
laws, sports with the lot of mortals? What this unjust necessity, which confounds the issue of actions,
be they those of prudence or those of folly? In what
consists the maledictions of Heaven denounced against
these countries? where is the divine curse that perpetuates this scene of desolation? Monuments of
past ages! say, have the heavens changed their laws,
and the earth its course? Has the sun extinguished
his fires in the region of space? Do the seas no longer send forth clouds? Are the rain and the dew
fixed in the air? Do the mountains retain their
springs? Are the streams dried up? and do the
plants no more bear fruit and seed? Answer, race of
falsehood and iniquity! has God troubled the primitive and invariable order which he himself assigned
to nature? Has heaven denied to the earth, and the
earth to its inhabitants, the blessings that were for-

merly dispensed? If the creation has remained the same, if its sources and its instruments are exactly what they once were, wherefore should not the present race have every thing within their reach that their ancestors enjoyed? Falsely do you accuse Fate and the Divinity! injuriously do you refer to God the cause of your evils. Tell me, perverse and hypocritical race! if these places are desolate, if powerful cities are reduced to solitude, is it he that has occasioned the ruin? Is it his hand that has thrown down these walls, sapped these temples, mutilated these pillars? or is it the hand of man? Is it the arm of God that has introduced the sword into the city, and set fire to the country, murdered the people, burned the harvests, rooted up the trees, and ravaged the pastures? or is it the arm of man? And when, after this devastation, famine has started up, is it the vengeance of God that has sent it, or the mad fury of mortals? When, during the famine, the people are fed with unwholesome provision, and pestilence ensues, is it inflicted by the anger of heaven, or brought about by human imprudence? When war, famine, and pestilence united, have swept away the inhabitants, and the land is become a desert, is it God who has depopulated it? Is it his rapacity that plunders the labourer, ravages the productive fields, and lays waste the country; or the rapacity of those who govern? Is it his pride that creates murderous wars; or the pride of kings and their ministers? Is it the venality of his decisions that overthrows the fortune of families, or the venality of the organs of the laws? Are they his passions that, under a thousand forms, torment individuals and nations; or the passions of human beings? And if, in the anguish of their misfortunes, they perceive not the remedies, is it the ignorance of God that is in fault, or their own ignorance? Cease, then, to accuse the decrees of Fate or the judgments of Heaven? If God is good, will he be

the author of your punishment? If he is just, will
he be the accomplice of your crimes? No, no; the
caprice of which man complains, is not the caprice of
destiny; the darkness that misleads his reason, is not
the darkness of God; the source of his calamities,
is not in the distant heavens, but near to him upon
the earth; it is not concealed in the bosom of the
Divinity; it resides in himself, man bears it in his
heart.

You murmur, and say, Why have an unbelieving
people enjoyed the blessings of heaven and of the
earth? Why is a holy and chosen race less fortunate
than impious generations? Deluded man! where is
the contradiction at which you take offence?—Where
the inconsistency in which you suppose the justice
of God to be involved? Take the balance of blessings and calamities, of causes and effects, and tell
me—When those infidels observed the laws of the
earth and the heavens, when they regulated their intelligent labours by the order of the seasons and the
course of the stars, ought God to have troubled the
equilibrium of the world to defeat their prudence?
When they cultivated with care and toil the face of
the country around you, ought he to have turned
aside the rain, to have withheld the fertilizing dews,
and caused thorns to spring up? When, to render
this parched and barren soil productive, their industry constructed aqueducts, dug canals, and brought
the distant waters across the deserts, ought he to
have blighted the harvest which art had created;
to have desolated a country that had been peopled in
peace; to have demolished the towns which labour
had caused to flourish; in fine, to have deranged and
confounded the order established by the wisdom of
man? And what is this *infidelity* which founded empires by prudence, defended them by courage, and
strengthened them by justice; which raised magnificent cities, formed vast ports, drained pestilential

marshes, covered the sea with ships, the earth with
inhabitants, and, like the creative spirit, diffused life
and motion through the world. If such is impiety,
what is true belief? Does holiness consist in destruction? Is then the God that peoples the air with
birds, the earth with animals, and the waters with reptiles; the God that animates universal nature, a God
that delights in ruins and sepulchres? Does he ask
devastation for homage, and conflagration for sacrifice? Would he have groans for hymns, murderers to
worship him, and a desert and ravaged world for his
temple? Yet such, *holy* and *faithful* generation, are
your works! These are the fruits of your *piety!* You
have massacred the people, reduced cities to ashes,
destroyed all traces of cultivation, made the earth a
solitude; and you demand the reward of your labours! Miracles are not too much for your advantage! For you the peasants that you have murdered
should be revived; the walls you have thrown down
should rise again; the harvests you have ravished
should flourish; the conduits that you have broken
down should be renewed; the laws of heaven and
earth, those laws which God has established for the
display of his greatness and his magnificence, those
laws anterior to all revelations and to all prophets,
those laws which passion cannot alter, and ignorance
cannot pervert, should be superseded. Passion knows
them not; ignorance, which observes no cause and
predicts no effect, has said in the foolishness of her
heart, "Every thing comes from chance; a blind
fatality distributes good and evil upon the earth;
success is not to the prudent, nor felicity to the
wise." Or else, assuming the language of hypocrisy,
she has said, "Every thing comes from God; and
it is his sovereign pleasure to deceive the sage, and to
confound the judicious." And she has contemplated
the imaginary scene with complacency. "Good!"
she hath exclaimed. "I then am as well endowed as

the science that despises me! The cold prudence which evermore haunts and torments me, I will render useless by a lucky intervention of Providence." Cupidity has joined the chorus. " I too will oppress the weak ; I will wring from him the fruits of his labour ; for such is the decree of Heaven, such the omnipotent will of Fate."—For myself, I swear by all laws human and divine, by the laws of the human heart, that the hypocrite and the deceiver shall be themselves deceived ; the unjust man shall perish in his rapacity, and the tyrant in his usurpation : the sun shall change its course, before folly shall prevail over wisdom and science, before stupidity shall surpass prudence in the delicate art of procuring to man his true enjoyment, and of building his happiness upon a solid foundation.

CHAP. IV.

THE HEMISPHERE.

THUS spoke the Apparition. Astonished at his discourse, and my heart agitated by a diversity of reflections, I was for some time silent. At length, assuming the courage to speak, I thus addressed him: O Genius of tombs and ruins ! your sudden appearance and your severity have thrown my senses into disorder, but the justness of your reasoning restores confidence to my soul. Pardon my ignorance. Alas! if man is blind, can that which constitutes his torment be also his crime ? I was unable to distinguish the voice of reason ; but the moment it was known to me, I gave it welcome. Oh ! if you can read my heart, you know how desirous it is of truth, and with what

c

ardour it seeks it; you know that it is in this pursuit I am now found in these remote places. Alas! I have wandered over the earth, I have visited cities and countries; and perceiving every where misery and desolation, the sentiment of the evils by which my fellow-creatures are tormented has deeply afflicted my mind! I have said to myself with a sigh: Is man, then, created to be the victim of pain and anguish? And I have meditated upon human evils, that I might find out their remedy. I have said, I will separate myself from corrupt societies; I will remove far from palaces where the soul is depraved by satiety, and from cottages where it is humbled by misery. I will dwell in solitude amidst the ruins of cities: I will enquire of the monuments of antiquity what was the wisdom of former ages: in the very bosom of sepulchres I will invoke the spirit that formerly in Asia gave splendour to states and glory to their people: I will enquire of the ashes of legislators what causes have erected and overthrown empires; what are the principles of national prosperity and misfortune; what the maxims upon which the peace of society and the happiness of man ought to be founded.

I stopped; and casting down my eyes, I waited the reply of the Genius. Peace and happiness, said he, descend upon him who practises justice! Young man, since your heart searches after truth with sincerity; since you can distinguish her form through the mist of prejudices which blind the eyes, your enquiry shall not be vain: I will display to your view this truth of which you are in pursuit; I will shew to your reason the knowledge which you desire; I will reveal to you the wisdom of the tombs, and the science of ages—Then approaching me, and placing his hand upon my head, Rise, mortal, said he, and disengage yourself from that corporeal frame with which you are encumbered.—Instantly, penetrated as with a celestial flame, the ties that fix us to the earth seemed to be loosened; and lifted by the wing of the Genius, I felt myself like a light vapour conveyed in the uppermost region. There, from above the atmosphere, looking down towards the earth I had quitted, I beheld a scene entirely new. Under my feet, floating in empty space, a globe similar to that of the moon, but smalle., and less luminous, presented to me one of his faces*; and this face had the appearance of a disk variegated with spots, some of them white and nebulous, others brown, green, and grey; and while I exerted my powers in discerning and discriminating these spots—Disciple of truth, said the Genius to me, have you any recollection of this spectacle? O Genius, I replied, if I did not perceive the moon in a different part of the heavens, I should suppose the orb below me to be that planet; for its appearance resembles perfectly the moon viewed through a telescope at the time of an eclipse: one might be apt to think the variegated spots to be seas and continents.

Yes, said he to me, they are the seas and continents of the very hemisphere you inhabit.

What, exclaimed I, is that the earth that is inhabited by human beings?

It is, replied he. That brown space which occupies irregularly a considerable portion of the disk, and nearly surrounds it on all sides, is what you call the main ocean, which, from the south pole advancing towards the equator, first forms the great gulf of Africa and India, then stretches to the east across the Malay Islands, as far as the confines of Tartary, while at the west it incloses the continents of Africa and of Europe, reaching to the north of Asia.

Under our feet, that peninsula of a square figure is the desert country of Arabia, and on the left you per-

* See Plate 1. representing half the terrestrial globe.

ceive that great continent, scarcely less barren in its
interior parts, and only verdant as it approaches the
sea, the inhabitants of which are distinguished by a
sable complexion*. To the north, and on the other
side of an irregular and narrow sea†, are the tracts of
Europe, rich in fertile meadows and in all the luxu-
riance of cultivation. To the right from the Cas-
pian, extend the rugged surface and snow-topt hills
of Tartary. In bringing back the eye again to the
spot over which we are elevated, you see a large white
space, the melancholy and uniform desert of Cobi,
cutting off the empire of China from the rest of the
world. China itself is that furrowed surface which
seems by a sudden obliquity to escape from the view.
Farther on, those vast tongues of land and scattered
points, are the peninsula, and islands of the Malayans, the unfortunate proprietors of aromatics and perfumes. Still nearer you observe a triangle which projects strongly into the sea, and is the too famous peninsula of India *(d)*. You see the crooked windings
of the Ganges, the ambitious mountains of Thibet,
the fortunate valley of Cassimere (12), the discourag-
ing deserts of Persia, the banks of the Euphrates and
the Tigris, the rough bed of the Jordan (4), and the
mouths of the solitary Nile. (See the Plate.)

O Genius, said I, interrupting him, the organ of a
mortal would in vain attempt to distinguish objects
at so great a distance. Immediately he touched my
eyes, and they became more piercing than those of
the eagle; notwithstanding which, rivers appeared to
me no more than meandering ribands, ridges of
mountains, irregular furrows, and great cities a nest
of boxes varied among themselves like the squares in
a chess-board.

The Genius proceeded to point out the different
objects to me with his finger, and to develope them

---

* Africa.   † The Mediterranean.

as he proceeded. These heaps of ruins, said he, that you observe in this narrow valley, laved by the Nile, are all that remain of the opulent cities that gave lustre to the ancient kingdom of Ethiopia (e). Here is the monument of its splendid metropolis, Thebes, with its hundred palaces (f), the progenitor of cities, the memento of human frailty. It was there that a people since forgotten, discovered the elements of science and art, at a time when all other men were barbarous, and that a race, now regarded as the refuse of society, because their hair is woolly, and their skin is dark, explored among the phenomena of nature, those civil and religious systems which have since held mankind in awe. A little lower the dark spots that you observe are the pyramids (1) whose masses have overwhelmed your imagination. Farther on, the coast (3) that you behold limited by the sea on one side, and by a ridge of mountains on the other, was the abode of the Phenician nations; there stood the powerful cities of Tyre, Sidon, Ascalon, Gaza, and Berytus. This stream of water, which seems to disembogue itself into no sea (4), is the Jordan; and these barren rocks were formerly the scene of events whose tale may not be forgotten. Here you find the desert of Horeb, and the hill of Sinai (5), where, by artifice which the vulgar were unable to penetrate, a subtle and daring leader gave birth to institutions of memorable influence upon the history of mankind. Upon the barren strip of land which borders upon this desert, you see no longer any trace of splendour; and yet here was formerly the magazine of the world. Here were the ports of the Indumeans (g), from whence the fleets of the Phenicians and the Jews, coasting the peninsula of Arabia, bent their voyages to the Persian gulf, and imported from thence the pearls of Havila, the gold of Saba and Ophir. It was here, on the side of Oman and Bahrain, that existed that site of magnificent and luxurious commerce, which, as it was transplanted from country to country, decided upon the fate of ancient nations. Hither were brought the vegetable aromatics, and the precious stones of Ceylon, the shawls of Cassimere the diamonds of Golconda, the amber of the Maldives, the musk of Thibet, the aloes of Cochin, the apes and the peacocks of the continent of India, the incense of Hadramut, the myrrh, the silver, the gold dust, and the ivory of Africa. From hence were exported, sometimes by the Black Sea, in ships of Egypt and Syria, those commodities, which constituted the opulence of Thebes, Sidon, Memphis and Jerusalem ; sometimes ascending the course of the Tygris and the Euphrates, they awakened the activity of the Assyrians, the Medes, the Chaldeans, and the Persians, and according as they were used or abused, cherished or overturned their wealth and prosperity. Hence grew up the magnificence of Persepolis, of which you may observe the mouldering columns (8); of Ecbatana (9), whose sevenfold walls are levelled with the earth; of Babylon (10), the ruins of which are trodden under foot of men *(h)*, of Nineveh (11), whose name seems to be threatened with the same oblivion that has overtaken its greatness; of Thapsacus, of Anatho, of Gerra, and of the melancholy and memorable Palmyra. O names, for ever glorious ! celebrated fields ! famous countries ! how replete is your aspect with sublime instruction ! How many profound truths are written on the surface of this earth ! Ye places that here witnessed the life of man, in so many different ages, aid my recollection while I endeavour to trace the revolutions of his fortune ! Say, what were the motives of his conduct, and what his powers ! Unveil the causes of his misfortunes, teach him true wisdom, and let the experience of past ages become a mirror of instruction, and a germ of happiness to present and future generations !

CHAP. V.

CONDITION OF MAN IN THE UNIVERSE.

AFTER a short silence, the Genius thus resumed his instructions :

I have already observed to you, O friend of truth, that man vainly attributes his misfortunes to obscure and imaginary agents, and seeks out remote and mysterious causes, from which to deduce his evils. In the general order of the universe, his condition is doubtless subjected to inconveniences, and his existence over-ruled by superior powers ; but these powers are neither the decrees of a blind destiny, nor the caprices of fantastic beings. Man is governed, like the world of which he forms a part, by natural laws, regular in their operation, consequent in their effects, immutable in their essence ; and these laws, the common source of good and evil, are neither written in the distant stars, nor concealed in mysterious codes : inherent in the nature of all terrestrial beings, identified with their existence, they are at all times and in all places present to the human mind ; they act upon the senses, inform the intellect, and annex to every action its punishment and its reward. Let man study these laws, let him understand his own nature, and the nature of the beings that surround him, and he will know the springs of his destiny, the causes of his evils, and the remedies to be applied.

When the secret power that animates the universe, formed the globe of the earth, he stamped on the beings which compose it essential properties, that became the rule of their individual action, the tie of their reciprocal connections, and the cause of the harmony of the whole. He hereby established a regular order of causes and effects, of principles and consequences, which, under an appearance of chance, governs the universe, and maintains the equilibrium of the world. Thus he gave to fire motion and activity, to air elasticity, to matter weight and density; he made air lighter than water, metals heavier than earth, wood less cohesive than steel; he ordered the flame to ascend, the stone to fall, the plant to vegetate; to man, whom he decreed to expose to the encounter of so many substances, and yet wished to preserve his frail existence, he gave the faculty of perception. By this faculty, every action injurious to his life gives him a sensation of pain and evil, and every favourable action a sensation of pleasure and good. By these impressions, sometimes led to avoid what is offensive to his senses, and sometimes attracted towards the objects that soothe and gratify them, man has been necessitated to love and preserve his existence. Self-love, the desire of happiness, and an aversion to pain, are the essential and primary laws that nature herself imposed on man, that the ruling power, whatever it be, has established to govern him: and these laws, like those of motion in the physical world, are the simple and prolific principle of every thing that takes place in the moral world.

Such then is the condition of man: on one side, subjected to the action of the elements around him, he is exposed to a variety of inevitable evils; and if in this decree Nature appears too severe, on the other hand, just and even indulgent, she has not only tempered those evils with an equal portion of benefits, she has moreover given him the power of augmenting the one, and diminishing the other. She has seemingly said to him, " Feeble work of my hands, I owe you nothing, and I give you life. The world in which I place you was not made on your account, and yet I grant you the use of it. You will find in it a

mixture of good and evil. It is for you to distinguish
them; you must direct your own steps in the paths
of flowers and of thorns. Be the arbitrator of your
lot; I place your destiny in your hands."——Yes,
man is become the artificer of his fate; it is himself
who has created in turn the vicissitudes of his fortune, his successes and his disappointment; and if,
when he reflects on the sorrows which he has associated to human life, he has reason to lament his weakness and his folly, he has perhaps still more right to
presume upon his force, and be confident in his energies, when he recollects from what point he has set
out, and to what height he has been capable of ele-
vating himself.

CHAP. VI.

ORIGINAL STATE OF MAN.

IN the origin of things, man, formed equally naked
both as to body and mind, found himself thrown by
chance upon a land confused and savage. An orphan,
deserted by the unknown power that had produced
him, he saw no supernatural beings at hand to adver-
tise him of wants that he owed merely to his senses,
and inform him of duties springing solely from those
wants. Like other animals, without experience of
the past, without knowledge of the future, he wandered in forests, guided and governed purely by the
affections of his nature. By the pain of hunger he
was directed to seek food, and he provided for his
subsistence; by the inclemencies of the weather, the
desire was excited of covering his body, and he made
himself cloathing; by the attraction of a powerful
pleasure, he approached a fellow-being, and perpetuated his species.

Thus the impressions he received from external objects, awakening his faculties, developed by degrees his understanding, and began to instruct his profound ignorance ; his wants called forth his industry ; his dangers formed his mind to courage ; he learned to distinguish useful from pernicious plants, to resist the elements, to seize upon his prey, to defend his life ; and his misery was alleviated.

Thus *self-love, aversion to pain, and desire of happiness*, were the simple and powerful motives which drew man from the savage and barbarous state in which nature had placed him : and now that his life is sown with enjoyment, that he can every day count upon some pleasure, he may applaud himself and say, " It is I who have produced the blessings that encompass me ; I am the fabricator of my own felicity ; a secure habitation, commodious raiment, an abundance of wholesome provision in rich variety, smiling valleys, fertile hills, populous empires, these are the works of my hand : but for me, the earth, given up to disorder, would have been nothing more than a poisonous swamp, a savage forest, and a hideous desert !" True, mortal creator ! I pay thee homage ! Thou hast measured the extent of the heavens, and counted the stars ; thou hast drawn the lightning from the clouds, conquered the fury of the sea and the tempest, and subjected all the elements to thy will ! But oh ! how many errors are mixed with these sublime energies !

CHAP. VII.

PRINCIPLES OF SOCIETY.

IN the mean time, wandering in woods and upon the borders of rivers, in pursuit of deer and of fish, the first human beings, hunters and fishermen, beset with dangers, assailed by enemies, tormented by hunger, by reptiles, and by the animals they chased, felt their individual weakness; and impelled by a common want of safety, and a common sentiment of the same evils, they united their powers and their strength. When one man was exposed to danger, numbers succoured and defended him; when one failed in provision, another shared with him his prey. Men thus associated for the security of their existence, for the augmentation of their faculties, for the protection of their enjoyment; and the principle of society was that of *self-love*.

Afterwards, instructed by the repeated experience of diverse accidents, by the fatigues of a wandering life, by the anxiety resulting from frequent scarcity, men reasoned with themselves, and said, " Why should we consume our days in search of the scattered fruits which a parsimonious soil affords? Why weary ourselves in the pursuit of prey that escape us in the woods or the waters? Let us assemble under our hand the animals that nourish us; let us apply our cares to the increase and defence of them. Their produce will afford as a supply of food, with their spoils we may clothe ourselves, and we shall live exempt from the fatigues of the day, and solicitude for the morrow." And aiding each other, they seized the nimble kid and the timid sheep; they tamed the

patient camel, the ferocious bull, and the impetuous
horse; and applauding themselves on the success of
their industry, they sat down in the joy of their hearts,
and began to taste repose and tranquillity: and thus
self-love, the principle of all their reasoning, was the
instigator to every art and every enjoyment.

Now that men could pass their days in leisure, and
the communication of their ideas, they turned upon
the earth, upon the heavens, and upon themselves an
eye of curiosity and reflection. They observed the
course of the seasons, the action of the elements, the
properties of fruits and plants; and they applied their
minds to the multiplication of their enjoyments. Remarking in certain countries the nature of seeds,
which contain within themselves the faculty of re-
producing the parent plant, they employed to their
own advantage this property of Nature; they committed to the earth barley, wheat, and rice, and reaped a
produce equal to their most sanguine hopes. Thus
they found the means of obtaining within a small
compass, and without the necessity of perpetual wandering, a plentiful and durable stock of provision: and
encouraged by this discovery, they prepared for themselves fixed habitations, they constructed houses, villages, and towns: they assumed the form of tribes
and of nations: and thus was *self-love* rendered the
parent of every thing that genius has effected, or human power performed.

By the sole aid then of his faculties, has man been
able to raise himself to the astonishing height of his
present fortune. Too happy would have been his
lot, had he, scrupulously observing the law imprinted
on his nature, constantly fulfilled the object of it!
But, by a fatal imprudence, sometimes overlooking
and sometimes transgressing its limits, he plunged in
an abyss of errors and misfortunes, and *self-love*, now
disordered, and now blind, was converted into a prolific source of calamities.

CHAP. VIII.

SOURCE OF THE EVILS OF SOCIETY.

IN reality, scarcely were the faculties of men expand-
ed, than, seized by the attraction of objects which
flatter the senses, they gave themselves up to unbri-
dled desires.   The sweet sensations which nature had
annexed to their true wants, to attach them to life, no
longer sufficed.   Not satisfied with the fruits which
the earth offered them, or their industry produced,
they were desirous of heaping up enjoyments, and
they coveted those which their fellow-creatures possessed.   A strong man rose up against a weak one to
tear from him the profit of his labour: the weak man
solicited the succour of a neighbour, weak like himself, to repel the violence.   The strong man in his
turn associated himself with another strong man, and
they said: " Why should we fatigue our arms in
producing enjoyments which we find in the hands of
the feeble, who are unable to defend themselves?   Let
us unite, and plunder them.   They shall toil for us,
and we shall enjoy in indolence the fruit of their exertions."   The strong thus associating for the purpose of oppression, and the weak for resistance, men
reciprocally tormented each other, and a fatal and
general discord was established upon the earth, in
which the passions, assuming a thousand new forms,
have never ceased to generate a regular train of calamities.

Thus that very principle of self-love, which, when
restrained within the limits of prudence, was a source
of improvement and felicity, became transformed,
in its blind and disordered state, into a contagious

D

poison. Cupidity, the daughter and companion of ignorance, has produced all the mischiefs that have desolated the globe.

Yes, ignorance and the love of accumulation, these are the two sources of all the plagues that infest the life of man! They have inspired him with false ideas of his happiness, and prompted him to misconstrue and infringe the laws of nature, as they related to the connexion between him and exterior objects. Through them his conduct has been injurious to his own existence, and he has thus violated the duty he owes to himself; they have fortified his heart against compassion, and his mind against the dictates of justice, and he has thus violated the duty he owes to others. By ignorance and inordinate desire, man has armed himself against man, family against family, tribe against tribe, and the earth is converted into a bloody theatre of discord and robbery. They have sown the seeds of secret war in the bosom of every state, divided the citizens from each other, and the same society is constituted of oppressors and oppressed, of masters and slaves. They have taught the heads of nations, with audacious insolence, to turn the arms of the society against itself, and to build upon mercenary avidity the fabric of political despotism: or they have taught a more hypocritical and deep-laid project, that imposed, as the dictate of heaven, lying sanctions and a sacrilegious yoke: thus rendering avarice the source of credulity. In fine, they have corrupted every idea of good and evil, just and unjust, virtue and vice: they have misled nations in a never-ending labyrinth of calamity and mistake. Ignorance and the love of accumulation!— These are the malevolent beings that have laid waste the earth; these are the decrees of fate that have overturned empires; these are the celestial maledictions that have struck those walls once so glorious, and converted the splendour of a populous city into a sad spectacle of ruins!—Since then it was from his own bosom all the evils proceeded that have vexed the life of man, it was there also he ought to have sought the remedies, where only they are to be found.

CHAP. IX.

THE ORIGIN OF GOVERNMENT AND LAWS.

IN truth, the period soon arrived when men, tired of the ills they occasioned each other, sighed after peace; and reflecting on the nature and causes of those ills, they said: " We mutually injure one another by our passions, and from a desire to grasp every thing, we in reality possess nothing. What one ravishes to-day, another tears from him to-morrow, and our cupidity rebounds upon our own heads. Let us establish arbitrators, who shall decide our claims and appease our variances. When the strong rises up against the weak, the arbitrator shall repel him ; and the life and property of each being under a common guarantee and protection, we shall enjoy all the blessings of nature."

Conventions, tacit or expressed, were thus introduced into society, and became the rule of the actions of individuals, the measure of their claims, and the law of their reciprocal relations. Chiefs were appointed to enforce the observance of the compact, and to these the people entrusted the balance of rights, and the sword to punish violations.

Then a happy equilibrium of powers and of action was established, which constituted the public safety. The names of equity and justice were acknowledged and revered. Every man, able to enjoy in peace the

fruits of his labour, gave himself up to all the energies of his soul; and activity, awakened and kept
alive by the reality or the hope of enjoyment, forced
art and nature to display all their treasures. The
fields were covered with harvests, the valleys with
flocks, the hills with vines, the sea with ships, and
man was happy and powerful upon the earth.

The disorder his imprudence had caused, his wisdom thus remedied. But this wisdom was still the
effect of the laws of nature in the organization of his
being. It was to secure his own enjoyments, that he
was led to respect those of another, and the desire of
accumulation found its corrective in enlightened self-
love.

Self-love, the eternal spring of action in every individual, was thus the necessary basis of all associations; and upon the observance of this natural law has
the fate of every nation depended. Have the factitious and conventional laws of any society accorded
with this law, and corresponded to its demands? In
that case every man, prompted by an overpowering
instinct, has exerted all the faculties of his nature, and
the public felicity has been the result of the various
portions of individual felicity. Have these laws,
on the contrary, restrained the effort of man in his
pursuit of happiness? In that case his heart, deprived of all its natural motives, has languished in inac-
tion, and the oppression of individuals has engendered
general weakness.

Self-love, impetuous and rash, renders man the
enemy of man, and of consequence perpetually tends
to the dissolution of society. It is for the art of legis-
lation, and for the virtue of ministers, to temper the
grasping selfishness of individuals, to keep each man's
desire to possess every thing in a nice equipoise, and
thus to render the subjects happy, in order that, in
the struggle of this with any other society, all the

members should have an equal interest in the preservation and defence of the commonwealth.

From hence it follows, that the internal splendour and prosperity of empires, have been in proportion to the equity of their governments; and their external power respectively, in proportion to the number of persons interested in the maintenance of the political constitution, and their degree of interest in that maintenance.

On the other hand, the multiplication of men by complicating their ties, having rendered the demarcation of their rights a point of difficult decision; the perpetual play of the passions, having given rise to unexpected incidents; the conventions that were formed having proved vicious, inadequate, or null; the authors of the laws having either misunderstood the object of them, or dissembled it, and the persons appointed to execute them, instead of restraining the inordinate desires of others, having abandoned themselves to the sway of their own avidity—society has, by these causes united, been thrown into trouble and disorder; and defective laws and unjust governments, the result of cupidity and ignorance, have been the foundation of the misfortunes of the people, and the subversion of states.

CHAP. X.

GENERAL CAUSES OF THE PROSPERITY OF ANCIENT STATES.

SUCH, O man, who enquirest after wisdom, have been the causes of the revolutions of those ancient states, of which you contemplate the ruins! Upon

whatever spot I fix my view, or to whatever period
my thought recur, the same principles of elevation
and decline, of prosperity and destruction, present
themselves to the mind. If a people were powerful,
if an empire flourished, it was because the laws of
convention were conformable to those of nature ; because the government procured to every man respectively the free use of his faculties, the equal security
of his person and property. On the contrary, if an
empire has fallen to ruin or disappeared, it is because
the laws were vicious or imperfect, or a corrupt government has checked their operation. If laws and
government, at first rational and just, have afterwards
become depraved, it is because the alternative of good
and evil derives from the nature of the heart of man,
from the succession of his inclinations, the progress of
his knowledge, the combination of events and circumstances as the history of the human species proves.

In the infancy of nations, when men still lived in
forests, all subject to the same wants, and endowed
with the same faculties, they were nearly equal in
strength ; and this equality was a circumstance high-
ly advantageous to the formation of society. Each
individual finding himself independent of every other,
no one was the slave, and no one had the idea of being
master of another. Untaught man knew neither servitude nor tyranny. Supplied with the means of pro-
viding sufficiency for his subsistence, he thought not
of borrowing from strangers. Owing nothing, and exacting nothing, he judged of the rights of others by
his own. Ignorant also of the art of multiplying enjoyments, he provided only what was necessary ; and
superfluity being unknown to him, the desire to en-
gross of consequence remained unexcited ; or if excited, as it attacked others in those possessions that
were wholly indispensable, it was resisted with energy,
and the very foresight of this resistance maintained a
salutary and immoveable equilibrium.

Thus original equality, without the aid of convention, maintained personal liberty, secured individual property, and produced order and good manners. Each man laboured separately and for himself; and his heart being occupied, he wandered not in pursuit of unlawful desires. His enjoyments were few, but his wants were satisfied: and as nature had made these wants less extensive than his ability, the labour of his hands soon produced abundance; abundance population; the arts delevoped themselves, cultivation extended, and the earth covered with numerous inhabitants, was divided into different domains.

The relations of men becoming complicated, the interior order of society was more difficult to maintain. Time and industry having created affluence, cupidity awoke from its slumber, and as equality, easy between individuals, could not subsist between families, the national balance was destroyed. It was necessary to supply the loss by means of an artificial balance; it was necessary to appoint chiefs, and establish laws; but as these were occasioned by cupidity, in the experience of primitive times they could not but partake of the origin from which they sprung. Various circumstances however concurred to temper the disorder, and make it indispensable for governments to be just.

States being at first weak, and having external enemies to fear, it was in reality of importance to the chiefs not to oppress the subject. By diminishing the interest of the citizens in their government, they would have diminished their means of resistance; they would have facilitated foreign invasion, and thus endangered their own existence for superfluous enjoyments.

Internally, the character of the people was repellant to tyranny. Men had too long contracted habits of independance; their wants were too limited, and

the consciousness of their own strength too inseparable from their minds.

States being closely knit together, it was difficult to
divide the citizens, in order to oppress some by means
of others.   Their communication with each other was
too easy, and their interests too simple and evident.
Beside, every man being at once proprietor and cultivator, he had no inducement to sell himself, and the
despot would have been unable to find mercenaries.

If dissensions arose, it was between family and family, one faction with another; and a considerable
number had still one common interest.   Disputes, it
is true, were in this case more warm, but the fear of
foreign invasion appeased the discord.   If the oppression of a party was effected, the earth being open
before it, and men still simple in their manners, finding every where the same advantages, the party mi-
grated and carried their independence to another
quarter.

Ancient states then enjoyed in themselves numerous means of prosperity and power.

As every man found his well-being in the constitution of his country, he felt a lively interest in its preservation; and if a foreign power invaded it, having
his habitation and his field to defend, he carried to
the combat the ardour of a personal cause, and his pa-
triotic exertions were prompted by self-defence.

As every action useful to the public excited its esteem and gratitude, each was eager to be useful, and
talents and civil virtues were multiplied by self-love.

As every citizen was called upon indiscriminately
to contribute his proportion of property and personal
effort, the armies and the treasures of the state were
inexhaustible.

As the earth was free, and its possession easy and
secure, every man was a proprietor, and the division
of property, by rendering luxury impossible, preserved
the purity of manners.

As every man ploughed his own field, cultivation was more active, provisions more abundant, and individual opulence constituted the public wealth.

As abundance of provision rendered subsistence easy, population rapidly increased, and states quickly arrived at their plenitude.

As the produce was greater than the consumption, the desire of commerce started up, and exchanges were made between different nations, which were an additional stimulus to their activity, and increased their reciprocal enjoyments.

In fine, as certain places in certain epochas combined the advantage of good government with that of being placed in the road of circulation and commerce, they became rich magazines of trade, and powerful seats of dominion. It was in this manner that the riches of India and Europe, accumulated upon the banks of the Nile, the Tigris, and the Euphrates, gave successive existence to the splendour of a thousand metropolisses.

The people, become rich, applied their superfluity of means to labours of public utility; and this was, in every state, the æra of those works, the magnificence of which astonishes the mind; those wells of Tyre *(i)* those artificial banks of the Euphrates, those conduits of Medea *(k)* those fortresses of the Desert, those aqueducts of Palmyra, those temples, those porticos.—And these immense labours were little oppressive to the nations that completed them, because they were the fruit of the equal and united effort of individuals free to act and ardent to desire.

The ancient states prospered, because social institutions were comfortable to the true laws of nature, and because the subjects of those states, enjoying liberty and the security of their persons and their property, could display all the extent of their faculties, and all the energy of self-love.

CHAP. IX.

GENERAL CAUSES OF THE REVOLUTIONS AND RUIN OF ANCIENT STATES.

IN the mean time the inordinate desire of accumulation had excited a constant and universal struggle among men; and this struggle, prompting individuals and societies to reciprocal invasions, occasioned perpetual commotions and successive revolutions.

At first, in the savage and barbarous state of the first human beings, this inordinate desire, daring and ferocious in its nature, taught rapine, violence, and murder; and the progress of civilization, was for a long time at a stand.

Afterwards, when societies began to be formed, the effect of bad habits communicating itself to laws and government, civil institutions became corrupt, and arbitrary and factitious rights were established, which gave the people depraved ideas of justice and morality.

Because one man, for example, was stronger than another, this inequality, the result of accident, was taken for the law of nature *(l)*; and because the life of the weak was in his power, and he did not take it from him, he arrogated over his person the absurd right of property, and individual slavery prepared the way for the slavery of nations.

Because the chief of a family could exercise an absolute authority in his own house, he made his inclinations and affections the sole rule of his conduct; he conferred and withheld the conveniencies and enjoyments of life without respect to the law of equality or justice, and paternal tyranny laid the foundation of political despotism *(m)*.

In societies formed upon such bases, time and industry having developed riches, inordinate desire, restricted by the laws, became artificial without being less active. Under the mask of union and civil peace, it engendered in the bosom of every state an intestine war; in which the citizens, divided into opposite corps of orders, classes, and families, aimed to appropriate to themselves, under the name of *supreme power*, the ability of grasping and controlling every thing at the will of their passions. It is this spirit of rapacity, the disguises of which are innumerable, but its operation and end uniformly the same, that has been the perpetual scourge of nations.

Sometimes opposing social compact, or destroying that which already existed, it has abandoned the inhabitants of a country to the tumultuous shock of all their jarring principles; and the dissolved states, under the name of *anarchy*, have been tormented by the passions of every individual member.

Sometimes a people, jealous of its liberty, having appointed agents to administer, these agents have assumed to themselves the powers of which they were only the guardians; have employed the public funds in corrupting elections, gaining partizans, and dividing the people against itself. By these means, from temporary, they have become perpetual, from elective, hereditary magistrates; and the state, agitated by the intrigues of the ambitious, by the bribes of the wealthy leaders of factions, by the venality of the indolent poor, by the empircism of declaimers, has been troubled with all the inconveniencies of *democracy*.

In one country, the chiefs equal in strength, mutually afraid of each other, have formed vile compacts and coalitions, and portioning out power, rank, honours, have arrogated to themselves privileges and immunities; have erected themselves into separate bodies and distinct classes; have tyrannised in common over the people, and, under the name of *aristo-cracy* the state has been tormented by the passions of the wealthy and the great.

In another country, tending to the same end by different means, *sacred impostors* have taken advantage of the credulity of the ignorant. In the secrecy of temples, and behind the veil of altars, they have made the Gods speak and act; have delivered oracles, worked pretended miracles, ordered sacrifices, imposed offerings, prescribed endowments; and under the name of *theocracy* and *religion*, the state has been tormented by the passions of priests.

Sometimes, weary of its disorders, or of its tyrants, a nation to diminish the sources of its evils, gave itself a single master. In that case, if the powers of the prince were limited, his only desire was to extend them; if indefinite, he abused the trust that was confided to him; and under the name of *monarchy*, the state was tormented by the passions of kings and princes.

Then the factious, taking advantage of the general discontent, flattered the people with the hope of a better master; they scattered gifts and promises, dethroned the despot to substitute themselves in his stead; and disputes for the succession or the division of power, have tormented the state with the disorders and devestations of *civil war*.

In fine, among these rivals, one individual more artful or more fortunate than the rest, gaining the ascendency, concentred the whole power in himself. By a singular phenomenon, one man obtained the mastery over millions of his fellow creatures, against their will, and without their consent; and thus the art of *tyranny* appears also to have been the offspring of inordinate desire. Observing the spirit of egotism that divided mankind, the ambitious adroitly foment-ed this spirit : he flattered the vanity of one, excited the jealousy of another, favoured the avarice of a third, inflamed the resentment of a fourth, irritated the passions of all. By opposing interests or prejudices, he sowed the seeds of divisions and hatred. He promised to the poor the spoil of the rich, to the rich the subjugation of the poor; threatened this man by that, one class by another; and insolating the citizens by distrust, he formed his own strength out of their weakness, and imposed upon them the yoke of *opinion*, the knots of which they tied with their own hands. By means of the army he extorted contributions; by the contributions he disposed of the army; by the corresponding play of money and places, he bound all the people with a chain that was not to be broken, and the states which they composed fell into the slow decay of *despotism*.

Thus did one and the same spring, varying its action under all the forms that have been enumerated, incessantly attack the continuity of states, and an eternal circle of vicissitudes have sprung from an eternal circle of passions.

This constant spirit of egotism operated two principal effects equally destructive: the one, that by dividing societies into all their fractions, a state of debility was produced, which facilitated their dissolution; the other, that always tending to concentre the power in a single hand, it occasioned a successive absorption of societies and states, fatal to their peace and to their common existence *(n)*.

Just as in a single state, the nation had been absorbed in a party, that party in a family, and that family in an individual, there also existed an absorption of a similar kind between state and state, attended with all the mischiefs in the relative situation of nations, that the other produced in the civil relation of individuals. One city subjected its neighbour city, and the result of the conquest was a province; province swallowed up province, and this produced a

E

kingdom; between two kingdoms a conquest took place, and thus furnished an empire of unwieldy bulk. Did the internal force of these states increase in proportion to their mass? On the contrary, it was diminished; and far from the condition of the people being happier, it became every day more oppressive and wretched, by causes inevitably flowing from the nature of things.

Because, as the boundaries of states became extended, their administration became more complicated and difficult; and to give motion to the mass, it was necessary to increase the prerogatives of the sovereign, and all proportion was thus annihilated between the duty of governors and their power.

Because despots, feeling their weakness, dreaded all those circumstances that developed the force of nations, and made it their study to attenuate it.

Because nations, estranged from each other by the prejudices of ignorance and the ferocity of hatred, seconded the perversity of governments, and employing a standing force for reciprocal offence, aggravated their slavery.

Because in proportion as the balance between states was broken, it became easy for the strong to overwhelm the weak.

Because, in proportion as state became blended with state, the people were stripped of their laws, their customs, every thing by which they were distinguished from each other, and thus lost the great mover, *selfishness*, which gave them energy.

And despots, considering empires in the light of domains, and the people as their property, abandoned themselves to depredations, and the licentiousness of the most arbitrary authority.

And all the force and wealth of nations were converted into a supply for individual expence and personal caprice; and kings, in the wearisomness of satiety, followed the dictates of every factitious and depraved taste *(o)*. They must have gardens constructed upon arches, and rivers carried to the summit of mountains; for them fertile fields must be changed into parks for deer; lakes formed where their was no water, and rocks elevated in those lakes; they must have palaces constructed of marble and porphyry, and the furniture ornamented with gold and diamonds, Millions of hands were thus employed in sterile labours; and the luxury of princes being imitated by their parasites, and descending step by step to the lowest ranks, became a general source of corruption and impoverishment.

And the ordinary tributes being no longer adequate to the insatiable thirst of enjoyment, they were augmented: the consequence of which was, that the cultivator, finding his toil increase without any indemnity, lost his courage; the merchant, seeing himself robbed, took a disgust to industry; the multitude, condemned to a state of poverty, exerted themselves no farther than the procurement of necessaries required, and every species of productive activity was at a stand.

And the surcharge of taxes rendering the possession of lands burthensome, the humble proprietor abandoned his field, or sold it to the man of opulence; and the mass of wealth centered in a few individuals. As the laws and institutions favoured this accumulation, nations were divided into a small body of indolent rich, and a multitude of mercenary poor. The people, reduced to indigence, debased themselves; the great, cloyed with superfluity, became depraved; and the number of citizens interested in the preservation of the state decreasing, its strength and existence were by so much the more precarious.

In another view, as there was nothing to excite emulation or encourage instruction, the minds of men sunk into profound ignorance.

The administration of affairs being secret and mysterious, there existed no means of reform or hope of better times; and as the chiefs ruled only by violence and fraud, the people considered them but as a faction of public enemies, and all harmony between the governed and the governors was at an end.

The states of opulent Asia become inervated by all these vices, it happened at length that the vagrant and poor inhabitants of the deserts and the mountains adjacent, coveted the enjoyments of the fertile plains, and, instigated by a common cupidity, they attacked polished empires, and overturned the thrones of despots. Such revolutions were rapid and easy, because the policy of tyrants had enfeebled the citizens, raised the fortresses, destroyed the warlike spirit of resistance, and because the oppressed subject was without personal interest, and the mercenary soldier without courage.

Hordes of barbarians having reduced whole nations to a state of slavery, it followed that empires, formed of a conquering and a vanquished people, united in their bosom two classes of men essentially opposite and inimical to each other. All the principles of society were dissolved. There was no longer either a common interest or public spirit: on the contrary, a distinction of casts and conditions was established, that reduced the maintenance of disorder to a regular system; and accordingly as a man was descended from this or that blood, he was born vassal or tyrant, live stock or proprietor.

The oppressors being in this case less numerous than the oppressed, it became necessary, in order to support this false equilibrium, to bring the science of tyranny to perfection. The art of governing was now nothing more than that of subjecting the many to the few. To obtain an obedience so contrary to instinct, it was necessary to establish the most severe penalties;

and the cruelty of the laws rendered the manners atrocious. The distinction of persons also establishing in the state two codes of justice, two species of rights, the people, placed between the natural inclinations of their hearts, and the oath they were obliged to pronounce, had two contradictory consciences; and their ideas of just and unjust had no longer any foundation in the understanding.

Under such a system the people fell into a state of depression and despair; and the accidents of nature increasing the preponderance of evil, terrified at this group of calamities, they referred the cause of them to superior and invisible powers; because they had tyrants upon earth, they supposed there to be tyrants in heaven; and superstition came in aid to aggravate the disasters of nations.

Hence originated gloomy and misanthropic systems of religion, which painted the gods malignant and envious like human despots. To appease them, man offered the sacrifice of all his enjoyments, punished himself with privations, and overturned the laws of nature. Considering his pleasures as crimes, his sufferings as expiations, he endeavoured to cherish a passion for pain, and to renounce self-love; he persecuted his senses, detested his life, and by a self-denying and unsocial system of morals, nations were plunged in the sluggishness of death.

But as provident nature had endowed the heart of man with inexhaustible hope, perceiving his desires disappointed of happiness here, he pursued it elsewhere; by a sweet illusion, he formed to himself another country, an asylum, where, out of the reach of tyrants, he should regain all his rights. Hence a new disorder arose. Smitten with his imaginary world, man despised the world of nature: for chimerical hopes he neglected the reality. He no longer considered his life but as a fatiguing journey, a painful dream; his body as a prison that withheld him from his felicity; the earth as a place of exile and pilgrimage, which he disdained to cultivate. A sacred sloth then established itself in the world: the fields were deserted, waste lands increased, empires were dispeopled, monuments neglected, and every where ignorance, superstition, and fanaticism, uniting their baleful effects, multiplied devastations and ruins.

Thus, agitated by their own passions, men whether in their individual capacity or as collective bodies, always rapacious and improvident, passing from tyranny to slavery, from pride to abjectness, from presumption to despair, have been themselves the eternal instruments of their misfortunes.

Such was the simplicity of the principles that regulated the fate of ancient states; such was the series of causes and effects consecutive and connected with each other, according to which they rose or fell in the scale of human welfare, just as the physical causes of the human heart were therein observed or infringed. A hundred divers nations, a hundred powerful empires, in their incessant vicissitudes, have read again and again these instructive lessons to mankind.—And these lessons are mute and forgotten! The diseases of past times have appeared again in the present! the heads of the different governments have practised again, without restraint, exploded projects of deception and despotism! The people have wandered as before in the labyrinths of superstition and ignorance!

And what, added the Genius, calling up his energies afresh, is the consequence of all this? Since experience is useless, since salutary examples are forgotten, the scenes which were acted before are now

about to be renewed; revolutions will again agitate
people and empires; powerful thrones will, as before,
be overturned; and terrible catastrophes remind the
human species, that the laws of nature, and the precepts of wisdom and truth, cannot be trampled upon
in vain.

———

CHAP. XII.

LESSONS TAUGHT BY ANCIENT, REPEATED IN MODERN TIMES.

IN this manner did the Genius address me. Struck
with the reasonableness and coherence of his discourse, and a multiplicity of ideas crowding upon my
mind, which, while they thwarted my habits, led my
judgment at the same time captive, I remained absorbed in profound silence. Meanwhile, as in this
sombre and thoughtful disposition I kept my eyes
fixed upon Asia, clouds of smoke and of flames at the
north, on the shores of the Black Sea, and in the fields
of the Crimea, suddenly attracted my attention. They
appeared to ascend at once from every part of the
peninsula, and passing by the isthmus to the continent, they pursued their course, as if driven by an
easterly wind, along the miry lake of Asoph, and
were lost in the verdant plains of the Coban. Observing more attentively the course of these clouds, I
perceived that they were preceded or followed by
swarms of living beings, which, like ants disturbed
by the foot of a passenger, were in lively action.
Sometimes they seemed to move towards and rush
against each other, and numbers after the concussion

remained motionless. Disquieted at this spectacle, I was endeavouring to distinguish the objects, when the Genius said to me: Do you see those fires which spread over the earth, and are you acquainted with their causes and effects?—O Genius! I replied, I see columns of flame and smoke, and as it were insects that accompany them; but discerning with difficulty, as I do, the masses of towns and monuments, how can I distinguish such petty creatures? I can see nothing more than that these insects seem to carry on a sort of mock battles; they advance, they approach towards each other, they attack, they pursue.—It is no mockery, said the Genius, it is the thing itself.—And what name, replied I, shall we give to these foolish animalculæ that destroy each other? Do they live only for a day, and is this short life further abridged by violence and murder?—The Genius then once more touched my eyes and my ears. Listen, said he to me, and observe—I immediately turned my eyes in the same direction, alas! said I, transpierced with anguish, these columns of flame, these insects, O Genius! they are men, and the ravages of war! These torrents of flame ascend from towns and villages set on fire! I see the horsemen that light them. I see them sword in hand overrun the country. Old men, women, and children, in confused multitudes, fly before them. I see other horsemen, who, with their pikes upon their shoulders, accompany and direct them: I can ever distinguish by their led horses, by their *kalpacks*, and by their tufts of hair *(p)*, that they are Tartars; and without doubt those who pursue them in triangular hats and green uniforms are Muscovites. I understand the whole: I perceive that the war has just broken out afresh between the empire of the Czars and the Sultans.—Not yet, replied the Genius; this is only the prelude. These Tartars have been, and would still be troublesome neighbours;

the Muscovites are riding themselves of them. Their country is an object of convenience to their less un-civilized enemies; it rounds and makes complete their dominions; and as the first step in the project that has been conceived, the throne of the Guerais is overturned.

In reality I saw the Russian flag hoisted over the Crimea, and their vessels scattered upon the Euxine.

Meanwhile, at the cries of the fugitive Tartars, the Musulman empire was in commotion. "Our bre-thren," exclaimed the children of Mahomet, "are driven from their habitations; the people of the pro-phet are outraged; infidels are in possession of a con-secrated land *(q)*, and profane the temples of Isla-mism? Let us arm ourselves to avenge the glory of God and our own cause."

A general preparation for war then took place in the two empires. Armed men, provisions, ammuni-tion, and all the murderous accoutrements of battle, were every where assembled. My attention was par-ticularly attracted by the immense crowds that in either nation thronged to the temples. On one side the Mussulmans, assembled before their mosques, washed their hands and feet, pared their nails, and combed their beard: then spreading carpets upon the ground, and turning themselves towards the south, with their arms sometimes crossed and sometimes ex-tended, they performed their genuflections and pros-trations. Recollecting the disasters they had expe-rienced during the last war, they cried: "God of cle-mency and pity, hast thou then abandoned thy faith-ful people? Why dost thou, who has promised to thy prophet the dominion of nations, and signalized religion by so many triumphs, deliver up true believ-ers to the sword of infidels;" And the Imans and the Santons said to the people: "It is the chastise-ment of your sins. You eat pork, you drink wine,

you touch things that are unclean: God has punished you. Do penance; purify yourselves; say your
creed*; fast from the rising of the sun to its setting;
give the tenth of your goods to the mosques; go to
Mecca; and God will make your arms victorious."
Then, assuming courage, the people gave a general
shout.   " There is but one God," said they in a
transport of rage, " and Mahomet is his prophet!
accursed be every one that believeth not!—Indulgent
God! grant us the favour to exterminate these Christians: it is for thy glory we fight, and by our death
we are martyrs to thy name."—And having offered
sacrifices, they prepared themselves for battle.

On the other hand, the Russians on their knees exclaimed: " Let us give thanks to God, and celebrate
his power: he has strengthened our arm to humble
his enemies. Beneficent God! incline thine ear to
our prayers. To please thee we will for three days
eat neither meat nor eggs. Permit us to exterminate
these impious Mahometans, and overthrow their empire, and we will give thee the tenth of the spoil, and
erect new temples to thy honour." The priests then
filled the churches with smoke, and said to the people: We pray for you, and God accepts our incense,
and blesses your arms. Continue to fast and to fight;
tell us the faults you have secretly committed; be-
stow our goods on the church; we will absolve you
of your sins, and you shall die in a state of grace."
And they sprinkled water on the people, distributed
among them little bones of departed saints to serve as
amulets and talismans; and the people breathed nothing but war and destruction.

Struck with this contrasting picture of the same
passions, and lamenting to myself their pernicious
consequences, I was reflecting on the difficulty the

* There is but one God, and Mahomet is his prophet.

common Judge would find in complying with such op
posite demands, when the Genius, from an impulse of
anger, vehemently exclaimed:

What madness is this which strikes my ear? What
blind and fatal insanity possesses the human mind?
Sacrilegious prayers, return to the earth from whence
you came! Ye concave heavens, repel these murderous vows, these impious thanksgivings! Is it thus,
O man, you worship the Divinity? And do you
think that he, whom you call Father of all, can receive with complacence the homage of free-booters
and murderers? Ye conquerors, with what sentiments
does he behold your arms reeking with blood that he
has created? Ye conquered, what hope can you
place in useless moans? Is he a man that he should
change, or the son of man that he should repent?
Is he governed like you by vengeance and compassion, by rage and by weariness! Base idea, how
much unworthy of the Being of Beings! Hear these
men, and you would imagine that God is a being capricious and mutable; that now he loves, and now he
hates; that he chastises one and indulges another;
that hatred is engendered and nourished in his bosom; that he spreads snares for men, and delights in
the fatal effects of imprudence; that he permits ill,
and punishes it; that he foresees guilt, and acqui-
esces; that he is to be bought with gifts like a partial
judge; that he reverses his edicts like an undiscerning
despot; that he gives and revokes his favours because
it is his will, and is to be appeased only by servility
like a savage tyrant. I now completely understand
what is the deceit of mankind, who have pretended
that God made man in his own image, and who have
really made God in theirs; who have ascribed to him
their weakness, their errors, and their vices; and in
the conclusion, surprised at the contradictory nature
of their own assertions, have attempted to cloke it

with hypocritical humility, and the pretended impotence of human reason, calling the delirium of their own understandings the sacred mysteries of heaven.

They have said, God is without variableness and they pray to him to change. They have said that he is incomprehensible, and they have undertaken to be interpreters of his will.

A race of impostors has made its appearance upon the earth, who, pretending to be in the confidence of God, and taking upon themselves the office of instructing the people, have opened the flood gates of falsehood and iniquity. They have affixed merit to actions which either are indifferent or absurd. They have dignified with the appellation of virtue the observance of certain postures, and the repitition of certain words and names. They have taught the impiety of eating certain meats on certain days rather than on others. It is thus the Jew would sooner die than work on the sabbath. It is thus the Persian would endure suffocation before he would blow the fire with his breath. It is thus the Indian places supreme perfection in smearing himself with cow-dung, and mysteriously pronouncing the word *Aum* *(r)*: It is thus the Mussulman believes himself purified from all his sins by the ablution of his head and his arms; and disputes, sabre in hand, whether he ought to begin the ceremony at the elbow *(s)* or the points of his fingers. It is thus the Christian would believe himself damned, were he to eat the juice of animal food instead of milk or butter. What sublime and truly celestial doctrines! What purity of morals, and how worthy of apostleship and martyrdom! I will cross the seas to teach these admirable laws to savage people and distant nations. I will say to them: " Children of nature, how long will you wander in the paths of ignorance? How long will you be blind to the true principles of morality

and religion? Visit civilized nations, and take lessons of pious and learned people. They will teach
you, that to please God, you must in certain months
of the year faint all day with hunger and thirst.
They will teach you how you may shed the blood of
your neighbour, and purify yourselves from the stain,
by repeating a profession of faith, and making a methodical ablution: how you may rob him of his
goods, and be absolved from the guilt, by sharing
them with certain persons whose profession it is to
live in idleness upon the labour of others."

Sovereign and mysterious Power of the Universe!
secret Mover of Nature! Universal Soul of every
thing that lives! infinite and incomprehensible Being,
whom, under so many forms, mortals have ignorantly
worshipped! God who in the immensity of the heavens dost guide revolving worlds, and people the
abyss of space with millions of suns: say, what appearance do those human insects, which I can with
difficulty distinguish upon the earth, make in thy
eyes? When thou directest the stars in their orbits,
what to thee are the worms that crawl in the dust?
Of what importance to thy infinite greatness are their
distinctions of sects and parties? And how art thou
concerned with the subtleties engendered by their
folly?

And you, credulous men, shew me the efficacy of
your practices! During the many ages that you have
observed or altered them, what change have your
prescriptions wrought in the laws of nature? Has the
sun shone with greater brilliance? Has the course
of the seasons at all varied? Is the earth more fruitful, are the people more happy? If God be good,
how can he be pleased with your penances? If he
be infinite, what can your homage add to his glory?
Inconsistent men, answer these questions!

Ye conquerors, who pretend by your arms to serve

F

God, what need has he of your aid? If he wishes to
punish, are not earthquakes, valcanoes, and the thun-
derbolt in his hand? And does a God of clemency
know no other way of correcting but by extermina-
tion?

Ye Mussulmans, if your misfortunes were the chastisements of heaven for the violation of the *fire precepts,* would prosperity be showered on the Franks
who laugh at these things? If it is by the laws of
the Koran that God judges the earth, what were the
principles by which he governed the nations that existed before the prophet, the numerous people who
drank wine, eat pork, and travelled not to Mecca, yet
to whom it was given to raise powerful empires? By
what laws did he judge the Sabeans of Ninevah and
of Babylon; the Persian, who worshipped fire; the
Greek and Roman idolators; the ancient kingdoms of
the Nile, and your own progenitors the Arabs and
Tartars? How does he at present judge the various
nations that are ignorant of your worship, the numerous casts of Indians, the vast empire of the Chinese,
the swarthy tribes of Africa, the islanders of the Atlantic Ocean, the colonies of America?

Presumptuous and ignorant men, who arrogate to
yourselves the whole earth, were God to summon at
once all past and present generations, what proportion would those Christian and Mussulman sects, calling themselves *universal,* bear in the vast assemblage?
What would be the judgment of his fair and impar-
tial justice respecting the actual mass of mankind?
It is in estimating the general system of his government that you wander among multiplied absurdities?
and it is there, that in reality, truth presents itself in
all its evidence. It is there that we trace the simple
but powerful laws of nature and reason; the laws of
the common mover, the general cause; of a God im-
partial and just, who, that he might send his rain

upon a country, asks not who is its prophet; who
causes his sun equally to shine on all tribes of men,
whether distinguished by a fair or sable complexion,
on the Jew as on the Mussulman, on the Christian as
on the Heathen; who multiplies the inhabitants of
every country with whom order and industry reign;
who gives prosperity to every empire where justice is
observed, where the powerful is restrained, and the
poor man protected by the laws; where the weak
live in safety, and where all enjoy the rights which
they derive from nature and an equitable compact.

Such are the principles by which nations are
judged! This is the true religion by which the fate
of empires is regulated, and which, O Ottomans, has
ever decided that of your own empire! Interrogate
your ancestors; ask them by what means they rose
to greatness, when, idolators, few in number and poor,
they came from the deserts of Tartary to encamp in
these fertile countries? Ask them if it was by islamism, at that period unknown to them, that they conquered the Greeks and Arabs; or by their courage,
prudence, moderation, and unanimity, the true powers of the social state? Then the Sultan himself administered justice and maintained order: then the
prevaricating judge and the rapacious governor were
punished, and the multitude lived in ease: the cultivator was secure from the rapine of the janizary, and
the fields were productive, the public roads were safe,
and commerce flourished. It is true you were a
league of robbers, but among yourselves you were just.
You subjugated nations, but you did not oppress
them. Vexed by their own princes they preferred
being your tributaries. " Of what importance is it
to me," said the Christian, " whether my master be
pleased with images or breaks them in pieces, provided he. is just towards me? God will judge his
doctrine in heaven." You were temperate and har-

dy; your enemies soft and effeminate: you were
skilled in the art of battle; they had forgotten its
principles: you had experienced chiefs, warlike and
disciplined troops; the hope of booty excited ardour;
bravery was recompensed; disobedience and cowardice punished, and all the springs of the human
heart were in action. You thus conquered a hundred nations, and out of the mass founded an immense
empire.

But other manners succeeded. The laws of nature, however, did not less operate in your misfortunes than in your prosperity. You destroyed your
enemies, and your grasping ambition, still in force,
preyed upon yourselves. Having become rich, you
commenced an internal contest respecting the division
and the enjoyment of your riches, and disorder was
generated through every class of your society. The
Sultan, intoxicated with his greatness, misunderstood
the object of his functions, and all the vices of arbitrary power presently unfolded themselves. Meeting
with no obstacle to his desires, he became a depraved
character. Weak, and arrogant at the same time, he
spurned the people, and would no longer be influenced
and directed by their voice. Ignorant, and yet flattered, he neglected all instruction, all study, and sunk
into total incapacity. Become himself unqualified for
the conduct of affairs, he committed the trust to
hirelings, and these hirelings deceived him. To satisfy their own passions, they stimulated and increased
his; they multiplied his wants, and his enormous luxury devoured every thing. He was no longer content
with the frugal table, the modest attire, and the simple habitation of his ancestors: the earth and sea
must be exhausted to satisfy his pride; scarce furs
must be fetched from the pole, and costly tissues
from the equator; he consumed at a meal the tribute
of a city, and in a day the revenue of a province. He

became infested with an army of women, eunuchs, and courtiers. He was told that the virtue of kings consisted in liberality; and the munificence and treasures of the people were delivered into the hands of parasites. In imitation of the master, the slaves were also desirous of having magnificient houses, furniture of exquisite workmanship, carpets richly embroidered, vases of gold and silver for the vilest uses; and all the wealth of the empire was swallowed up in the *Serai*.

To supply this inordinate luxury the slaves and the women sold their influence; and venality introduced a general depravation. They sold the favour of the prince to the Visier, and the visier sold the empire. They sold the law to the Cadi, and the Cadi sold justice. They sold the altar to the priest, and the priest sold heaven. And gold obtaining every thing, nothing was left unpractised to obtain gold. For gold, friend betrayed friend; the child his father; the servant his master; the wife her honour; the merchant his conscience; and there no longer existed in the state either good faith, manners, concord, or stability.

The Pacha, who purchased his office, presently had recourse to the system of farming it for a revenue, and exercising upon it every species of extortion. He sold the collection of the taxes, the command of the troops, the administration of the districts; and, in proportion as every employment was temporary, rapine, diffusing itself from rank to rank, was rapid and precipitate. The excisemen oppressed the merchant by his exactions, and trade was annihilated. The Aga stript the husbandman, and cultivation was degraded. The labourer, robbed of his little capital, had not wherewith to sow his field: taxes nevertheless became due, and he was unable to pay them; he was threatened with corporal punishment, and driven to the expedient of a loan: specie, for want of security, was withdrawn from circulation; the interest of money became enormous, and usury aggravated the misery of the poor.

Inclement seasons, periods of dearth, had rendered the harvests abortive, but government would neither forgive nor postpone its demands. Distress began its career: a part of the inhabitants of the villages took refuge in the cities; the burthen upon those that remained became greater; their ruin was consummated, and the country depopulated.

Driven to the last extremity by tyranny and insult, certain villages broke out into rebellion. The Pacha considered the event as a subject of rejoicing; he made war upon them, took their houses by storm, ransacked their goods, and carried off their cattle. The soil became a desert, and he exclaimed, "What care I: I shall be removed from it to-morrow."

Yet again, the want of cultivation led one step farther. Periodical rains or swelling tides overflowed the banks, and covered the country with swamps: these swamps exhaled a putrid air, which spread chronical diseases, pestilence, and sickness, of a thousand forms, and was followed by a still farther decrease of population, by penury and ruin.

Oh! who can enumerate all the evils of this tyrannical system of government?

Sometimes the Pachas make war of themselves, and to avenge their personal quarrels, provinces are laid waste. Sometimes, dreading their masters, they aim at independence, and draw upon their subjects the chastisement of their revolt. Sometimes, fearing these very subjects, they call to their aid and keep in pay foreign troops; and to be sure of them, they indulge them in every kind of robbery. In one place, they commence an action against a rich man, and plunder him upon false pretences. In another, they suborn witnesses, and impose a fine for an imaginary offence. On all occasions they excite the hatred of sects against each other, and encourage informations for the sake of increasing their own corrupt advantages. They extort from men their property; they attack their persons, and when their imprudent avarice has heaped into one mass the riches of a province, the supreme government, with execrable perfidy, pretending to avenge the oppressed inhabitants, draws to itself their spoil in the spoil of the culprit, and wantonly and vainly expiate in blood the crime of which it was itself the accomplice.

O iniquitous beings, sovereigns or ministers, who sport with the life and property of the people! was it you who gave breath to man, that you take it from him? is it you who fertilize the earth, that you dissipate its fruits? Do you fatigue your arms with ploughing the field? Do you expose yourselves to the heat of the sun, and endure the torment of thirst in cutting down the harvest and binding it into sheaves? Do you watch like the shepherd in the nocturnal dew? Do you traverse deserts like the indefatigable merchant? Alas! when I have reflected on the cruelty and insolence of the powerful, my indignation has been roused, and I have said in my anger, What! will there never appear upon the earth a race of men who shall avenge the people and punish tyrants? A small number of robbers devour the multitude, and the multitude suffer themselves to be devoured! O degraded people, awake to the recognition of your rights! authority proceeds from you; yours is all the power. Vainly do kings command you *in the name of God* and *by their lance:* soldiers, obey not the summons. Since God supports the Sultan, your succour is useless; since the sword of heaven suffices him, he has no need of yours; let us see what he can do of himself.—The soldiers have laid down their arms; and lo, the masters of the world are as feeble as the meanest of their subjects! Ye people, know then that those who govern you are your chiefs and not you masters; your guardians appointed by yourselves, and not your proprietors; that your wealth is your own, and to you they are accountable for the administration of it; that kings or subjects, God has made all men equal, and no human being has a right to oppress his fellow-creature.

But this nation and its chiefs acknowledge not these sacred truths.—Be it so; they will suffer the consequences of their error. The decree is gone forth; the day approaches when this colosus of power shall be dashed to pieces, and fall, crushed by its own weight. Yes, I swear by the ruins of so many demolished empires, that the crescent shall undergo the same fate as the states whose mode of government it has imitated! A foreign people shall drive the Sultans from their metropolis; the throne of Orkhan shall be subverted; the last shoot of his race shall be cut off; and the horde of the Oguzians (*t*), deprived of their chief, shall be dispersed like that of the Nogaians. In this dissolution the subjects of the empire, freed from the yoke that held them together, will resume their ancient distinctions, and a general anarchy will take place, as happened in the empire of the Sophis (*u*), till there shall arise among the Arabs, the Armenians, or the Greeks, legislators who shall form new states. Oh! were a sagacious and hardy race of men to be found, what materials of greatness and glory are here!—But the hour of destiny is arrived. The cry of war strikes my ear, and the catastrophe is about to commence. In vain the Sultan draws out his armies; his ignorant soldiers are beaten and scattered. In vain he calls upon his subjects: their hearts are callous; his

subjects reply: " It is decreed; and what is it to
us who is to be master? we cannot loose by the
change." In vain these true believers invoke heaven
and the prophet; the prophet is dead, and heaven
without pity answers: " Cease to call upon me. You
are the authors of your calamities, find yourselves
their remedy. Nature has established laws, it becomes you to practice them. Examine and reflect
upon the events that take place, and profit by experience. It is the folly of man that works his destruction; it is his wisdom that must save him. The
people are ignorant; let them get understanding;
their chiefs are depraved, let them correct their vices and amend their lives, for such is the decree of
nature: *Since the evils of society flow from* IGNO-
RANCE *and* INORDINATE DESIRE, *men will never
cease to be tormented till they shall become intelligent and
wise; till they shall practice the art of justice, founded on a knowledge of the various relations in which
they stand, and the laws of their own organization**."

*A singular moral phenomenon made its appearance in Eu-
rope in the year 1788. A great nation, jealous of its liberty,
contracted a fondness for a nation the enemy of liberty; a nation friendly to the arts for a nation that detests them; a mild
and tolerant nation for a persecuting and fanatic one; a social
and gay nation for a nation whose characteristics are gloom and
misantrophy: in a word, the French were smitten with a passion
for the Turks: they were desirous of engaging in a war for
them, and that at a time when a revolution in their own country was just at its commencement. A man who perceived the
true nature of the situation, wrote a book to dissuade them
from the war: it was immediately pretended that he was paid
by the government, which in reality wished the war, and which
was upon the point of shutting him up in a state prison. Another man wrote to recommend the war: he was applauded, and
his word was taken in payment for the science, the politeness,
and importance of the Turks. It is true that he believed in his
own thesis, for he had found among them people who cast a
nativity, and alchemists who ruined his fortune; as he found

CHAP. XIII.

WILL THE HUMAN RACE BE EVER IN A BETTER
CONDITION THAN AT PRESENT.

OPPRESSED with sorrow at the predictions of the Genius, and the severity of his reasoning: unhappy nations, cried I, bursting into tears! Unhappy my own lot! I now despair of the felicity of man! since his evils flow from his own heart, since he must himself apply the remedy, woe for ever to his existence! For what can restrain the inordinate desire of the powerful? Who shall enlighten the ignorance of the weak? Who shall instruct the multitude in the knowledge of its rights, and force the chiefs to discharge the duties of their station? Individual will not cease to oppress individual, one nation to attack another nation, and never will the day of prosperity and glory again dawn upon these countries. Alas! conquerors will come; they will drive away the oppressors, and will establish themselves in their place; but, succeeding to their power, they will succeed also to their rapacity, and the earth will

---

Martinists at Paris, who enabled him to sup with Sesostris, and Magnetisers who concluded with destroying his existence. Notwithstanding this, the Turks were beaten by the Russians, and the man who then predicted the fall of their empire, persists in the prediction. The result of this fall will be a complete change of the political system, as far as it relates to the coast of the Mediterranean. If, however, the French become important in proportion as they become free, and if they will make use of the advantage they will obtain their progress may easily prove of the most honourable sort, inasmuch as, by the wise decrees of fate, the true interest of mankind evermore accords with their true morality.

have changed its tyrants, without lessening the tyranny.

Then turning towards the Genius: O Genius! said I, despair has taken hold of my heart. While you have instructed me in the nature of man, the depravity of governors, and the abjectness of those who are governed, you have given me a disgust to life; and since there is no alternative but to be the accomplice or the victim of oppression, what has the virtuous man to do but to join his ashes to those of the tombs.

The Genius, fixing upon me a look of severity mixed with compassion, was silent. After a few minutes he replied: Is it then in dying that virtue consists? The wicked man is indefatigable in the consummation of vice, and the just disheartened at the first obstacle which stands in the way of doing good! But such is the human heart: success intoxicates it to presumption, disappointment dejects and terrifies it. Always the victim of the sensation of the moment, it judges not of things by their nature but by the impulse of passion. Mortal, who despairest of the human race, upon what profound calculation of reasonings and events is your judgment formed? Have you scrutinized the organization of sensible beings, to determine with precision whether the springs that incline them to happiness are weaker than those which repel? or rather, viewing at a glance the history of the species, and judging of the future by the example of the past, have you hence discovered with certainty, that all proficiency is impossible? Let me ask: Have societies, since their origin, made no step towards instruction and a better state of things? Are men still in the woods, destitute of every thing, ignorant, stupid, and ferocious? Are there no nations advanced beyond the period, when nothing was to be seen upon the face of the globe but savage freebooters or savage slaves? If individuals have at certain times, and in certain places, become better, why should not the mass improve? If particular societies have attained a considerable degree of perfection, why should not the progress of the general society advance? If first obstacles have been overcome, why should succeeding ones be insurmountable.

But you are of opinion that the human race is degenerating? Guard yourself against the illusion and paradoxes of misanthrophy. Dissatisfied with the present, man supposes in the past a perfection which does not exist, and which is merely the discoloration of his chagrin. He praises the dead from enmity to the living, and employs the bones of the fathers as an instrument of chastisement against the children.

To establish this principle of a retrograde perfection, it is necessary that we should contradict the testimony of facts and reason. Nor is this all; the facts of history might indeed be equivocal, but it is farther necessary that we should contradict the living fact of the nature of man; that we should assert that he is born with a perfect science in the use of his senses; that, previous to experience, he is able to distinguish poison from aliment; that the sagacity of the infant is greater than that of his bearded progenitor; that the blind man can walk with more assurance than the man endued with sight; that man, the creature of civilization, is less favoured by circumstances than the cannibal; in a word, that there is no truth in the existing gradation of instruction and experience.

Young man, believe the voice of tombs and the testimony of monuments. There are countries which have doubtless fallen off from what they were at certain epochas: but if the understanding were to analyse thoroughly the wisdom and felicity of their inhabitants at those periods, their glory would be found to have less of reality than of splendour; it would be seen, that even in the most celebrated states of antiquity, there existed enormous vices and cruel abuses, the precise cause of their instability; that in general the principles of government were atrocious; that, from people to people, audacious robbery, barbarous wars, and implacable animosities were prevalent (x); that natural right was unknown: that morality was perverted by senseless fanaticism and deplorable superstition; that a dream, a vision, an oracle, were the frequent occasion of the most terrible commotions. Nations are not perhaps yet free from the power of these evils; but their force is at least diminished, and the experience of past times has not been wholly lost. Within the three last centuries especially, the light of knowledge has been increased and disseminated; civilization, aided by various happy circumstances, has perceptibly advanced, and even inconveniencies and abuses have proved advantageous to it; for if conquest have extended kingdoms and states beyond due bounds, the people of different countries, uniting under the same yoke, have lost that spirit of estrangement and division which made them all enemies to one another. If the hands of power have been strengthened, an additional degree of system and harmony has at least been introduced in its exercise. If wars have become more general in the mass of their influence and operation, they have been less destructive in their details. If the people carry to their combat less personality and less exertion, their struggless are less sanguinary and ferocious. If they are less free, they are less turbulent; if they are more effeminate, they are more pacific. Despotism itself seems not to have been unproductive of advantages: for if the government has been absolute, it has been less perturbed and tempestuous; if

thrones have been regarded as hereditary property,
they have excited less dissension, and exposed the
people to fewer convulsions: in fine, if despots, with
timid and mysterious jealousy, have interdicted all
knowledge of their administration, all rivalship for
the direction of affairs, the passions of mankind,
excluded from the political career, have fixed upon
the arts and the science of nature ; the sphere of
ideas has been enlarged on every side ; man, devoted
to abstract studies, has better understood his place
in the system of nature, and his social relations ;
principles have been more fully discussed, objects
more accurately discerned, knowledge more widely
diffused, individuals made more capable, manners
more sociable, life more benevolent and pleasing ; the
species at large, particularly in certain countries,
have been evidently gainers ; nor can this improvement fail to proceed, since its two principal obstacles,
those which have hitherto rendered it so slow, and
frequently retrograde, the difficulty of transmitting
ideas from age to age, and communicating them rapidly from man to man, have been removed.

With the people of antiquity, every canton and
every city, having a language peculiar to itself,
stood aloof from the rest, and the result was favourable to ignorance and anarchy : they had no communication of ideas, no participation of discoveries,
no harmony of interests or of will, no unity of action
or conduct.   Beside, the only means of diffusing
and transmitting ideas being that of speech, fugitive
and limited, and that of writing, slow of execution,
expensive, and acquired by few, there resulted an extreme difficulty as to instruction in the first instance,
the loss of advantages one generation might derive
from the experience of another, instability, retrogra-
dation of science, and one unvaried scene of chaos
and childhood.

On the contrary, in the modern world, and particularly in Europe, great nations having allied themselves by a sort of universal language, the firm of opinion has been placed upon a broad basis; the minds of men have sympathised, their hearts have enlarged: we have seen agreement in thinking, and concord in acting; in fine, that sacred art, that memorable gift of celestial genius, the press, furnished a means of communicating, of diffusing at one instance any idea to millions of the species, and of giving it a permanence which all the power of tyrants has been able neither to suspend nor suppress. Hence has the vast mass of instruction perpetually increased; hence has the atmosphere of truth continually grown brighter, and a strength of mind been produced that is in no fear of counteraction. And this improvement is the necessary effect of the laws of nature; for by the law of sensation, man as invincibly tends to make himself happy, as the flame to ascend, the stone to gravitate, the water to gain its level. His ignorance is the obstacle which misleads him as to the means, and deceives him respecting causes and effects. By force of experience he will become enlightened; by force of errors he will set himself right; he will become wise and good, because it is his interest to be so: and ideas communicating themselves through a nation, whole classes will be instructed, science will be universally familiar, and all men will understand what are the principles of individual happiness, and of public felicity. They will understand what are their respective relations, their rights, and their duties, in the social order; they will no longer be the dupes of inordinate desire; they will perceive that morality is a branch of the science of physics, composed it is true, of elements complicated in their operation, but simple and invariable in their nature, as being no other than the elements of human organization itself. They will feel the necessity of being moderate and just, because therein consists the advantage and security of each; that to wish to enjoy at the expence of another is a false calculation of ignorance, because the result of such proceeding, are reprisals, enmity, and revenge; and that dishonesty is invariably the offspring of folly.

Individuals will feel that private happiness is allied to the happiness of society.

The weak, that instead of dividing their interests, they ought to unite, because equality constitutes their strength.

The rich, that the measure of enjoyment is limited by the constitution of the organs and that lassitude follows satiety.

The poor, that the highest degree of human felicity consists in peace of mind and the due employment of time.

Public opinion, reaching kings on their thrones, will oblige them to keep themselves within the bounds of a regular authority.

Chance itself, serving the cause of nations, will give them sometimes incapable chiefs, who, through weakness, will suffer them to become free; and sometimes enlightened chiefs, who will virtuously emancipate them:

Individuality will be a term of greater comprehension, and nations, free and enlightened, will hereafter become one complex individual, as single men are now: the consequences will be proportioned to the state of things. The communication of knowledge will extend from society to society, till it comprehends the whole earth. By the law of imitation the example of one people will be followed by others, who will adopt its spirit and its laws. Despots themselves, perceiving that they can no longer maintain their power without justice and beneficence, will be induced, both from necessity and rivalship, to soften the rigour of

their government; and civilization will be universal.
—Among nations there will be established an equilibrium of force, which, confining them within the
limits of just respect for their reciprocal rights, will
put an end to the barbarous practice of war, and
induce them to submit to civil arbitration the decision of their disputes (*y*); and the whole species
will become one grand society, one individual family
governed by the same spirit, by common laws, and
enjoying all the felicity of which human nature is
capable.

This great work will doubtless be long accomplishing, because it is necessary that one and the same
motion should be communicated to the various parts of
an immense body, that the same leaven should assimilate
an enormous mass of heretogeneous elements: but
this motion will effectually operate. Already society
at large, having passed through the same stages as
particular societies have done, promises to lead to
the same results. At first, disconnected in its parts,
each individual stood alone; and this intellectual solitude .constituted its age of anarchy and childhood.
Divided afterwards into sections of irregular size, as
chance directed, which have been called states and
kingdoms, it has experienced the fatal effects which
result from the inequality of wealth and conditions;
and the aristocracy by which great empires have
domineered over their dependencies, have formed its
second age. In process of time, these paramount
chiefs of the globe have disputed with each other for
superiority, and then was seen the period of factions
and civil broils. And now the parties, tired of their
discords and feeling the want of laws, sigh for the
epocha of order and tranquility. Let but a virtuous
chief arise, a powerful and just people appear, and
the earth will arrive at supreme power. It waits a
legislative people; this is the object of its wishes and

its prayers, and my heart hears its voice.—Then turning to the quarter of the West: Yes, continued he, a hollow noise already strikes my ear; the cry of liberty, uttered upon the farther shore of the Atlantic, has reached to the old continent. At this cry a secret murmur against oppression is excited in a powerful nation; a salutary alarm takes place respecting its situation; it enquires what it is and what it ought to be; it examines into its rights, its resources, and what has been the conduct of its chiefs. One day, one reflection more—and an immense agitation will arise, a new age will make its appearance, an age of astonishment to vulgar minds, of surprise and dread to tyrants, of emancipation to a great people, and of hope to the whole world.

CHAP. XIV.

GRAND OBSTACLE TO IMPROVEMENT.

THE Genius stopt. My mind, however, pre-occu-pied with gloomy forebodings, yielded not to persua-sion; but fearful of offending him by opposition, I made no reply. After a short interval; fixing on me a look that transpierced my soul: You are silent, said he, and your heart is agitated with thoughts which it dares not utter!—Confused and terrified: O Genius, I made answer, pardon my weakness: truth alone has doubtless proceeded from your lips; but your celestial intelligence can distinguish its traits, where to my gross faculties there appear nothing but clouds. I acknowledge it, conviction has not penetrated my soul, and I feared that my doubts might give you offence.

And what is doubt, replied he, that it should be

regarded as a crime? Has man the power of thinking
contrary to the impressions that are made upon him?
If a truth be palpable, and its observance important,
let us pity the man who does not perceive it: his
punishment will infallibly spring from his blindness.
If it be uncertain and equivocal, how is he to find
in it what does not exist? To believe without evidence
and demonstration is an act of ignorance and folly.
The credulous man involves himself in a labyrinth
of contradictions; the man of sense examines and
discusses every question, that he may be consistent
in his opinions; he can endure contradiction, because
from the collision evidence arises. Violence is the
argument of falsehood; and to impose a creed
authoritatively, is the index and proceeding of a
tyrant.

Emboldened by these sentiments, I replied: O
Genius, since my reason is free, I strive in vain to
welcome the flattering hope with which you would
console me. The sensible and virtuous soul is prone
enough to be hurried away by dreams of fancied
happiness; but a cruel reality incessantly recals its
attention to suffering and wretchedness. The more
I meditate on the nature of man, the more I examine
the present state of society, the less possible does it
appear to me that a world of wisdom and felicity
should ever be realized. I survey the face of our
whole hemisphere, and no where can I perceive the
germ of a happy revolution. All Asia is buried in
the most profound darkness. The Chinese, subjected
to an insolent despotism (z), dependent for their
fortune upon the decision of lots, and held in awe by
strokes of the bamboo, inslaved by the immutability
of the code, and by the irremediable vice of their
language, offer to my view an abortive civilization
and a race of automata. The Indian, fettered by
prejudice, and manacled by the inviolable institution

of his casts, vegetates in an incurable apathy. The Tartar, wandering or fixed, at all times ignorant and ferocious, lives in the barbarity of his ancestors. The Arab, endowed with a happy genius, loses its force and the fruit of his labour in the anarchy of his tribes, and the jealousy of his families. The African, degraded from the state of man, seems irremediably devoted to servitude. In the north I see nothing but serfs, reduced to the level of cattle, the live stock of the estate upon which they live (1). Ignorance, tyranny, and wretchedness, have every where struck the nations with stupor; and vicious habits, depraving the natural senses, have destroyed the very instinct of happiness and truth. In some countries of Europe, indeed, reason begins to expand its wings; but even there, is the knowledge of individual minds common to the nation? Has the superiority of the government been turned to the advantage of the people? And these people, who call themselves polished, are they not those who three centuries ago filled the earth with their injustice? Are they not those who, under the pretext of commerce, laid India waste, dispeopled a new continent, and who at present subject Africa to the most inhuman slavery? Can liberty spring up out of the bosom of despots, and justice be administered by the hands of rapacity and avarice! O Genius! I have beheld civilized countries, and the illusion of their wisdom has vanished from my sight. I saw riches accumulated in the hands of a few individuals, and the multitude poor and destitute. I saw all right and power concentrated in certain classes, and the mass of the people passive and dependent. I saw the palaces of princes, but no incorporation of individuals as such, no common-hall of nations. I perceived the deep attention that was given to the interests of government; but no public interest, no sympathetic spirit. I saw that the whole science of those who command consisted in prudently oppressing; and the refined servitude of polished nations only appeared to me the more irremediable.

With one obstacle in particular my mind was sensibly struck. In surveying the globe, I perceived that it was divided into twenty different systems of religious worship. Each nation has received, or formed for itself, opposite opinions, and ascribing to itself exclusively the truth, has imagined every other to be in error. But if, as is the fact, in this discordance the majority deceive themselves with sincerity, it follows that the human mind as readily imbibes falsehood as truth; and in that case how is it to be enlightened? How are prejudices to be extirpated that first take root in the mind? How is the bandage to be removed from the eyes, when the first article in every creed, the first dogma of all religions, is the proscription of doubt, of examination, and of the right of private judgment? How is truth to make itself known? If she resort to the demonstration of argument, pusillanimous man appeals against evidence to his conscience. If she call in the aid of divine authority, already prepossessed, he opposes an authority of a similar kind, and treats all innovation as blasphemy. Thus, in his blindness, rivetting the chains upon himself, does he become the sport of his ignorance and passions. To dissolve these fatal shackles, a miraculous concurrence of happy circumstances would be necessary. It would be necessary that a whole nation, cured of the delirium of superstition, should no longer be liable to the impressions of fanaticism; that, freed from the yoke of a false doctrine, it should voluntarily embrace the genuine system of morality and reason; that it should become at once courageous and prudent, wise and docile; that every individual, acquainted with his rights, should scrupulously observe their limits; and the poor should know how to resist seduction, and the rich the allurements of avarice; that there should be found upright and disinterested chiefs; that its tyrants should be seized with a spirit of madness and folly; that the people, recovering their powers, should perceive their inability to exercise them, and consent to appoint delegates; that having first created their magistrates, they should know both how to respect and how to judge them; that in the rapid renovation of a whole nation pervaded with abuse, each individual, removed from his former habits, should suffer patiently the pains and self-denials annexed; in fine that the nation should have the courage to conquer its liberty, the wisdom to secure it, the power to defend it, and the generosity to communicate it. Can sober judgment expect this combination of circumstances! Should fortune in the infinite variety of her caprices produce them; is it likely that I should live to see that day? Will not this frame long before that have mouldered in the tomb?

Here, oppressed with sorrow, my heart deprived me of utterance. The Genius made no reply; but in a low tone of voice I heard him say to himself: " Let us revive the hope of this man; for if he who loves his fellow-creatures be suffered to despair, what is to become of nations? The past is perhaps but too much calculated to deject him. Let us then anticipate futurity; let us unveil the astonishing age that is about to rise, that virtue, seeing the end of its wishes, animated with new vigour, may redouble its efforts to hasten the accomplishment of it."

CHAP. XV.

NEW AGE.

SCARCELY had the Genius uttered to himself these words than an immense noise proceeded from the West; and turning my eyes to that quarter, I perceived at the extremity of the Mediterranean, in the country of one of the European nations, a prodigious movement, similar to what exists in the bosom of a large city when, pervaded with sedition, an innumerable people, like waves, fluctuate in the streets and public places. My ear, struck with their cries, which assended to the very heavens, distinguished at intervals these phrases:

" What is this new prodigy? What this cruel and mysterious scourge? We are a numerous people, and we want strength! We have an excellent soil, and we are destitute of provision! We are active and labourious, and we live in indigence! We pay enormous tributes, and we are told that they are not sufficient! We are at peace without, and our persons and property are not safe within! What then is the secret enemy that devours us!"

From the midst of the concourse, some individual voices replied: "Erect a standard of distinction, and let all those who, by useful labours, contribute to the support and maintenance of society, gather round it, and you will discover the enemy that preys on your vitals."

The standard being erected, the nation found itself suddenly divided into two bodies of unequal magnitude and dissimilar appearance; the one innumerable and nearly integral, exhibited, in the general poverty

of their dress, and in their meagre and sunburnt
faces, the marks of toil and wretchedness; the other
a petty groupe, a valueless faction, presented, in their
rich attire, embroidered with gold and silver, and in
their sleak and ruddy complexions, the symptoms of
leisure and abundance.   Considering these men more
attentively, I perceived that the large body was constituted of labourers, artisans, tradesmen, and every
profession useful to society, and that in the lesser
groupe there were none but priests, courtiers, public
accountants, commanders of troops: in short, the civil,
military, or religious agents of government.

The two bodies being front to front assembled, and
having looked with astonishment at each other, I saw
the feelings of indignation and resentment spring up
in the one, and a sort of panic in the other; and the
large said to the small body:

Why stand you apart? Are you not of our
number?

No, replied the groupe; you are the people; we
are a privileged class; we have laws customs and rites
peculiar to ourselves.

People.   And what labour do you perform in the
society.

Privileged Class. None: we are not made to labour.
People.   How then have you acquired your wealth.
Privileged Class. By taking the pains to govern
you.

People.   To govern us! and is this what you call
governing? We toil, and you enjoy; we produce, and
you dissipate; wealth flows from us, and you absorb
it.—Privileged men, class distinct from the people,
form a nation apart and govern yourselves (2).

Then deliberating on their new situation, some
among the groupe said: Let us join the people, and
partake their burthens and cares; for they are men
like ourselves.   Others replied: To mix with the

herd would be degrading and vile: they are born to serve us, who are men of a superior race. The civil governors said: the people are mild and naturally servile; let us speak to them in the name of the King and the law, and they will return to their duty. People; the King decrees, the sovereign ordains.

People. The King cannot decree any thing which the safety of the people does not demand; the sovereign cannot ordain but according to law.

Civil Governors. The law calls upon you for submission.

People. The law is the general will; and we will a new order.

Civil Governors. You are in that case rebels.

People. A nation cannot be a rebel; tyrants only are rebels.

Civil Governors. The King is on our side, and he enjoins you to submit.

People. Kings cannot be separated from the nation in which they reign. Our King cannot be on your side; you have only the phantom of his countenance.

Then the military governors advanced, and they said: The people are timorous; it is proper to threaten them; they will yield to the influence of force.— Soldiers, chastise this insolent multitude.

People. Soldiers, our blood flows in your veins! will you strike your brothers? If the people be destroyed, who will maintain the army?

And the soldiers, grounding their arms, said to their chiefs: We are part of the people; we whom you call upon to fight against them.

Then the ecclesiastical governors said: There is but one resource left. The people are superstitious: it is proper to overawe them with the name of God and religion.

Priests. Our dear brethren, our children, God has commissioned us to govern you.

People. Produce the patent of his commission.

Priests. You must have faith; reason leads men into guilt,

People. And would you govern us without reason?

Priests. God is the God of peace; religion enjoins you to obey.

People. No; justice goes before peace; obedience implies a law, and renders necessary the cognizance of it.

Priests. This world was intended for trial and suffering.

People. Do you then shew us the example of suffering.

Priests. Would you live without Gods or Kings?

People. We abjure tyranny of every kind.

Priests. You must have mediators, persons who may act in your behalf.

People. Mediators with God, and mediators with the King! Courtiers and priests, your services are too expensive; henceforth we take our affairs into our own hands.

Then the smaller groupe exclaimed: It is over with us; the multitude are enlightened. And the people replied: You shall not be hurt; we are enlightened, and we will commit no violence. We desire nothing but our rights: resentment we cannot but feel, but we consent to pass it by: we were slaves, we might now command; but we ask only to be free, and free we are.

—

CHAP. XVI.

A FREE AND LEGISLATIVE PEOPLE.

I NOW reflected with myself that public power was at a stand, that the habitual government of this

people was annihilated, and I shuddered at the
idea of their falling into the dissolution of anarchy.
But taking their affairs immediately into their
consideration, they quickly dispelled my apprehensions.

"It is not enough," said they, "that we have
freed ourselves from parasites, and tyrants, we must
prevent for ever the revival of their power. We are
human beings, and we know, by dear-bought experience, that every human being incessantly grasps at
authority, and wishes to enjoy it at the expence
of others. It is therefore necessary to guard ourselves
beforehand against this unfortunate propensity, the
prolific parent of discord; it is necessary to establish
rules by which our rights are to be determined and
our conduct governed But in this investigation
abstruse and difficult questions are involved, which
demand all the attention and faculties of the wisest
men. Occupied in our respective callings, we have
neither leisure for these studies, nor are we compe-
tent of ourselves to the exercise of such functions.
Let us select from our body certain individuals, to
whom the employment will be proper. To them let
our common powers be delegated, to frame for us
a system of government and laws: let us constitute
them the representatives of our interests and our
wills; and that this representation may be as accurate
as possible, and have comprehended in it the whole
diversity of our wills and interests, let the individuals
that comprise it be numerous, and citizens like ourselves."

The selection being made, the people thus addressed their delegates: "We have hitherto lived in a
society formed by chance, without fixed clauses,
without free conventions, without stipulation of
rights, without reciprocal engagements; and a multitude of disorders and evils have been the result of
this confused state of things. We would now, with

mature deliberation, frame a regular compact; and we have made choice of you to draw up the articles of it. Examine then with care what ought to be its basis and principles. Investigate the object and tendency of every association; observe what are the rights which every individual brings into it, the powers he cedes for the public good, and the powers which he reserves entire to himself. Communicate to us equitable laws and rules of conduct. Prepare for us a new system of government, for we feel that the principles, which to this day have guided us, are corrupt. Our fathers have wandered in the paths of ignorance, and we from habit have trod in their steps. Every thing is conducted by violence, fraud, or delusion; and the laws of morality and reason are still buried in obscurity. Do you unfold the chaos; discover the time, order, and connexion of things; publish your code of laws and rights; and we will conform to it."

And this people raised an immense throne in the form of a pyramid, and seating upon it the men they had chosen, said to them: " We raise you this day above us, that you may take a more comprehensive view of our relations, and be exalted above the atmosphere of our passions.

" But remember that you are citizens like ourselves; that the power which we confer upon you belongs to us; that we give it as a trust for which you are responsible, not as exclusive property, or hereditary right; that the laws which you make, you will be the first to submit to; that to-morrow you will descend from your stations, and rank again with us; that you will have acquired no distinguishing right, but the right to our gratitude and esteem. And oh! with what glory will the universe, that reveres so many apostles of error, honour the first assembly of enlightened and reasonable men, who shall have declared the immutable principles of justice to mankind, and consecrated, in the very face of tyrants, the rights of nations."

———

CHAP. XVII.

UNIVERSAL BIAS OF ALL RIGHT AND ALL LAW.

THESE men, chosen by the people to investigate the true principles of morality and reason, then proceeded to the object of their mission; and, after a long examination, having discovered a universal and fundamental principle, they said to their constituents: "We have employed our faculties in the investigation you demand of us, and we conceive the following to be the primordial bias and physical origin of all justice and all right.

"Whatever be the active power, the moving cause, that directs the universe, this power having given to all men the same organs, the same sensations, and the same wants, has thereby sufficiently declared that it has also given them the same rights to the use of its benefits; and that in the order of nature all men are equal.

"Secondly, inasmuch as this power has given to every man the ability of preserving and maintaining his own existence, it clearly follows, that all men are constituted independent of each other, that they are created free, that no man can be subject and no man sovereign, but that all men are the unlimited proprietors of their own persons.

"Equality, therefore, and liberty, are two essential attributes of man, two laws of the Divinity, not less essential and immutable, than the physical properties of inanimate nature.

H 3

" Again, from the principle, that every man is the unlimited master of his own person, it follows, that one inseparable condition in every contract and engagement is the free and voluntary consent of all the persons therein bound.

" Farther, because every individual is equal to every other individual, it follows, that the balance of receipts and payments, in political society, ought to be rigorously in equilibrium with each other; so that from the idea of equality immediately flows that other idea of equity and justice*.

" Finally, equality and liberty constitute the physical and unalterable basis of every union of men in society, and of consequence the necessary and generating principle of every law and regular system of government (3).

" It is because this basis has been invaded, that the disorders have been introduced among you, as in every other nation, which have at length excited you to resistance.   It is by returning once more to a conformity with this rule, that you can reform abuses and reconstitute a happy order of society.

" We are bound, however, to observe to you, that from this regeneration there will result an extreme shock to be endured in your habits, in your fortunes, and in your prejudices. Vicious contracts must be dissolved, unjust prejudices abolished, imaginary distinctions surrendered, and iniquitous descriptions of property abrogated : in fine, you must set out once more from the state of nature.   Consider whether you are capable of these mighty sacrifices."

They concluded : and, while I reflected upon the inherent cupidity of the human heart, I was induced to believe that the people would reject a melioration

* The etymology of the words themselves trace out to us this connexion : *equilibrium, equalitas, equitas,* are all of one family, and the physical idea of *equality* in the scales of a balance is the source and type of all the rest.

presented under such austere colours. I was mistaken. Instantly a vast crowd of men thronged towards the throne, and solemnly abjured all riches and all distinctions. " Unfold to us, (cried they, the laws of equality and liberty : we disclaim all future possession that is not held in the sacred name of justice. *Equality, liberty, justice,* these are our inviolable code : these names shall inscribe our standard."

Immediately the people raised a mighty standard, varied with three colours, and upon which those three words were written. They unfurled it over the throne of the legislators, and now for the first time the symbol of universal and equal justice appeared upon the earth. In front of the throne the people built an altar, on which they placed golden scales, a sword, and a book with this legend : TO EQUAL LAW, THE PROTECTOR, AND THE JUDGE. They then drew round the throne a vast amphitheatre, and the nation seated itself to hear the publication of the law. Millions of men, in act of solemn appeal to heaven, lifted up their hands together, and swore, " that they would live equal, free, and just ; that they would respect the rights and property of each other ; that they would yield obedience to the law and its Ministers regularly appointed."

A sight like this, so full of sublimity and energy, so interesting by the generous emotions it implied, melted me into tears ; and addressing myself to the Genius, I said : " Now may I live ! for after this there is nothing which I am not daring enough to hope."

CHAP. XVIII.

CONSTERNATION AND CONSPIRACY OF TYRANTS.

MEANWHILE, scarcely had the solemn cry of liberty and equality resounded through the earth, than astonishment and apprehension were excited in the different nations. In one place, the multitude, moved by desire, but wavering between hope and fear, between a sense of their rights and the habitual yoke of slavery, betrayed symptoms of agitation: in another, kings suddenly roused from the sleep of indolence and despotism, were alarmed for the safety of their thrones: every where those classes of civil and religious tyrants, who deceive princes and oppress the people, were seized with rage and consternation; and, concerting plans of perfidy, they said to one another: " Woe be to us, should this fatal cry of liberty reach the ear of the multitude, and this destructive spirit of justice be disseminated."—And seeing the standard waving in the air: " What a swarm of evils, cried they, are included in these three words! If all men are equal, where is our exclusive rights to honours and power? If all men are or ought to be free, what becomes of our slaves, our vassals, our property? If all are equal in a civil capacity, where are our privileges of birth and succession, and what becomes of nobility? If all are equal before God, where will be the need of mediators, and what is to become of the priesthood? Ah! let us accomplish, without a moment's delay, the destruction of a germ so prolific and contagious! let us employ the whole force of our art against this calamity. Let us sound the alarm to kings, that they may join in our cause. Let us divide the people; let us engage them in war, and turn aside their attention by conquests and national jealousy.   Let us excite their apprehensions respecting the power of this free nation. Let us form a grand league against the common enemy. Let us pull down the sacrilegious standard, demolish this throne of rebellion, and quench this fire of revolution in its outset."

And in reality the civil and religious tyrants of the people entered into a general combination, and having gained, either by constraint or seduction, multitudes on their side, they advanced in an hostile manner against the free nation.   Surrounding the altar and throne of natural law, they demanded, with loud cries : " What is this new and heretical doctrine ? What this impious altar, this sacrilegious worship ? True believers and loyal subjects ! Would you not suppose that to-day truth has been first discovered, and that hitherto you have been involved in error ? Would you not suppose that these men, more fortunate than yourselves, have alone the privilege of being wise ? And you, rebel and guilty nation, do you not feel that your chiefs mislead you ? That they adulterate the principles of your faith, and overturn the religion of your fathers ? Tremble lest the wrath of heaven be lighted against you ; and hasten by speedy repentance to expatiate your error."

But inaccessible to seduction as to terror, the free nation kept silence : it maintained an exact discipline in arms, and continued to exhibit an imposing attitude.

And the legislators said to the chiefs of nations : " If when we went on with our eyes hood-winked, our steps did not fail to be enlightened, why now that the bandage is removed, should we conceive that we are involved in darkness ? If we, who prescribe to mankind to exert their faculties, deceive and mislead them, what can be expected from those who desire only to maintain them in blindness? Ye chiefs of nations, if you possess truth, communicate it: we shall receive it with gratitude: for with ardour we pursue it, and with interest shall engage in the discovery. We are men, and may be deceived; but you also are men, and as fallible as ourselves. Assist us in this labyrinth, in which the human species has wandered for so many ages; assist us to dissipate the illusion of evil habits and prejudice. Enter the lists with us in the shock of opinions which dispute for our acceptance, and engage with us in tracing the pure and proper character of truth. Let us terminate to-day the long combat of error; let us establish between it and truth a solemn contest: let us call in men of every nation to assist us in the judgment: let us convoke a general assembly of the world; let them be judges in their own cause; and in the successive trial of every system, let no champion and no argument be wanting to the side of prejudice or of reason. In fine, let a fair examination of the result of the whole give birth to universal harmony of minds and opinions."

CHAP. XIX.

GENERAL ASSEMBLY OF THE PEOPLE.

THUS spoke the legislators of this free people; and the multitude, seized with the spirit of admiration, which every reasonable proposition never fails to inspire, shouted their applause, and the tyrants remained alone, overwhelmed with confusion.

A scene of a new and astonishing nature then presented itself to my view. All the people and nations of the globe, every race of men from every climate, advancing on all sides, seemed to assemble in one inclosure, and form in distinct groupes an immense congress. The motley appearance of this innumerable crowd, occasioned by their diversity of dress, of features, and of complexion, exhibited a most extraordinary and most attractive spectacle.

On one side I could distinguish the European with his short and close habit, his triangular hat, smooth chin, and powdered hair; and on the opposite side the Asiatic with a flowing robe, a long beard, a shaved head, and a circular turban. Here I observed the inhabitants of Africa, their skin of the colour of ebony, their hair woolly, their body girt with white and blue fish-skin, and adorned with bracelets and collars of corals, shells, and glass-beads; there the northern tribes, inveloped in bags of skin; the Laplander with his piked bonnet and his snow-shoes; the Samoiede with glowing limbs and with a strong odour; the Tongouse with his bonnet shaped like a horn, and carrying his idols pendant from his neck; the Yakoute with his freckled skin; the Calmuck with flattened nose and with little eyes, forced as it were to have no correspondence with each other. Farther in the distance were the Chinese, attired in silk, and with their hair hanging in tresses; the Japanese of mingled race; the Malayans with spreading ears, with a ring in their nose, and with a vast hat of the leaves of the palm-tree (4): and the *Tatoued* inhabitants of the islands of the ocean and of the continent of the Antipodes *. The contemplation of one species thus infinitely varied, of one understanding thus modified with extravagance, of one organization assuming so contrary appearances, gave me a very complicated sensation, and excited in me a thousand thoughts (5). I contemplated with astonishment this gradation of colour, from a bright carnation to a brown scarcely less bright, a dark brown, a muddy brown, bronze, olive, leaden, copper, as far

* The country of the *Papons*, or New Guinea.

as to the black of ebony and jet. I observed the Cassimerean, with his rose-coloured cheek, next in vicinity to the sun-burnt Hindoo; the Georgian standing by the Tartar; and I reflected upon the effect of climate, hot or cold, of soil mountainous or deep, marshy or dry, wooded or open. I compared the dwarf of the pole with the giant of the temperate zone; the lank Arab with the pot-bellied Hollander; the squat figure of the Samoiede with the tall and slender form of the Slavonian and the Greek; the greasy and woolly head of the Negro with the shining locks of the Dane; the flat-faced Calmuck, with his eyes angle-wise to each other and his nose crushed, to the oval and swelling vissage, the large blue eyes, and the aquiline nose, of the Circassian and the Abassin. I contrasted the painted linens of India with the workmanlike cloths of Europe; the rich furs of Silesia: the various clothing of savage nations, skins of fishes, platting of reeds, interweaving of leaves and feathers, together with the blue stained figures of serpents, stars, and flowers, with which their skin is varied. Sometimes the general appearance of this multitude reminded me of the enamelled meadows of the Nile and the Euphrates, when after rains and inundations, millions of flowers unfold themselves on all sides; and sometimes it resembled, in murmuring sound and busy motion, the innumerable swarms of grasshoppers which alight in the spring like a cloud upon the plains of Hauran.

At sight of so many living and percipient animals, I recollected, on one side, the immense multitude of thoughts and sensations which were crowded into this space; and on the other, reflected on the contest of so many opinions and prejudices, and the struggle of many capricious passions; and I was struck with astonishment, admiration, and apprehension. When the legislators, having enjoined silence, presently fixed my attention on themselves.

" Inhabitants of the earth, (said they), a free and powerful nation addresses you in the name of justice and of peace, and offers, as the sure pledge of its sincerity, its conviction and experience.   We were for a long time tormented with the same evils as you; we have inquired into their origin, and we have found them to be derived from violence and injustice, which the inexperience of past ages established into laws, and the prejudices of the present generation have supported and cherished.   Then, abolishing every factious and arbitrary institution, and ascending to the source of reason and of right, we perceived that there existed in the order of the universe, and in the physical constitution of man, eternal and immutable laws, which waited only his observance to render him happy.   O men of different climes ! look to the heavens that gave you light, to the earth that nourishes you ! Since they present to you all the same gifts ; since the Power that directs their motions has bestowed on you **the** same life, the same organs, the same wants, has it not also given you the same right to the use of its benefits ? Has it not hereby declared you all to be equal and free ? What mortal then shall dare refuse to his fellow-creature that which is granted him by nature ? O nations ! let us banish all tyranny and discord ; let us form one society, one vast family ; and, since mankind are all constituted alike, let there henceforth exist but one law, that of nature ; one code, that of reason ; one throne, that of justice ; one altar, that of union."

They ceased : and the multitude rended the skies with applause and acclamation ; and in their transports made the earth resound with the words *equality, justice, union !* But different feelings presently succeeded to this first emotion.   The doctors and chiefs of the people exciting in them a spirit of disputation, there arose a kind of murmur, which, spreading from groupe to groupe, was converted into uproar,

I

and from uproar into disorder of the first magnitude. Every nation assumed exclusive pretensions, and claimed the preference for its own opinions and code.

"You are in error," said the parties, pointing to each other; "we alone are in possession of reason and truth: ours is the true law, the genuine rule of justice and right, the sole means of happiness and perfection: all other men are either blind or rebellious." And the agitation became extreme.

But the legislators having proclaimed silence; "People (said they), by what impulse of passion are you agitated: Where will this quarrel conduct you? What advantage do you expect from this dissension? For ages has the earth been a field of disputation, and torrents of blood have been shed to decide the controversy: What profit have you reaped from so many combats and tears? When the strong has subjected the weak to his opinion, has he thereby furthered the cause of evidence and truth? O nations, take counsel of your own wisdom! If disputes arise between families, or individuals, by what mode do you reconcile them; do you not appoint arbitrators?" "Yes," exclaimed the multitude unanimously. Treat then the authors of your present dissensions in a similar manner. Command those, who call themselves your instructors, and who impose on you their creed, to discuss in your presence the arguments on which it is founded. Since they appeal to your interests, understand in what manner your interests are treated by them. And you, chiefs and doctors of the people, before you involve them in the discordance of your opinions, let the reasons for and against these opinions be fairly discussed. Let us establish a solemn controversy, a public investigation of truth, not before the tribunal of a rail individual, or a prejudiced party, but in presence of the united information and interests of mankind; and let the natural sense of the whole species be our arbitrator and judge."

CHAP. XX.

INVESTIGATION OF TRUTH.

THE people having by shouts expressed their approbation, the legislators said : " That we may proceed in this grand work with order and regularity, let a spacious amphitheatre be formed in the sand before the altar of union and peace : let each system of religion, and each particular sect, erect its proper and distinguishing standard in points of the circumference ; let its chiefs and its doctors place themselves round it, and let their followers be ranged in a right line terminated by the standard."

The amphitheatre being traced out, and order proclaimed, a prodigious number of standards were instantly raised, similar to what is seen in a commercial port, when on days of festivity, the flags of a hundred nations stream from a forest of masts. At sight of this astonishing diversity, I addressed myself to the Genius : I scarcely supposed the earth, said I, to be divided into more than eight or ten different systems of religion, and I then despaired of conciliation : how can I now hope for concord when I behold thousands of different parties !—These, however, replied the Genius, are but a part of what exist; and yet they would be intolerant.

As the groupes advanced to take their stations, the Genius, pointing out to me the symbols and attributes of each, thus explained to me their meaning.

That first groupe, said he, with a green standard, on which you see displayed a cross, a bandage, and a sabre, is formed of the followers of the Arabian prophet. To believe in a God (without knowing what he is); to have faith in the words of a man (without understanding the language in which he speaks); to travel into a desert in order to pray to the Deity (who is every where); to wash the hands with water (and not abstain from blood); to fast all day (and practise intemperance at night); to give alms of their own property (and to plunder the property of their neighbour): such are the means of perfection instituted by Mahomet, such the signals and characteristics of his true followers; and whoever professes not these tenets, is considered as a reprobate, has the sacred anathema denounced against him, and is devoted to the sword. A God of clemency, the author of life, has, according to them, instituted these laws of oppression and murder; has instituted them for the whole universe, though he has condescended to reveal them but to one man: has established them from all eternity, though they were made known by him but yesterday. These laws are sufficient for all the purposes of life, and yet a volume is added to them; this volume was to diffuse light, to exhibit evidence, to lead to perfection and happiness, and yet, in the very life-time of its prophet, its pages, every where abounding with obscure, ambiguous, and contradictory passages, needed explanation and commentaries; and the persons who undertook to interpret them, varying in opinion, became divided into sects and parties opposite and inimicable to each other. One maintains that Ali is the true successor, and another takes the part of Omar and Aboubekre. This denies the eternity of the Koran, that the necessity of ablutions and prayers. The Carmite proscribes pilgrimage, and allows the use of wine; the Hakemite preaches the doctrine of transmigration, and thus are there sects to the number of seventy-two, of which you may enumerate the different standards (6). In this discordance, each ascribing the evidence exclusively to itself, and stigmatizing the rest with heresy and rebellion, has turned against them its sanguinary zeal. And this religion, which celebrates a beneficent and merciful God, the common parent of the whole human race, converted into a torch of discord and an incentive to war, has never ceased for twelve hundred years to whelm the earth in blood, and spread ravage and desolation from one extremity of the ancient hemisphere to the other (7).

The men you see distinguished by their vast white turbans, their hanging sleeves and long rosaries, are the Imans, the Mollas, and the Muftis; and not far from them are the Dervises with a pointed bonnet, and the Santons with their sacred tonsure. They utter with vehemence their several confessions of faith; they dispute with eagerness respecting the more or less important sources of impurity; the mode of performing ablutions; the attributes and perfections of God; the Chaitan and the good and evil Genii; death; the resurrection; the interrogatory which succeeds the tomb; the passage of the perilous bridge, and its hair-breadth escapes; the balance of good and bad works; the pains of hell, and the joys of paradise.

By the side of these, that still more numerous groupe, with standards of a white ground strewed with crosses, consists of the worshippers of Jesus. Acknowledging the same God as the Mussulmans, founding their belief on the same books, admitting like them a first man, who lost the whole human race by eating an apple, they yet feel towards them a holy horror; and from motives of *piety*, these two sects reciprocally treat each other as *impious* men and blasphemers. Their chief point of dissension is, that the Christian, after admitting the unity and indivisibility of God, proceeds to divide him into three persons, making of each an entire and complete God, and yet preserving an identical whole : he adds, that this Being, who fills the universe, reduced himself to the stature and form of a man, and assumed material, perishable, and limited organs, without ceasing to be immaterial, eternal, and infinite.   The Mussulman, on the contrary, not able to comprehend these mysteries, though he readily conceives of the eternity of the Koran, and the mission of the prophet, treats them as absurdities, and rejects them as the visions of a disordered brain.   Hence result the most implacable animosities.

Divided among themselves, the Christian sects are not less numerous than those of the Mussulman religion ; and the quarrels that agitate them are by so much the more violent, since the objects for which they contend being inaccessible to the senses, and of consequence incapable of demonstration, the opinions of each sectary can have no other foundation than that of his will or caprice.   Thus agreeing that God is an incomprehensible and unknown being, they nevertheless dispute respecting his essence, his mode of acting, and his attributes.   Agreeing that his supposed transformation into man is an enigma above the human understanding, they still dispute respecting the confusion or the distinction of two wills and two natures, the change of substance, the real or fictitious presence, the mode of incarnation, &c. &c. Hence innumerable sects, of which two or three hundred have already perished, and three or four hundred others still exist, and are represented by that multitude of colours in which your sight is bewildered. The first in order, surrounded by a groupe absurd and discordant in their attire, red, purple, black, white, and speckled, with heads wholly or partially shaved, or with their hair short, with red caps, square caps, here with mitres, there with beards, is the standard of the Roman Pontiff, who, applying to the priest-hood the pre-eminence of his city in the civil order, has erected his supremacy into a point of religion, and made of his pride an article of faith.

At the right you see the Greek Pontiff, who, proud of the rivalship set up by his metropolis, op-poses equal pretensions, and supports them against the Western church, by the superior antiquity of that of the East. At the left, are the standards of two recent chiefs *, who, throwing off a yoke that was be-come tyrannical, have, in their reform, erected altars against altars, and gained half Europe from the Pope. Behind them are the inferior sects into which these grand parties are again subdivided, the Nestorians, the Eutycheans, the Jacobites, the Iconoclasts, the Anabaptists, the Presbyterians, the Wiclifites, the Osiandrins, the Manicheans, the Pietists, the Ada-mites, the Enthusiasts, the Quakers, the Weepers, together with a hundred others (8); all of distinct parties, of a persecuting spirit when strong, tolerant when weak, hating each other in the name of a God of peace, forming to themselves an exclusive paradise in a religion of universal charity, each dooming the rest, in another world, to endless torments, and rea-lizing here the imaginary hell of futurity.

Next to this groupe, observing a single standard of a hyacinth colour, round which were gathered men in all the various dresses of Europe and Asia : Here, said I to the Genius, we shall at least find unanimity. —At first sight, replied he, and from an incidental and temporary circumstance this would seem to be the case : but do you not know what system of wor-ship it is ?—Then perceiving in Hebrew letters the monogram of God, and branches of the palm-tree in the hands of the Rabbins : Are not these, said I, the

* Luther and Calvin.

children of Moses, dispersed over the earth, and who, holding every nation in abhorrence, have been themselves universally despised and persecuted ?—Yes, replied the Genius, and it is for this very reason that, having neither time nor liberty to dispute, they have preserved the appearance of unanimity. But in their re-union, no sooner shall they compare their principles, and reason upon their opinions, than they will be divided, as formerly, at least into two principal sects*, one of which, taking advantage of the silence of their legislator, and confining itself to the literal sense of his books, will deny every dogma not therein clearly understood, and of consequence will reject, as inventions, the immortality of the soul, its transmigration into an abode of happiness or seat of pain, its resurrection, the last judgment, the existence of angels, the revolt of a fallen spirit, and the poetical system of a world to come : and this favoured people, whose perfection consists in the cutting off a morsel of their flesh, this atom of people, that, in the ocean of mankind, is but as a small wave, and that pretends that the whole was made for them alone, will farther reduce by one half, in consequence of their schism, their already trivial weight in the balance of the universe.

The Genius then directed my attention to another groupe, the individuals of which were clothed in white robes, had a veil covering the mouth, and were ranged round a standard of the colour of the clouds gilded by the rising sun. On this standard was painted a globe, one hemisphere of which was black and the other white. The fate of these disciples of Zoroaster (9), continued he, this obscure remnant of a people once so powerful, will be similar to that of the Jews. Dispersed as they are at present among other nations, and persecuted by all, they receive with-

* The Sadducees and Pharisees.

out discussion the precepts that are taught them : but so soon as their Mobed and their Destours (10) shall be restored to their full prerogatives, the controversy will be revived respecting the good and the bad principle, the combats of Ormuz, God of light, and Abrimanes, God of darkness ; the literal or allegorical senses of these combats ; the good and evil Genii ; the worship of fire and the elements ; pollution and purification ; the resurrection of the body, or the soul, or both (11) ; the renovation of the present world, or the production of a new which is to succeed it.   The Parses will ever divide themselves into sects, by so much the more numerous as their families shall have contracted different manners or opinions during their dispersion.

Next to these are standards, which exhibit upon a blue ground monstrous figures of human bodies, double, triple, or quadruple, with the heads of lions, boars, and elephants, and tails of fishes, tortoises, &c. These are the standards of the Indian sects, who find their Gods amidst the animal creation, and the souls of their kindred in reptiles and insects.   These men anxiously support hospitals for the reception of hawks, serpents, and rats, and look with horror upon their brethren of mankind ! they purify themselves with the dung and urine of a cow, and consider themselves as polluted by the touch of a heretic ! They wear a net over their mouths, lest by accident a fly should get down their throat, and they should thus interrupt the progress of a purified spirit in its purgatory ; but with all this humanity in unintelligible cases, they think themselves obliged to let a Paria (12) perish with hunger rather than relieve him ! They worship the same Gods, but inlist themselves under hostile standards.

This first standard, separated from the rest, and on which you see represented a figure with four heads, is the standard of Brama, who, though the creator of the universe, has neither followers nor temples, and who, reduced to serve as a pedestal to the Lingam (13), receives no other mark of attention than a little water sprinkled every morning over his shoulder by the Bramin, and a barren song in his praise.

The second standard, on which you see painted a kite, his body scarlet and his head white, is that of the Vichenou, who, though the preserver of the universe, has passed a part of his life in malevolent actions. Sometimes you see him under the hideous forms of a boar and a lion, tearing the entrails of mankind; sometimes under that of a horse (14), soon to appear upon the face of the earth, with a sabre in his hand, to destroy the present inhabitants of the world, to darken the stars, to drive the planets from their spheres, to shake the whole earth, and to oblige the mighty serpent to vomit a flame which shall consume the globes.

The third standard is that of Chiven, the destroyer of all things, the God of desolation, and who nevertheless has for his emblem the instrument of production; he is the most detestable of the three, and he has the greatest number of followers. Proud of his attribute and character, his partizans in their devotions (15) express every sort of contempt for the other Gods, his equals and his brothers, and imitating the inconsistency that characterises him, they profess modesty and chastity, and at the same time publicly crown with flowers, and bathe with milk and honey, the obscene image of the Lingam.

Behind them came the less magnificent standards of a multitude of Gods, male, female, and hermaphrodite, related to and connected with the three principal, who pass their lives in intestine war, and are in this respect imitated by their worshippers. These Gods have need of nothing, and receive offerings without ceasing. Their attributes are omnipotence and ubiquity, and a Bramin with some petty charm imprisons them in an image, or in a pitcher, and retails their favours according to his will and pleasure.

At a still greater distance you will observe a multitude of other standards, which upon a yellow ground, common to them all, have different emblems figured, and are the standards of one God, who, under various names, is acknowledged by the nations of the East. The Chinese worship him under the name of *Fot* (16); the Japanese denominate him *Budso*; the inhabitants of Ceylon, *Beddhou*; the people of Laos, *Chekia*; the Peguan, *Phta*; the Siamese, *Sommon-Kodom*; the people of Thibet, *Budd* and *La*; all of them agree as to most points of his history; they celebrate his penitence, his sufferings, his fasts, his functions of mediator and expiator, the enmity of another God his adversary, the combats of that adversary and his defeat: but they disagree respecting the means of recommending themselves to his favour, respecting rites and ceremonies, respecting the dogmas of their interior and their public doctrine. Thus the Japanese Bonze, in a yellow robe, and with his head uncovered, preaches the eternity of souls and their successive transmigration into different bodies; while his rival, the Sintoist, denies that the soul can exist independently of the senses (17), and maintains that it is the mere result of the organization with which it is connected, and with which it perishes, as the sound of a flute is annihilated when you break it in pieces. Near him the Siamese, with shaved eyebrows, and with the Talipat screen in his hand (18), recommends alms-giving, purifications, and offerings, at the very time that he believes in blind necessity and immutable fate. The Chinese Ho-Chang sacrifices to the souls of his ancestors, while his neighbour, the follower of Confucius, pretends to discover his future destiny by the tossing of counters and the conjunction of the stars (19). Observe this infant at-

tended by a numerous crowd of priests with yellow
garments and bonnets: he is the grand Lama, and
the God of Thibet has just become incarnate in his
person (20). He however has a rival on the banks of
the Baikal; nor is the Calmuc Tartar in this repect
any way behind the Tartar of La-sa. They are
agreed in this important doctrine, that God can become incarnate only in a human body, and scorn the
stupidity of the Indian, who looks down with reverence upon cow-dung, though they themselves preserve with no less awe the excrements of their pontiff (21).

As these standards passed, an innumerable crowd
of others presented themselves to our eyes, and the
Genius exclaimed: I should never come to a conclusion, were I to detail to you all the different systems
of belief which divide these nations. Here the Tartar Hordes adore, under the figure of animals, insects,
and birds, the good and the evil Genii, who, under a
principal but indolent divinity, govern the universe,
by their idolatry, giving us an image of the ancient
paganism of the western world. You see the strange
dress of their Chamans, a robe of leather fringed with
little bells and rattles, embroidered with idols of iron,
claws of birds, skins of serpents, and heads of owls:
they are agitated with artificial convulsions, and with
magical cries evoke the dead to deceive the living.
In this place you behold the sooty inhabitants of Africa, who, while they worship their *Fetiches*, entertain the same opinions. The inhabitant of Juida
adores God under the figure of an enormous serpent,
which for their misfortune the swine reward as a delicious morsel (22). The Teleutean dresses the figure
of his God in a variety of gaudy colours, like a Russian soldier; and the Kamchadale, finding that every
thing goes on ill in this world, and under his climate,
represents God to himself under the figure of an ill-

natured and arbitrary old man (23), smoking his
pipe and sitting in his *traineau* employed in the hunting of foxes and martins. In fine, there are a hundred other savage nations, who, entertaining none of
these ideas of civilized countries respecting God, the
soul, and a future state, exercise no species of worship, and yet are not less favoured with the gifts of
nature, in the irreligion to which nature has destined
them.

———

CHAP. XXI.

PROBLEM OF RELIGIOUS CONTRADICTIONS.

THE different groupes having taken their stations,
and profound silence succeeding to the confused uproar of the multitude, the legislators said: " Chiefs
and doctors of the people! you perceive how the various nations of mankind, living apart, have hitherto
pursued different paths, each believing its own to be
that of truth. If truth, however, is one, and your
opinions are opposite, it is manifest that some of you
must be in error: and since so many men deceive
themselves, what individual shall dare say, I am not
mistaken? Begin, then, by being indulgent respecting your disputes and dissentions. Let us all seek
truth, as if none of us had possession of it. The opinions which to this day have governed the earth,
produced by chance, desseminated in obscurity, admitted without discussion, credited from a love of novelty and imitation, have in a manner clandestinely
usurped their empire. It is time, if they are founded
in reality, to give them the solemn stamp of certainty, and to legitimate their existence. Let us this day

K

cite them to a common and general examination; let each make known his creed; let the united assembly be the judge, and let us acknowledge that to be the only true one, which is proper for the whole human race."

Then, in order of position, the first standard at the left being desired to speak: "There can be no doubt," said they, " that ours is the only true and infallible doctrine. In the first place, it is revealed by God himself."

" So also is ours," exclaimed all the other standards, " and there can be no room for doubt."

" But it is at least necessary to explain it,' said the legislators, " for it is impossible for us to believe any thing of which we are ignorant."

" Our doctrine," resumed the first standard, " is proved by numerous facts, by a crowd of miracles, by resurrections from the dead, by torrents suddenly dried up, mountains removed from their situations, &c. &c."

" We also," cried the rest, " are in possession of miracles without number;" and each began to recite the most incredible things.

" Their miracles," replied the first standard, " are imaginary, or the prestiges of the evil spirit who has deluded them."

To this it was answered by the others: " They are yours on the contrary, that are imaginary;" and each speaking of himself, added: " Ours are the only true ones, all other miracles are false."

" Have you living witnesses of their truth?" the legislators asked.

" No," they universally answered; " they are ancient facts, of which the witnesses are dead, but these facts are recorded."

" Be it so," replied the legislators: " but as they contradict each other, who shall reconcile them?"

" Just arbitrators!" cried one of the standards, " as a

proof that our witnesses have seen the truth, they died in confirmation of it; and our creed is sealed with the blood of martyrs."

" So also is ours," exclaimed the rest: " we have thousands of martyrs, who have died in the most agonizing tortures, without in a single instance abjuring the truth." And the Christians of every sect, the Mussulmans, the Indians, the Japanese recounted endless legends of confessors, martyrs, penitents, &c.

One of these parties having denied the martyrology of the others: " We are ready," cried they, " to die ourselves to prove the infallibility of our creed."

Instantly a crowd of men of every sect and of every religion, presented themselves to endure whatever torments might be inflicted on them; and numbers of them began to tear their arms, and to beat their head and their breast, without discovering any symptom of pain.

But the legislators putting a stop to this violence: " O men!" said they to them, " hear with composure the words we address to you. If you die to prove that two and two make four, will this truth gain additional confirmation by your death?"

" No," was the general answer.

" If you die to prove they are five, will this make them five?"

" No," they again replied.

" What, then, does your persuasion prove, since it makes no alteration in the existence of things. Truth is one; your opinions are various; many of you must therefore be mistaken. And since man, as is evident, can persuade himself of error, how can his persuasion be regarded as the demonstration of evidence: Since error has its martyrs, what is the signet of truth? Since the evil spirit works miracles, what is the distinguishing characteristic of the Divinity?

Beside, why this uniform resort to incomplete and insufficient miracles? Why not rather, instead of these violations of nature, change the opinions of rational beings? Why murder and terrify men, instead of enlightening and instructing them?

"O credulous mortals, and obstinate in your credulity! as we are none of us certain of what passed yesterday, of what is passing this very day before our eyes, how can he swear to the truth of what happened two thousand years ago? Weak, and at the same time proud beings! the laws of nature are immutable and profound, our understandings full of illusion and frivolity, and yet we would decide upon and comprehend every thing. But in reality it is easier for the whole human race to fall into error, than an atom of the universe to change its nature."

"Well then," said one of the doctors, "let us leave the evidence of facts, since such evidence is equivocal, and let us attend to the proofs of reason, and the intrinsic merit of the doctrine itself."

An Iman of the law of Mahomet, with a look of confidence, then advanced in the sand, and having turned himself towards Mecca, and uttered with emphasis his confession of faith: "Let God be praised!" said he, in a grave and authoritative voice; "the light shines in all its splendour, and the truth has no need of examination." Then exhibiting the Koran: "Behold the light and the truth in their genuine colours! In this book every doubt is removed, it will conduct the blind man safely, who shall receive without discussion the divine word, given to the prophet to save the simple and confound the wise. God hath appointed Mahomet to be his minister upon earth; he has delivered up the world to him, that he might subdue by his sword such as refuse to believe in his law. Infidels dispute his authority, and resist the truth: their obduracy proceeds from God, who has hardened their hearts that he might inflict upon them the most dreadful chastisements *."

Here a violent murmur from all sides interrupted the Iman. "What man is this," cried every groupe, "who thus gratuitously commits outrage? By what right does he pretend, as conqueror and tyrant, to impose his creed on mankind? Has not God created us as well as him with eyes, understanding, and reason? Have we not an equal right to make use of them in determining what we ought to reject, and what to believe? If he have the right to attack, have not we the right to defend ourselves? If he be content to believe without examination, are we therefore not to employ our reason in the choice of our creed?

" And what is this *splendid* doctrine which fears the *light?* What this apostle of a God of clemency who preaches only carnage and murder? What this God of justice who punishes a blindness which himself has caused? If violence and persecution are the arguments of truth, mildness and charity must they be the indices of falsehood?"

A man advancing from the next groupe, then said to the Iman: "Admitting that Mahomet is the apostle of the better doctrine, the prophet of the true religion, condescend to tell us, in practising this doctrine, whom we are to follow, his son-in-law Ali, or his vicars Omar and Aboubekre (24)?"

At the mention of these names a terrible schism arose among the Mussulmans. The partisans of Omar and of Ali treating each other as heretics and blasphemers, were equally lavish of execrations. The dispute even became so violent, that it was necessary

* This passage contains the sense and nearly the very words of the first chapter of the Koran; and the reader will observe in general, that, in the pictures that follow, the writer has endeavoured to give as accurately as possible the letter and spirit of the opinions of each party.

for the neighbouring groupes to interpose to prevent their coming to blows.

Some degree of tranquillity being at length restored, the legislators said to the Imans : " You see what are the consequences which result from your principles! were they carried into practise, you would by your enmity destroy each other till not an individual would remain : and is it not the first law of God, that man should live ?" Then addressing themselves to the other groupes : " this spirit of intolerance and exclusion," said they, " is doubtless shocking to every idea of justice, and destroys the whole basis of morals and society : shall we not, however, before we entirely reject this code, agree to hear some of its dogmas recited, that we may not decide from forms only, without having investigated the religion itself ?"

The groupes having consented to the proposal, the Iman began to explain to them how God, who before time had spoken to the nations sunk in idolatry by twenty-four thousand prophets, had at length sent the last, the extract and perfection of all the rest, Mahomet, in whom was vested the salvation of peace : he informed them that to prevent the word of truth from being any more perverted by infidels, the Divine clemency had written with his own fingers the chapters of the Koran ; and that the Koran, by virtue of its character of the word of God, was, like its author, uncreated and eternal. He proceeded to explain to them the dogmas of Islamism ; that this book had been transmitted from heaven, leaf by leaf in twenty-four thousand miraculous visions of the angel Gabriel ; that the angel announced his approach by a small still knocking, which threw the prophet into a cold sweat ; that Mahomet had in one night traversed ninety heavens, mounted upon the animal called Borak, one-half woman and one-half horse ; that being endowed with the gift of miracles, he walked in the sunshine unattended by a shadow, caused with a single word trees already withered to resume their verdure, filled the wells and the cisterns with water, and cut in two equal parts the body of the moon; that, authorised by a commission from heaven, he had propagated, sword in hand, a religion the most worthy of God for its sublimity, the most suitable to man for the simplicity of its injunctions, consisting indeed only of eight or ten principal doctrines, such as the unity of God; the authority of Mahomet the only prophet of God; our duty to pray five times in a day; to fast one month in the year; to repair to Mecca once at least in our lives; to pay the tenth of all that we possess; to drink no wine, to eat no pork, and to make war upon the infidels (25); upon which conditions every Mussulman, being himself an apostle and a martyr, should enjoy in this life a thousand blessings, and in the world to come, after a solemn trial, his soul being weighed in the balance of good works, his absolution pronounced by the two black angels, and his progress performed over the bridge that crosses the infernal pit, as narrow as a hair and as keen as a razor, should be received in the seat of delights, bathed in rivers of milk and honey, embalmed in the perfumes of India and Arabia, and live in uninterrupted commerce with those chaste females, the celestial Houris, who present a perpetually renewed virginity to the elect, who preserve a perpetual vigour.

An involuntary smile was visible in the countenance of every one at this relation; and the various groupes, reasoning upon these articles of belief, unanimously said: " Is it possible for reasonable beings to have faith in such reveries? Might not one suppose that a chapter had just been read to us from the *Thousand and One Nights?*

A Samoiede advancing in the sand then said: " The paradise of Mahomet is in my opinion excellent: but

one of the means of obtaining it puzzles me extreme-
ly. If, as this prophet ordains, it is necessary to abstain from meat and drink between the rising and setting of the sun, how in our country is such a fast prac-
ticable, where the sun continues above the horizon
for six months together ?"

To vindicate the honour of their prophet, the
Mussulman doctors denied the possibility of this;
but a hundred people bearing testimony to the fact,
the infallibility of Mahomet sustained a violent
shock.

" It is singular," said a European, " that God
should continually have revealed what was going on
in heaven, without ever having informed us of what
passes upon earth."

" Their pilgrimage," said an American, " is to me
an insuperable difficulty. For let us suppose a generation to be twenty-five years, and the number of
males existing on the globe to be a hundred millions:
in this case, each being obliged to travel to Mecca
once during his life, there would be annually engaged
in the pilgrimage four millions of men; and as it
would be impracticable for them to return in the
same year, the number would be doubled, or, in other
words, would amount to eight millions. Where are
provisions, accommodation, water, and vessels to be
found for this universal procession ? What numerous
miracles would it not be necessary to work !"

" The proof," said a Catholic Divine, " that the
religion of Mahomet is not a revealed religion, is,
that the majority of ideas upon which it is founded
existed for a long time before it, and that it is
nothing more than a confused mixture formed out
of the truths of our holy religion and that of the
Jews, which an ambitious man has made serve his
projects of dominion, and his worldly views. Turn
over the pages of his book : you will see little else
than the histories of the Old and New Testament
travestied into the most absurd tales, and the rest a

tissue of vague and contradictory declamation, and ridiculous or dangerous precepts. Analyze the spirit of these precepts, and the conduct of their apostle : you will find a subtle and daring character, which to arrive at its end, works, it is true, with admirable skill upon the passions of those whom it wishes to govern. It addresses itself to simple and credulous men, and it tells them of prodigies : they are ignorant and jealous, and it flatters their vanity by despising science ; they are poor and rapacious, and it excites their avidity by the hope of plunder ; having nothing at first to give them on earth, it creates treasures in heaven; it makes them long for death, as the supreme blessing; the dastardly it threatens with hell; to the brave it promises paradise; the weak it strengthens by the principle of fatality; in short, it produces the attachment it requires, by every allurement of the senses, and the fascination of all the passions.

" How different is the character of the Christian doctrine ? and how much does its empire, established on the wreck of every natural inclination and the extinction of all the passions, prove its celestial origin ! How forcibly does its mild and compassionate morality attest its emanation from the Divinity ! Many of its dogmas, it is true, are beyond the reach of human understanding, and impose on reason a respectful silence ; but this very circumstance the more fully confirms its revelation, since the faculties of men could never have invented such sublime mysteries." Then, with the Bible in one hand, and the Four Evangelists in the other, the doctor began to relate that in the beginning, God (after having passed an eternity without doing any thing) conceived at length the design (without apparent motive) of forming the world out of nothing: that having in six days created the whole universe, he found himself tired on the seventh : that having placed the first pair of human beings in a delightful garden to make them completely happy, he nevertheless forbade them to taste of the fruit of one tree which he planted within their reach: that these first parents having yielded to temptation, all their race (as yet unborn), were condemned to suffer the penalty of a fault which they had no share in committing: that after permitting the human species to damn themselves for four or five thousand years, this God of compassion ordered his well-beloved son, engendered without a mother, and of the same age as himself, to descend upon the earth in order to be put to death, and this for the salvation of mankind, the majority of whom have nevertheless continued in the road to sin and damnation: that to remedy this inconvenience, this God, the son of a woman, who was at once a mother and a virgin, after having died and risen again, commences a new existence every day, and under the form of a morsel of dough is multiplied a thousand fold at the pleasure of the basest of mankind. Having explained these dogmas, he was going on to treat of the doctrine of the sacraments, of absolution and anathema, of the means of purifying men from crimes of every sort with a drop of water and the muttering half a dozen words; but he had no sooner pronounced the names of indulgence, papal prerogative, sufficient grace, and effectual grace, than he was interrupted by a thousand voices at once. It is a horrid corruption, cried the Lutherans, to pretend to sell for money the pardon of sin; it is contrary to the sense of the gospel, said the Calvinists, to talk of the real presence in the Sacrament. The Pope, exclaimed the Jansenists, has no power to decide upon any thing without a council. Thirty sects at once mutually accused each other of heresy and blasphemy, and their voices were so confused that it was no longer possible to distinguish a word they uttered.

After some time, silence being at length restored, the Mussulmans said to the legislators: " Since you have rejected our doctrine as containing things incredible, can you possibly admit that of the Christians, which is still more contrary to justice and common sense? An immaterial and infinite God to transform himself into a man? To have a son as old as himself! This God-man to become bread, which is eaten and undergoes digestion! What absurdities have we equal to these? Is it to these men belong the exclusive right of exacting a blind obedience? And will you accord to them privileges of faith, to our detriment?"

Some savage tribes then advanced: "What," said they, "because a man and a woman ate an apple six thousand years ago, is the whole human race to be involved in damnation? And do you call God just? What tyrant ever made the children responsible for the sins of their fathers? How can one man answer for the actions of another? Would not this be overthrowing every principle of equity and reason?"

"Where," exclaimed others, "are the witnesses and proofs of all these pretended facts? It is impossible to receive them without evidence. The most trivial action in a court of judicature requires two witnesses, and are we to believe all this upon mere tradition and hearsay?"

A Jewish Rabbin then addressing the assembly, said: "For the general facts we are indeed sureties; but as to the form and application of those facts, the case is different, and the Christian is here condemned out of their own mouth. They cannot deny that we are the stock from which they are descended, the trunk upon which they have been grafted; from whence it follows, by an inevitable dilemma, that either our law is from God, and then theirs is a heresy, since it differs from ours; or our law is not from God, and then whatever proves its falsehood is destructive of theirs."

" But there is a proper line of distinction," said the Christian, " to which it is necessary to attend. Your law is of God as typical and preparative, not as final and absolute; you are but the image, of which we are the reality."

" We are r t ignorant," replied the Rabbin, " that such are your pretensions; but they are perfectly supposititious and false. Your system rests entirely on mystical (2d), visionary, and allegorical interpretations. You pervert the letter of our books, substitute continually for the true sense of a passage the most chimerical ideas, and find in them whatever is agreeable to your fancy, just as a roving imagination discovers figures in the clouds. You have thus imagined a spiritual Messiah, where our prophets speak only of a political king. You have interpreted into a redemption of the human race, what refers solely to the re-establishment of our nation. Your pretended conception of the virgin is derived from a phrase which you have wrested from its true meaning. You construe every thing as you please. You even find in our books your doctrine of the Trinity, though they contain not the most indirect allusion to it, and though the idea was an invention of profane nations, and admitted into your code, together with a multitude of other opinions of every worship and sect of which it is composed, during the chaos and anarchy of the three first ages."

At these words, transported with indignation, and crying out sacrilege! blasphemy! the Christian doctors were disposed to lay violent hands upon the Jew: and a motley groupe of monks, some in black, some in white, advancing with a standard on which *pincers, a gridiron,* and *a funeral pile,* and the words, *justice, charity,* and *mercy,* were painted*, exclaimed: " It is proper to make an example of this impious heretic,

* This description answers exactly to the colours of the Iu-

and to burn him alive for the glory of God!" And already they had pictured to their imaginations the scene of torture, when the Mussulmans in a tone of irony said to them: "Such is the religion of peace, whose humble and humane spirit you have so loudly vaunted! Such that evangelical charity which combats incredulity with no other weapon than mildness, and opposes only patience to injuries! Hypocrites, it is thus you deceive nations! It is in this manner you have propagated your destructive errors! When weak, you have preached liberty, toleration, and peace; when power has been in your hands, you have practised violence and persecution!"——And they were beginning to recite the wars and murders of Christianity, when the legislators, demanding silence, assuaged for a while the discord.

"It is not," replied the monks in a tone of affected mildness and humility, "ourselves that we would avenge, we are desirous only of defending the cause and glory of God."

"And what right have you," said the Imans, "to constitute yourselves his representatives more than we? Have you privileges that we are not favoured with? Are you beings of a different nature from us?"

"To take upon ourselves to defend God, is to insult his wisdom and power," said another groupe, "does he not know better than mortals what is becoming his dignity?"

"Certainly," rejoined the monks; "but his ways are secret."

"You, however," said the Rabbins, "will always find the difficulty insuperable of proving that you enjoy the exclusive privilege of comprehending them." And the Jews, proud of finding their cause supported, fondly pleased themselves with the idea that

quisition of Spanish Jacobins; and is a proof of what has been before observed, that the writer has endeavoured to give a just picture of each party.

L

their books would be triumphant; when the Mobed*
of the Parses begged leave to speak.

" We have heard," said he to the legislators, " the
account of the Jews and Christians respecting the
origin of the world, and though they have introduced
various corruptions, they have related a number of
facts which our religion admits; but we deny that
they are to be attributed to the Hebrew legislator.
It was not he who made known to mankind these sublime dogmas, these celestial events: it was not to
him that God revealed them, but to our holy prophet
Zoroaster; and proofs of this are to be found in the
very books in question. If you examine with attention the detail of laws, of rights, and of precepts established by Moses, you will no where find the most
tacit indication of what constitutes at present the basis of the Jewish and Christian theology. You will
perceive no trace either of the immortality of the soul,
or a life to come, or hell, or paradise, or the revolt of
the principal angel, author of all the evils which
have afflicted the human race, &c. These ideas were
unknown to Moses, and this appears from indisput-
able evidence, since it was not till four hundred years
after him that they were first promulgated by Zoroaster in Asia (27)."

The Mobed added, addressing himself to the Rabbins: " It was not till the epocha, till after the age
of your first kings, that these ideas appeared in your
writings; and then their appearance was furtive and
gradual, according as there grew a political relation
between your ancestors and ours. It was particularly
at the period when, conquered and dispersed by the
kings of Nineveh and Babylon, your progenitors re-
sorted to the banks of the Tigris and the Euphrates,
and resided in our country for three successive generations, that they imbibed our manners and opinions,

* High priest.

which before they had regarded with aversion, as contrary to their law. When our king, Cyrus, had delivered them from slavery, they felt attached to us from sentiments of gratitude; they became our disciples and imitators, and introduced our peculiar doctrines into the corrected publication of their sacred books (28); for your Genesis in particular was never the work of Moses, but a compilation digested after the return from the Babylonish captivity, and containing in it the Chaldean opinions respecting the origin of the world.

" At first the pure followers of the law, opposing to the emigrants the letter of the text and the absolute silence of the prophet, endeavoured to overpower these innovations; but they ultimately prevailed, and our doctrines, modified according to your ideas, gave rise to a new sect. You expected a king, the restorer of your political independence; we announced a God, the regenerator of the world, and the saviour of mankind. These ideas blended together, constituted the tenets of the Essenians, and through them became the basis of Christianity. Jews, Christians, Mahometans, however lofty may be your pretensions, you are, in your spiritual and immaterial system, only the blundering followers of Zoroaster !"

Having thus commenced his discourse, the Mobed went on to the detail of his religion; and supporting his sentiments by quotations from the Zadder and the Zendavesta, he recounted in the same order as they are found in the book of Genesis, the creation of the world in six *gahans* (29); the formation of a first man and a first woman in a peculiar and celestial habitation, under the reign of perfect good; the introduction of evil into the world by the great lizard, the emblem of Ahrimanes; the revolt and combat of this magnificent genius of darkness, against Ormuz the benevolent God of light; the distribution of angels into white and black, good and ill; their hierarchy

consisting of cherubim, seraphim, thrones, dominions,
&c.; the end of the world at the close of six thousand
years; the coming of the Lamb, the regenerator of
nature; the new world; the life to come in an abode
of felicity or anguish; the passage of souls over the
bridge of the abyss; the celebration of the mysteries
of Mithra; the unleavened bread that is set apart for
the initiated: the baptism of new-born children; extreme unction and auricular confession (30); in a
word, he repeated so many articles analogous to those
of the three preceding religions, that his discourse
seemed to be a commentary or a continuation of the
Koran or the Apolypse.

But the Jewish, Christian, and Mahometan doctors
excepted to this detail, and treating the Parses as idolatrous worshippers of fire, charged them with falsehood, invention, and alteration of facts. A violent
dispute then arose respecting the dates of events,
their order and succession, respecting the origin of
opinions, their transmission from one people to another, the authenticity of the books which establish
them, the epocha when these books were composed,
the character of their compilers, the value of their
testimony; and the various parties proving, each
against the rest, contradictions, improbabilities, and
the counterfeit nature of their books, accused one
another of having founded their creed upon popular
rumours, upon vague traditions, upon absurd fables,
invented by folly, and admitted without examination
by unknown, ignorant, or partial writers, at doubtful
periods, and different from those to which their partisans referred them.

A loud rumour was now excited under the standards
of the various Indian sects: and the Bramins, entering
their protest against the claims of the Jew and the
Parses, said: " What are these upstart and almost
unknown people, who thus arrogantly consider themselves as the founders of nations, and the deposi-

tories of the sacred archieves? To hear their calculations of five or six thousand years, one would
suppose that the world was but of yesterday, whereas
our monuments prove a duration of many thousand
centuries. And in what respect are their books
preferable to ours? Are then the Vedes, the Chastres,
the Pourans, inferior to the Bible, the Zendavesta,
the Sadder (31)? Is not the testimony of our progenitors and our Gods, of equal value with that of
the Gods and progenitors of the western world? Oh!
were we permitted to reveal to profane men the mysteries of our religion! Did not a sacred veil justly
hide our doctrine from every eye."

The Bramins suddenly observing a profound silence:
" How," said the legislators, " can we admit your
doctrine, if you refuse to make it known? How could
its first authors propagate it, when, having sole possession of it, they regarded even their own people as
profane? Has heaven revealed it that it might be
kept a secret?

The Bramins however persisted in their silence;
and a European at this moment offering to speak, remarked, that their secrecy was at present an empty
form, that their sacred books were divulged and their
doctrine explained: he accordingly undertook to recapitulate its several articles.

Beginning with an abstract of the four Vedes, the
twenty-eight Pourans, and the five or six Chastres,
he recounted how an immaterial, infinite, eternal and
round Being, after having passed an unlimited portion
of time in self-contemplation, desirous at length of
manifesting himself, separated the faculties of male
and female which were in him, and operated an
act of generation of which the Lingam remains the
emblem; how from this first act were born three
divine powers, of the names of Brama, Bichen, or
Vichenou, and Chib or Chiven (32), the first deputed
to create, the second to preserve, the third to destroy

L 3

or change the form of the universe. He then detailed the history of their exploits and adventures, and related how Brama, proud of having created the world and the eight Bobouns (or spheres) of probation, and of being preferred to his equal Chib, this pride occasioned between them a combat, in which the globes or celestial orbits were broken to pieces, as if they had been a basket of eggs: how Brama, overcome in this contest, was reduced to serve as a pedestal to Chib, metamorphosed into the Lingam: how Vichenou, the preserver of the universe, had, in the discharge of his function, assumed nine animal and mortal forms, how under the first, that of a fish, he saved from the universal deluge a family by whom the earth was repeopled; afterwards, in the shape of a tortoise (33), drew from the sea of milk the mountain *Mandreguiri* (the Pole); then, under that of a boar, tore the entrails of the giant *Erenniachessen,* by whom the earth had been sunk in the abyss of *Djole,* from which he delivered it; how he became incarnate under the form of the Black Shepherd, and bearing the name of *Chris-en* rescued the world from the venemous serpent Calengam, whose head he crushed, after having himself received a wound in his heel.

Passing to the history of the secondary Genii, unfolded to the assembly how the Eternal, for the display of his glory, had created divers orders of angels, whose office it was to sing his praises and direct the universe: that a part of these angels had revolted under the conduct of an ambitious chief, who wished to usurp the power of God, and take the reins of Government into his own hands: that God precipitated them into a world of darkness as a punishment for their misdeeds: that at last, touched with compassion, he consented to withdraw them from thence, and to receive them again into favour, after previously subjecting them to a long state of probation : that for this purpose, having created fifteen orbits or regions of planets, and bodies to inhabit them, he obliged these rebellious angels to undergo eighty-seven transmigrations: that the souls, thus purified, returned to their primitive source, to the ocean of life from which they had emanated : that as all living beings contained a portion of this universal soul, it was an act of great criminality to deprive them of it. He was proceeding to develope the rights and ceremonies of this religion, when, speaking of offerings and libations of milk and butter to Gods of wood and of brass, he was interrupted by a universal murmur mixed with loud bursts of laughter.

Each of the different groupes reasoned in its own particular manner respecting this system. "They are idolaters," said the Mussulmans, " it is our duty to exterminate them."—" They are mad," said the followers of Confucius, it is our duty to cure them."—" What absurd Gods," cried the rest, "a set of fat monkeys begrimmed with smoke, whom they wash like children in clouts, and from whom they drive away the flies, lured by the taste of honey, who would otherwise defile them with their excrements."

At these words a Bramin, bursting with indignation, exclaimed : " These are inscrutable mysteries, the profound emblems of truth, which you are not worthy to know."

" And how comes it." replied a Lama of Thibet, " that you are more worthy than we ? Is it because you pretend to be sprung from the head of Brama, while the rest of mankind derive their origin from the less noble parts of his body? If you would support the fable of your origin, and the vain distinctions of your casts, prove that you are of a nature different from us ; prove at least by historical testimony the allegories you maintain ; nay, prove that you are really the authors of this system; for on our part we are able to prove, if that were necessary, that you have only stolen and disfigured it; that you have borrowed the ancient paganism of the western world, and blended it by an absurd conceit with the purely spiritual nature of our Gods (34), a nature which stoops not to address itself to the senses, and was wholly unknown to the world till the mission of Beddou."

Instantly innumerable voices demanded to be informed of this nature, and to hear of that God with whose very name the majority of them were unacquainted. In pursuance of this demand, the Lama resumed:

"In the beginning," said he, "there was one God, self existent, who passed through a whole eternity, absorbed in the contemplation of his own reflections, ere he determined to manifest those perfections to created beings, when he produced the matter of the word. The four elements, at their production, lay in a state of mingled confusion, till he breathed upon the face of the waters, and they immediately became an immense bubble, shaped like an egg, which when complete became the vault or globe of the heavens in which the world is inclosed (35). No sooner was the earth and the bodies of animals produced, than God, the source of motion, bestowed upon them as a living soul a portion of his substance. Thus the soul of every living thing, being only a fraction or separate part of the universal soul, no percipient being is liable to perish, but merely changes its form and mould as it passes successively into different bodies. But of all the substantial forms, that of men is most pleasing to the Divine Being, as most resembling his uncreated perfections; and man, when, by withdrawing himself from the commerce of the senses, he becomes absorbed in the contemplation of his own nature, discovers the Divinity that

resides in it, and himself becomes worthy of Divinity.
Thus is God incessantly rendering himself incarnate;
but his greatest and most solemn incarnation was
three thousand years ago, in the province of Cassi-
mère, under the name of Fôt or Beddou, for the
purpose of teaching the doctrine of self-denial and
self-annihilation." The Lama proceeded to detail
the history of Fôt, observing, that he had sprung
from the right intercostal of a virgin of the royal
blood, who, when she became a mother, did not the
less continue to be a virgin: that the king of the
country, uneasy at his birth, was desirous to put him
to death, and caused all the males who were born at
the same period to be massacred: that being saved
by shepherds, Beddou lived in the desert to the age
of thirty years, at which time he opened his commission, preaching the doctrine of truth and casting
out devils: that he performed a multitude of the most
astonishing miracles, spent his life in fasting and the
severest mortifications, and at his death bequeathed
to his disciples the volume in which the principles
of his religion are contained. The Lama then began
to read—

" He that forsaketh his father and his mother,"
says Fôt, " to follow me, shall become a perfect Samanean (a heavenly being).

" He that keepeth my precepts to the fourth degree of perfection, shall acquire the power of flying
in the air, of moving earth and heaven, of protracting
or shortening his life, and of rising again.

" The Samanean looks with contempt on riches,
and makes use only of such things as are strictly necessary. He mortifies the flesh, subdues his passions,
fixes his desires and affections on nothing terrestrial,
meditates without ceasing upon my doctrine, endures
injuries with patience, and bears no enmity against
his neighbour.

" Heaven and earth," says Fôt, " shall pass away;

despise therefore your bodies which are composed of the four perishable elements: and think only of your immortal soul.

" Hearken not to the suggestions of the flesh: fear and sorrow are the produce of the passions: stifle the passions, and fear and sorrow will thus be destroyed.

" Whosoever dies," says Fôt, " without having received my doctrine, becomes again and again an inhabitant of the earth, till he shall have embraced it."

The Lama was going on with his extracts, when the Christians interrupted him, observing, that his religion was an alteration of theirs; that Fôt was Jesus himself disfigured; and that the Lamas were nothing more than a degenerate sect of the Nestorians and Manicheans.

But the Lama (36), supported by all the Chamans, Bonzes, Gonnis, Talapoins of Siam, of Ceylon, of Japan, and of China, demonstrated to the Christians, from their own theologians, that the doctrine of the Samaneans was known through the East upwards of a thousand years before Christianity existed; that their name was cited previous to the reign of Alexander; and that of Boutta or Beddou could be traced to a more remote antiquity than that of Jesus—" And now," said they, retorting upon the Christians, " do you prove to us that you are not yourselves degenerated Samaneans; that the man whom you consider as the author of your sect is not Fôt himself in a different form. Demonstrate his existence by historical monuments of so remote a period as those which we have adduced (37); for as it appears to be founded on no authentic testimony, we absolutely deny its truth; and we maintain, that your gospels are taken from the books of the Mithriacs of Persia, and the Essenians of Syria, who were themselves only reformed Samaneans (38)."

These words excited a general outcry on the part

of the Christians, and a new dispute more violent than any preceding one was on the point of taking place, when a group of Chinese Chamans, and Talapoins of Sion came forward, pretending that they could easily adjust every difference, and produce in the assembly an uniformity of opinion; and one of them speaking for the rest, said: "It is time that we should put an end to all those frivolous disputes, by drawing aside the veil and exposing to your view the *interior* and *secret* doctrine which Fôt himself, on his death-bed, revealed to his disciples (39). These various theological opinions are mere chimeras; these accounts of the attributes, actions and life of the Gods, are nothing more than allegories and mysterious symbols, under which moral ideas, and the knowledge of the operations of nature in the action of the elements and the revolutions of the planets, are ingeniously depicted.

"The truth is, that there is no reality in any thing; that all is illusion, appearance, and dream; that the moral metempsychoses is nothing more than a figurative sense of the physical metempsychosis, of that successive motion by which the elements of which a body is composed, and which never perish, pass, when the body itself is dissolved, into a thousand others, and form new combinations. The soul is merely the vital principle resulting from the properties of matter, and the action of the elements in bodies, in which they create a spontaneous movement. To suppose that this result of organization, which is born with it, developed with it, sleeps with it, continues to exist when organization is no more, is a romance that may be pleasing enough, but that is certainly chimerical. God himself is nothing more than the principal mover, the occult power diffused through every thing that has being, the sum of its laws and its properties, the animating principle; in a word, the soul of the universe; which, by reason of the infinite diversity of its connections and operations, considered sometimes as simple and sometimes as multiple, sometimes as active and sometimes as passive, has ever presented to the human mind an insolvable enigma. What we can comprehend with great perspicuity is, that matter does not perish; that it possesses essential properties, by which the world is governed in a mode similar to that of a living and organized being; that, with respect to man, the knowledge of its laws is what constitutes his wisdom; that in their observance consist virtue and merit; and evil, sin, vice, in the ignorance and violation of them; that happiness and misfortune are the respective result of this observance or neglect, by the same necessity that occasions light substances to ascend, heavy ones to fall, and by a fatality of causes and effects, the chain of which extends from the smallest atom to the stars of greatest magnitude and elevation (40)."

A crowd of Theologians of every sect instantly exclaimed that this doctrine was rank materialism; and those who professed it impious Atheists, enemies both of God and man, who ought to be extirpated from the earth. "Strange reasoning," replied the Chamans. "Supposing us to be mistaken, which is by no means impossible, since it is one of the attributes of the human mind to be subject to illusion, what right have you to deprive beings like yourselves of the life which God has given them? If heaven considers us as culpable, and looks upon us with horror, why does it dispense to us the same blessings as to you? If it treats us with endurance, what right have you to be less indulgent? Pious men, who speak of God with so much certainty and confidence, condescend to tell us what he is; explain, so that we may comprehend them, those abstract and metaphysical beings which you call God and the soul; substances without matter, existence without body, life without organs or sensations. If you discover these beings by means of your senses, render them in like manner perceptible to us. If you speak of them only upon testimony and tradition, show us a uniform recital, and give an identical and determinate basis to your creed."

There now arose a warm controversy between the Theologians respecting the nature of God and his mode of acting and manifesting himself; respecting the soul and its union with the body, whether it has existence previous to the organs, or from the time of their formation only; respecting the life to come and another world; and every sect, every school, every individual, differing from the rest as to all these points, and assigning for its dissent plausible reasons and respectable but opposite authorities, they were all involved in an inextricable labyrinth of contradictions.

At length, the legislators having restored silence, recalled the dispute to its true object, and said: "Leaders and instructors of the people, you came hither for the purpose of investigating truth; and at first every one of you, confident in his own infallibility, demanded an implicit faith: presently, however, you felt the contrariety of your opinions, and consented to submit them to a fair comparison and a common rule of evidence. You proceeded to expose your proofs: you began with the allegation of facts; but it presently appeared that every religion and every sect had its miracles and its martyrs, and had an equal cloud of witnesses to boast, who were ready to prove the rectitude of their sentiments by the sacrifice of their lives. Upon this first point therefore the balance remained equal.

"You next passed to proofs of reasoning: the same arguments were alternately applied to the support of opposite propositions; the same assertions, equally gratutious, were successively advanced and repelled; every one was found to have an equal reason for denying his assent to the system of the others. A farther consequence that arose from thus confronting your system was, that notwithstanding their dissimilitude in some points, their resemblance in others was not less striking. Each of you claimed the first deposit and the original discovery; each of you taxed his neighbour with adulteration and plagiarism; and a previous question to the embracing of any of your doctrines appeared to result from the history of opinions.

"A still greater embarrassment arose when you entered into the explication of your doctrines: the more assiduous were your endeavours, the more confused did they appear! they rested upon a basis inaccessible to human understanding, of consequence you had no means to judge of their validity, and you readily admitted that, in asserting them, you were the echoes of your fathers. Hence it became important to know how they had come into the hands of that former generation, who had no means of learning them different from yourselves. Thus the transmission of theological ideas from country to country, and their first rise in the human understanding, were equally mysterious, and the question became every moment more complicated with metaphysical subtlety and antiquarian research.

But as these opinions, however extraordinary, have some origin; as all ideas, even the most abstracted and fantastical, have in nature some physical model, we must ascend to that origin in order to discover what this model is, and how the understanding came by those ideas of Deity, the soul and immaterial beings, that are so obscure, and which form the foundation of so many religious systems; we must trace their lineal descent and the alterations they have undergone in their various successions and ramifications. If, therefore, there are in this assembly men who have made these objects their peculiar study, let them come forward and endeavour to dispel, in the presence of the nations of the earth, the obscurity of opinions in which for so long a period they have all wandered."

—

CHAP. XXII.

ORIGIN AND GENEALOGY OF RELIGIOUS IDEAS.

AT these words a new groupe, formed in an instant, of individuals from every standard, but undistinguished by any, advanced in the sand; and one of the members, speaking in the name of the general body, said:

"Legislators, friends of evidence and of truth!

"That the subject of which we treat should be involved in so many clouds, is by no means astonishing, since, beside the difficulties that are peculiar to it, thought itself has, till this moment, ever had shackles imposed upon it, and free enquiry, by the intolerance of every religious system, been interdicted. But now that thought is unrestrained, and may develope all its powers, we will expose in the face of day, and submit to the common judgment of assembled nations, such rational truths as unprejudiced minds have by long and laborious study discovered: and this, not with the design of imposing them as a creed, but from a desire of provoking new lights, and obtaining better information.

"Chiefs and instructors of the people, you are not ignorant of the profound obscurity in which the nature, origin, and history of the dogmas you teach are inveloped. Imposed by force and authority, inculcated by education, maintained by the influence of example, they were perpetuated from age to age, and habit and inattention strengthened their empire.

M 2

But if man, enlightened by experience and reflection, summoned to the bar of mature examination the prejudices of his infancy, he presently discovers a multitude of incongruities and contradictions, which awaken his sagacity, and call forth the exertion of his reasoning powers.

"At first, remarking the various and opposite creeds into which nations are divided, we are led boldly to reject the infallibility claimed by each; and arming ourselves alternately with their reciprocal pretensions, to conceive that the senses and the understanding emanating directly from God, are a law not less sacred, and a guide not less sure, than the indirect and contradictory codes of the prophets.

"If we proceed to examine the texture of the codes themselves, we shall observe that their pretended divine laws, that is to say, laws immutable and eternal, have risen from the complexion of times, of places, and of persons; that these codes issue one from another in a kind of genealogical order mutually borrowing a common and similar fund of ideas, which every institutor modifies agreeably to his fancy.

"If we ascend to the source of those ideas, we shall find that it is lost in the night of time, in the infancy of nations, in the very origin of the world, to which they claim alliance; and there, immersed in the obscurity of chaos, and the fabulous empire of tradition, they are attended with so many prodigies as to be seemingly inaccessible to the human understanding. But this prodigious state of things gives birth itself to a ray of reasoning, that resolves the difficulty; for if the miracles held out in systems of religion have actually existed; if, for instance, metamorphoses, apparitions, and the conversations of one or more Gods, recorded in the sacred books of the Hindoos, the Hebrews, and the Parses, are indeed events in real history, it follows that nature in those times was perfectly unlike the nature that we are acquainted with now; that men of the present age are totally different from the men that formerly existed; and, consequently, that we ought not to trouble our heads about them.

"On the contrary, if those miraculous facts have had no real existence in the physical order of things, they must be regarded solely as productions of the human intellect: and the nature of man, at this day, capable of making the most fantastic combinations, explains the phenomenon of those monsters in history. The only difficulty is to ascertain how and for what purpose the imagination invented them. If we examine with attention the subjects that are exhibited by them, if we analyze the ideas which they combine and associate, and weigh with accuracy all their concomitant circumstances, we shall find a solution perfectly conformable to the laws of nature. Those fabulous stories have a figurative sense different from their apparent one, they are founded on simple and physical facts: but these facts, being ill conceived and erroneously represented, have been disfigured and changed from their original nature by accidental causes dependent on the human mind, by the confusion of signs made use of in the representation of objects, by the equivocation of words, the defect of language, and the imperfection of writing. These Gods, for example, who act such singular parts in every system, are no other than the physical powers of nature, the elements, the winds, the meteors, the stars, all which have been personified by the necessary mechanism of language, and the manner in which objects are conceived by the understanding. Their life, their manners, their actions, are only the operation of the same powers, and the whole of their pretended history no more than a description of their various phenomena, traced by the first naturalist that observed them, but taken in a contrary sense by the vulgar, who did not understand it, or by succeeding generations, who forgot it.   In a word, all the theological dogmas respecting the origin of the world, the nature of God, the revelation of his laws, the manifestation of his person, are but recitals of astronomical facts, figurative and emblematical narratives of the motion and influence of the heavenly bodies. The very idea itself of the Divinity, which is at present so obscure, abstracted, and metaphysical, was in its origin merely a composite of the powers of the material universe, considered sometimes analytically, as they appear in their agents and their phenomena, and sometimes synthetically, as forming one whole, and exhibiting an harmonious relation in all its parts.   Thus the name of God has been bestowed sometimes upon the wind, upon fire, water, and the elements; sometimes upon the sun, the stars, the planets, and their influences; sometimes upon the universe at large, and the matter of which the world is composed, sometimes upon abstract and metaphysical properties, such as space, duration, motion, and intelligence; but in every instance, the idea of a deity has not flowed from the miraculous revelation of an invisible world, but has been the natural result of human reflection, has followed the progress and undergone the changes of the successive improvement of intellect, and has had for its subject the visible universe and its different agents.

" It is then in vain that nations refer the origin of their religion to heavenly inspiration; it is in vain that they pretend to describe a supernatural state of things as first in the order of events: the original barbarous state of mankind, attested by their own monuments (41), belies all their assertions.   These assertions are still more victoriously refuted by considering this great principle, *that man receives no ideas*

but through the medium of his senses (42): for from
hence it appears, that every system which ascribes
human wisdom to any other source than experience
and sensation, includes in it υς εςον πϱοϲεϱου, and represents the last results of understanding as earliest
in the order of time. If we examine the different
religious systems which have been formed respecting
the actions of the Gods, and the origin of the world,
we shall discover at every turn an anticipation in the
order of narrating things, which could only be suggested by subsequent reflection. Reason, then, emboldened by these contradictions, hesitates not to
reject whatever does not accord with the nature of
things, and accepts nothing for historical truth that
is not capable of being established by argument and
ratiocination. Its ideas and suggestions are as follow:

"Before any nation received from a neighbour
nation dogmas already invented; before one generation inherited the ideas of another, none of these complicated systems had existence. The first men, the
children of nature, whose consciousness was anterior
to experience, and who brought no preconceived
knowledge into the world with them, were born without any idea of those articles of faith which are the
result of learned contention; of those religious rites
which had relation to arts and practices not yet in
existence; of those precepts which suppose the passions already developed: of those laws which have
reference to a language and a social order hereafter to
be produced; of that God, whose attributes are ab-
stractions of the knowledge of nature, and the idea of
whose conduct is suggested by the experience of a
despotic government; in fine, of that soul and those
spiritual existences which are said not to be the object
of the senses, but which, however, we must for ever
have remained unacquainted with, if our senses had
not introduced them to us. Previously to arriving at

these notions, an immense catalogue of existing facts must have been observed. Man, originally savage, must have learned from repeated trials the use of his organs. Successive generations must have invented and refined upon the means of subsistence; and the understanding, at liberty to disengage itself from the wants of nature, must have risen to the complicated art of comparing ideas, digesting reasonings, and seizing upon abstract similitudes.

SECT. I.   *Origin of the idea of God: Worship of the elements, and the physical powers of nature.*

"IT was not till after having surmounted those obstacles, and run a long career in the night of history, that man, reflecting on his state, began to perceive his subjection to forces superior to his own and independant of his will. The sun gave him light and warmth; fire burned, thunder terrified, the winds buffetted, water overwhelmed him; all the various natural existences acted upon him in a manner not to be resisted. For a long time, an automaton, he remained passive, without enquiring into the cause of this action; but the very moment he was desirous of accounting to himself for it, astonishment seized his mind; and passing from the surprise of a first thought to the reverse of curiosity, he formed a chain of reasoning.

"At first considering only the action of the elements upon him, he inferred, relatively to himself, an idea of weakness, of subjection, and relatively to them, an idea of power, of domination; and this idea was the primitive and fundamental type of all his conceptions of the Divinity.

"The action of the natural existences, in the second place, excited in him sensations of pleasure or pain, of good or evil; by virtue of his organization, he conceived love or aversion for them, he desired or dreaded their presence; and fear or hope was the principle of every idea of religion.

"Afterwards, judging every thing by comparison, and remarking in those beings a motion spontaneous like his own, he supposed there to be a will, an intelligence inherent in that motion, of nature similar to what existed in himself: and hence, by way of inference, he started a fresh argument.—Having experienced that certain modes of behaviour towards his fellow-creatures wrought a change in their affections and governed their conduct, he applied those practices to the powerful beings of the universe. "When my fellow-creature of superior strength," said he to himself, "is disposed to injure me, I humble myself before him, and my prayer has the art of appeasing him. I will pray to the powerful beings that strike me. I will supplicate the faculties of the winds, the planets, the waters, and they will hear me. I will conjure them to avert the calamities, and to grant me the blessings which are at their disposal. My tears will move, my offerings propitiate them, and I shall enjoy complete felicity."

"And, simple in the infancy of his reason, man spoke to the sun and the moon, he animated with his understanding and his passions the great agents of nature: he thought by vain sounds and useless practices to change their inflexible laws. Fatal error! He desired that the water should ascend, the mountains be removed, the stone mount in the air; and substituting a fantastic to a real world, he constituted for himself beings of opinion, to the terror of his mind and the torment of his race.

"Thus the ideas of God and religion sprung, like all others, from physical objects, and were in the understanding of man the produce of his sensations, his wants, the circumstances of his life, and the progressive state of his knowledge.

"As these ideas had natural beings for their first models, it resulted from hence that the Divinity was originally as various and manifold as the forms under which he seemed to act: each being was a Power, a Genius, and the first men found the universe crowded with innumerable Gods.

"In like manner the ideas of the Divinity having had for motors the affections of the human heart, they underwent an order of division calculated from the sensations of pain and pleasure, of love and hatred: the powers of nature, the Gods, the Genii, were classed into benign and maleficent, into good and evil ones: and this constitutes the universality of these two ideas in every system of religion.

"These ideas, analogous to the condition of their inventors, were for a long time confused and gross. Wandering in woods, beset with wants, destitute of resources, men in their savage state had no leisure to make comparisons and draw conclusions. Suffering more ills than they tasted enjoyments, their most habitual sentiment was fear, their theology terror, their worship confined to certain modes of salutation, of offerings which they presented to beings whom they supposed to be ferocious and greedy like themselves. In their state of equality and independance, no one took upon him the office of mediator with Gods as insubordinate and poor as himself. No one having any superfluity to dispose of, there existed no parasite under the name of priest, nor tribute under the name of victim, nor empire under the name of altar; their dogma and morality, jumbled together, were only self-preservation; and their religion, and arbitrary idea without influence on the mutual relations existing between men, was but a vain homage paid to the visible powers of nature.

" Such was the first and necessary origin of every idea of the Divinity."

The orator then addressing the savage nations, said : " We appeal to you, who have received no foreign fictitious ideas, whether your conceptions have not been formed precisely in this manner? We ask you also, learned theologians, if such be not the unanimous record of all the monuments of antiquity (43)?"

SECT. II. *Second system: Worship of the Stars, or Sabeism.*

" BUT those same monuments offer us a more methodical and more complicated system, that of the worship of all the stars, adored at one time under their proper form, at another under emblems and figurative symbols. This worship was also the effect of the knowledge of man in physics, and derived immediately from the first causes of the social state; that is to say, from wants and arts of the first degree, the elements as it were in the formation of society.

" When men began to unite in society, they found it necessary to enlarge the means of their subsistence, and consequently to apply themselves to agriculture; and the practice of agriculture required the observation and knowledge of the heavens (44). It was necessary to know the periodical return of the same operations of nature, the same phenomena of the same skies; it was necessary to regulate the duration and succession of the seasons, months and years. In order to this it was requisite to become acquainted with the march of the sun, which in its zodiacal revolution showed itself the first and supreme agent, of all creation; then of the moon, which by its changes and returns regulated and distributed time; finally of the stars, and even of the planets, which, by their appearance and disappearance on the horizon and the nocturnal hemisphere, formed the minutest divisions. In a word, it was necessary to establish an entire system of astronomy, to form an almanac; and from this labour there quickly and spontaneously resulted a new manner of considering the dominant and governing powers. Having observed that the productions of the earth bore a regular and constant connection with the phenomena of the heavens; that the birth, growth, and decay of each plant, were allied to the appearance, exaltation and decline of the same planet, the same groupe of stars; in short, that the languor or activity of vegetation seemed to depend on celestial influences, men began to infer from this an idea of action, of power, in those bodies, superior to terrestrial beings; and the stars dispensing scarcity or abundance, became powers, Genii (45), Gods, authors of good and evil.

" As the state of society had already introduced a methodical hierarchy of ranks, employments and conditions, men, continuing to reason from comparison, transferred their new acquired notions to their theology, and the result was a complicated system of gradual Divinities, in which the sun, as the first God, was a military chief, a political king; the moon, a queen, his consort; the planets, servants, bearers of commands, messengers: and the multitude of stars, a nation, an army of heroes, of Genii, appointed to govern the world under the command of their officers; every individual had a name, functions, attributes, drawn from its connections and influences, and even a sex derived from the gender of its appellation (46).

" As the state of society had introduced certain usages and complex practices, worship, leading the van, adopted similar ones. Ceremonies, simple and private at first, became public and solemn; offerings

were more rich and more numerous; rites more methodical; places of assembly, chapels, and temples,
were erected; officers, pontiffs, created to administer; forms and epochas were settled; and religion
became a civil act, a political tie. But in this developement it altered not its first principles, and the
idea of God was still that of physical beings, operating good or ill, that is to say, impressing sensations
of pain or pleasure: the dogma was the knowledge
of their laws or modes of acting; virtue and sin the
observance or infringement of those laws; and morality, in its native simplicity, a judicious practice of
all that is conducive to the preservation of existence,
to the well-being of the individual and of his fellow-
creatures (47).

" Should it be asked at what epoch this system
took birth, we shall answer, supported by the authority of the monuments of astronomy itself, that its
principles can be traced back with certainty to a period of nearly seventeen thousand years (48).   Should
we farther be asked to what people or nation it ought
to be attributed, we shall reply that those self-same
monuments, seconded by unanimous tradition, attribute it to the first tribes of Egypt.   And when reason finds in that region a concurrence of all the physical circumstances calculated to give rise to; when
it finds at once a zone of heaven, in the vicinity of
the tropic, equally free from the rains of the equator
and the fogs of the north (49); when it finds there
the central point of the antique sphere: a salubrious
climate; an immense yet mangeable river; a land
fertile without art, without fatigue; inundated, without pestilential exhalations; situate between two
seas which lave the shores of the richest countries—
it becomes manifest that the inhabitant of the districts of the Nile, inclined to agriculture from the
nature of his soil; to commerce, from the facility of
communication; to geometry, from the annual neces-

N

sity of measuring his possessions; to astronomy, from the state of his heaven, ever open to observation: must first have passed from the savage to the social state, and consequently attained that physical and moral knowledge proper to civilized man.

" It was thus, upon the distant shores of the Nile, and among a nation of sable complexion, that the complex system of the worship of the stars, as connected with the produce of the soil and the labours of agriculture, was constructed. The worship of the stars, under their proper forms, or their natural attributes, was a simple process of the human understanding; but in a short time the multiplicity of objects, their relations, their action and re-action, having confounded the ideas and the signs that represented them, a consequence resulted as absurd in its nature as pernicious in its tendency.

SECT. III. *Third system; Worship of symbols, or idolatry.*

" From the instant this agricolar race had turned an eye of observation on the stars, they found it necessary to distinguish individuals or groupes, and to assign to each a proper name. A considerable difficulty here presented itself; for, on the one hand, the celestial bodies, similar in form, offered no peculiar character by which to denominate them: and, on the other hand, language, poor and in a state of infancy, had no expressions for so many new and metaphysical ideas. The usual stimulus of genius, necessity, conquered all obstacles. Having remarked that in the annual revolution, the renewal and periodical appearance of the productions of the earth were constantly connected with the rising and setting of certain stars, and with their position relatively to the

sun, the mind, by a natural mechanism, associated in
its thought terrestrial and celestial objects, which had
in fact a certain alliance; and applying to them the
same sign, it gave to the stars, and the groupes it
formed of them, the very names of the terrestrial objects to which they bore affinity (50).

" Thus the Ethiopian of Thebes called stars of inundation, or of *Aquarius*, those under which the river
began to overflow*; stars of the ox or bull, those
under which it was convenient to plough the earth;
stars of the lion, those under which that animal, driven by thirst from the deserts, made his appearance
on the banks of the Nile; stars of the sheaf, or of the
harvest maid, those under which the harvests were
got in; stars of the lamb, stars of the goat, those
under which those valuable animals brought forth
their young; and this was a first part of the difficulty
resolved.

" On the other hand, man, having remarked in the
beings that surrounded him certain qualities peculiar
to each species, and having invented a name by
which to design them, speedily discovered an ingeni-
ous mode of generalizing his ideas, and transferring
the name already invented to every thing bearing a
similar or analogous property or agency, enriched
his language with a multiplicity of metaphors and
tropes.

" Thus the same Ethiopian, having observed that
the return of the inundation answered constantly to
the appearance of a very beautiful star towards the
scource of the Nile, which seemed to warn the husbandman against being surprised by the waters, he
compared this action with that of the animal, who by
barking gives notice of danger, and called this star
the dog, the barker *(Syrius)*.   In the same manner
he called stars of the crab, those which shewed them-

* This must have been June.   See Note (46.)

selves when the sun, having reached the bounds of
the tropic, returned backwards and sideways like the
crab, or *Cancer ;* stars of the wild goat, those which,
the sun being arrived at its greatest altitude, at the
top of the horary gnomon, imitated the action of that
animal, who delights in climbing the highest rocks;
stars of the balance, those which, the days and
nights being of the same length, seemed to observe
an equilibrium like that instrument; stars of the
scorpion, those which were perceptible when certain
regular winds brought a burning vapour like the poison of the scorpion.   In the same manner he called
by the name of rings and serpents the figured traces
of the orbits of the stars and planets (51); and this
was the general means of appellation of all the heavenly bodies, taken in groupes or individually, according to their connection with rural and terrestrial
operations, and the analogies which every nation
found them to bear to the labours of the fields, and
the objects of their climate and soil.

" From this proceeding it resulted, that abject and
terrestrial beings entered into association with the
superior and powerful beings of the heavens; and
this association became more rivetted every day by
the very constitution of language and the mechanism
of the mind.   Men would say, by a natural metaphor,
" The bull spreads upon the earth the germins of fecundity (in spring), and brings back abundance by the
revival of vegetation.   The lamb (or ram) delivers
the heavens from the malevolent Genii of winter; and
saves the world from the serpent (emblem of the wet
season).   The scorpion pours out his venom upon the
earth, and spreads diseases and death, &c."

" This language, understood by every body, was at
first attended with no inconvenience ; but, in process
of time, when the almanac had been regulated, the
people, who could do without further observation of
the skies, lost sight of the motive which led to the

adoption of these expressions; and the allegory still remaining in the practices of life, became a fatal stumbling-block to the understanding and reason. Habituated to join to symbols the ideas of their models, the mind finally confounded them; then those same animals, which the imagination had raised to heaven, descended again on the earth; but in this return, decked in the livery and invested with the attributes of stars, they imposed upon their own authors. The people, imagining that they saw their Gods before them, found it a more easy task to offer up their prayers. They demanded of the ram of their flock the influence which they expected from the celestial ram; they prayed the scorpion not to pour out his venom upon nature; they revered the fish of the river, the crab of the sea and the scarabeus of the slime; and by a series of corrupt but inseparable analogies, they lost themselves in a labyrinth of consequent absurdities.

" Such was the origin of this ancient and singular worship of animals; such the train of ideas by which the character of the Divinity became common to the meanest of the brute creation; and thus was formed the vast, complicated, and learned theological system, which, from the banks of the Nile, conveyed from country to country by commerce, war, and conquest, invaded all the old world; and which, modified by times, by circumstances, and by prejudices, is still to be found among a hundred nations, and subsists to this day as the secret and inseparable basis of the theology of those even who despise and reject it."

At these words, murmurs being heard in various groupes: " I repeat it," continued the orator. " People of Africa! hence, for example, has arisen among you the adoration of your *Feteches*, plants, animals, pebbles, bits of wood, before which your ancestors would never have been so absurd as to prostrate themselves, if they had not seen in them talismans, partaking of the nature of the stars (52). Nations of Tartary! this is equally the origin of your *Marmouzets*, and of the whole train of animals with which your Chamans ornament their magic robes. This is the origin of those figures of birds and serpents, which all the savage nations, with mystic and sacred ceremonies, imprint on their skin. Indians! it is in vain you cover yourselves with the veil of mystery: the hawk of your God Vichenou is but one of the thousand emblems of the sun in Egypt, and his incarnations in a fish, boar, lion, turtle, together with all his monstrous adventures, are nothing more than the metamorphoses of the same star, which, passing successively through the signs of the twelve animals*, was supposed to assume their forms, and to act their astronomical parts (53). Japanese! your bull, which breaks the egg of the world, is merely that of the heavens, which, in times of yore, opened the age of the creation, the equinox of Spring. Rabbins, Jews! that same bull is the *Apis* worshipped in Egypt, and which your ancestors adored in the idol of the golden calf. It is also your bull, children of Zoroaster! that, sacrificed in the symbolic mysteries of Mithra, shed a blood fertilizing to the world. Lastly, your bull of the Apocalypse, Christians! with his wings the symbol of the air, has no other origin: your lamb of God, immolated, like the bull of Mithra, for the salvation of the world, is the self-same sun in the sign of the celestial ram, which, in a subsequent age, opening the equinox in his turn, was deemed to have rid the world of the reign of evil, that is to say, of the serpent, of the large snake, the mother of winter and emblem of the Ahrimanes or Satan of the Persians, your institutors. Yes, vainly does your imprudent zeal consign idolaters to the torments of the Tartarus

---

* The Zodiac.

which they have invented : the whole basis of your
system is nothing more than the worship of the star
of day, whose attributes you have heaped upon your
chief personage. It is the sun, which, under the
name of Orus, was born, like your God, in the arms of
the celestial virgin, and passed through an obscure,
indigent, and destitute childhood, answering to the
season of cold and frost. It is the sun, which, under
the name of Osiris, persecuted by Typhon and the tyrants of the air, was put to death, laid in a dark tomb,
the emblem of the hemisphere of winter, and which,
rising afterwards from the inferior zone to the highest point of the heavens, awoke triumphant over giants and the destroying angels. Ye priests, from
whom the murmurs proceed, you wear yourselves its
signs all over your bodies. Your tonsure is the disk
of the sun; your stole its Zodiac (54); your rosaries
the symbols of the stars and planets. Pontiffs and
prelates! your mitre, your croiser, your mantle, are
the emblems of Osiris; and that crucifix of which
you boast the mystery, without comprehending it, is
the cross of Serapis, traced by the hands of Egyptian
priests on the plan of the figurative world, which,
passing through the equinoxes and the tropics, became the emblem of future life and resurrection, because it touched the gates of ivory and horn through
which the soul was to pass in its way to heaven."

Here the doctors of the different groupes looked
with astonishment at one another, but none of them
breaking silence, the orator continued.

"Three principal causes concurred to produce
this confusion of ideas. First, the necessity, on account of the infant stage of language, of making use
of figurative expressions to depict the relations of
things; expressions that, passing afterwards from a
proper to a general, from a physical to a moral sense,
occasioned, by their equivocal and synonymous terms
a multiplicity of mistakes.

" Thus having at first said, that the sun surmounted and passed in its course through the twelve animals, they afterwards supposed that it combated, conquered, and killed them, and from this was composed the historical life of Hercules.

" Having said that it regulated the period of rural operations, of seed time and of harvest; that it distributed the seasons, ran through the climates, swayed the earth, &c. it was taken for a legislative king, a conquering warrior, and hence they formed the stories of Osiris, of Bacchus, and other similar Gods.

" Having said that a planet entered into a sign, the conjunction was denominated a marriage, adultery, incest (55): having farther said, that it was buried, because it sunk below the horizon, returned to light and gained its state of eminence, they gave it the epithet of dead, risen again, carried into heaven, &c.

" The second cause of confusion was the material figures themselves, by which thoughts were originally painted, and which, under the name of hieroglyphics, or sacred characters, were the first invention of the mind. Thus to denote an inundation, and the necessity of preserving one's-self from it, they painted a boat, the vessel Argo; to express the wind, they painted a bird's wing; to specify the season, the month, they delineated the bird of passage, insect, or animal, which made its appearance at that epoch; to express winter they drew a hog, or a serpent which are fond of moist and miry places. The combination of these figures had also a meaning, and was substituted for words and phrases * (56). But as there was nothing fixed or precise in this sort of language, as the number of those figures and their combinations became excessive and burdensome to the memory, confusions and false interpretations were the first and obvious result. Genius having afterwards invented

* See the example cited in note (45).

the more simple art of applying signs to sounds, of which the number is limited, and of painting the word instead of the thought, hieroglyphic pictures were, by means of alphabetical writing, brought into disuse; and from day to day their forgotten significations made way for a variety of illusions, equivoques, and errors.

"Lastly, the civil organization of the first states was a third cause of confusion. Indeed, when the people began to apply themselves to agriculture, the formation of the rural calendar requiring continual astronomical observations, it was necessary to chuse individuals whose province it should be to watch the appearance and setting of certain stars, to give notice of the return of the inundation, of particular winds and rains, and the proper time for sowing every species of grain. These men, on account of their office, were exempted from the common occupations, and the society provided for their subsistence. In this situation, solely occupied in making observations, they soon penetrated the great phenomena of nature, and dived into the secret of various of her operations. They became acquainted with the course of the stars and planets; the connection which their absence and return had with the productions of the earth and the activity of vegetation: the medicinal or nutritive properties of fruits and plants; the action of the elements, and their reciprocal affinities. But as there were no means of communicating this knowledge otherwise than by the painful and laborious one of oral instruction, they imparted it only to their friends and kindred; and hence resulted a concentration of science in certain families, who, on this account, assumed to themselves exclusive privileges, and a spirit of corporation and separate distinction fatal to the public weal. By this continued succession of the same labours and enquiries, the progress of knowledge it is true was hastened, but, by the mystery that accompanied it, the people, plunged daily in the thickest darkness, became more superstitious and more slavish. Seeing human beings produce certain phenomena, announce, as it were at will, eclipses and comets, cure diseases, handle noxious serpents, they supposed them to have intercourse with celestial powers; and, to obtain the good or have the ills averted which they expected from those powers, they adopted these extraordinary human beings as mediators and interpreters. And thus were established in the very bosom of states sacrilegious corporations of hypocritical and deceitful men, who arrogated to themselves every kind of power; and priests, being at once astronomers, divines, naturalists, physicians, necromancers, interpreters of the Gods, oracles of the people, rivals of kings of their accomplices, instituted under the name of religion an empire of mystery, which to this very hour has proved ruinous to the nations of mankind."

At these words the priest of all the groupes interrupted the orator; with loud cries, they accused him of impiety, irreligion, blasphemy, and were unwilling he should proceed: but the legislators having observed, that what he related was merely a narrative of historical facts; that if those facts were false or forged, it would be an easy matter to refute them; and that if every one were not allowed the perfect liberty to declare his opinion, it would be impossible to arrive at truth—he thus went on with his discourse.

"From all these causes, and the perpetual association of dissimilar ideas, there followed a strange mass of disorders in theology, morality, and tradition. And first, because the stars were represented by animals, the qualities of the animals, their likings, their sympathies, their aversions, were transferred to the Gods and supposed to be their actions. Thus the God *Ichneumon* made war against the God crocodile;

the God wolf wanted to eat the God sheep; the God
stork devoured the God serpent; and the Deity became a strange, whimsical, ferocious being, whose
idea misled the judgment of man, and corrupted both
his morals and his reason.

"Again, as every family, every nation in the spirit
of its worship adopted a particular star or constellation for its patron, the affections and antipathies of
the emblematical brute were transferred to the sectaries of this worship; and the partisians of the God
dog were enemies to those of the God wolf; the worshippers of the God bull abhorred those who fed upon
beef, and religion became the author of combats and
animosities, the senseless cause of frenzy and superstition (57).

"Farther, the names of the animal stars having,
on account of this same patronage, been conferred on
nations, countries, mountains, and rivers, those objects were also taken for Gods; and hence there
arose a medley of geographical, historical, and mythological beings, by which all tradition was involved
in confusion.

"In fine, from the analogy of their supposed actions the planetary gods having been taken for men,
heroes, and kings; kings and heroes took in their
turn the actions of the Gods for models, and became,
from imitation, warlike, conquering, sanguinary,
proud, lascivious, indolent; and religion consecrated
the crimes of despots, and perverted the principles
of governments.

SECT. IV. *Fourth system; Worship of two principles, or Dualism.*

"Meanwhile the astronomical priests, enjoying
in their temples peace and abundance, made every

day fresh progress in the sciences; and the system of the world gradually displaying itself before their eyes, they started successively various hypotheses as to its agents and effects, which became so many systems of theology.

"The navigators of the maritime nations, and the caravans of the Asiatic and African Nomades, having given them a knowledge of the earth from the Fortunate Islands to Serica, and from the Baltic to the sources of the Nile, they discovered, by a comparison of the different Zones, the rotundity of the globe, which gave rise to a new theory. Observing that all the operations of Nature, during the annual period, were summed up in two principal ones, that of producing and that of destroying; that upon the major part of the globe, each of these operations was equally accomplished from one to the other equinox; that is to say, that during the six months of summer all was in a state of procreation and increase, and during the six months of winter all in a state of langour and nearly dead, they supposed nature to contain two contrary powers always struggling with and resisting each other; and considering in the same light the celestial sphere, they divided the pictures, by which they represented it, into two halves or hemispheres, so that those constellations which appeared in the summer heaven formed a direct and superior empire, and those in the winter heaven an opposite and inferior one. Now as the summer constellations were accompanied with the season of long, warm, and unclouded days, together with that of fruits and harvests, they were deemed to be the powers of light, fecundity, and creation; and by transition from a physical to a moral sense, to be Genii, angels of science, beneficence, purity, virtue: in like manner the winter constellations, being attended with long nights and the polar fogs, were regarded as genii of darkness, destruction, death, and, by similar transition,

as angels of wickedness, ignorance, sin, vice. By
this disposal, heaven was divided into two domains,
two factions: and the analogy of human ideas opened
already a vast career to the flights of imagination;
but a particular circumstance determimed, if it did
not occasion, the mistake and illusion. (Consult
Plate II. at the end of the volume.)

"In the projection of the celestial sphere drawn by
astronomical priests (58), the Zodiac and the constellations disposed in a circular order, presented
their halves in diametrical opposition: the winter
hemisphere was adverse, contrary, opposite to, being
the Antipodes of, that of summer. By the continued
metaphor these words were converted into a moral
sense, and the adverse angels and Genii became rebels
and enemies (59). From that period the whole astronomical history of the constellations was turned
into a political history; the heavens became a human
state, where every thing happened as it does on earth.
Now as the existing states, for the most part despotic, had their monarchs, and as the sun was the apparent sovereign of the skies, the summer hemisphere (empire of light), and its constellations (a nation of white angels), had for king an enlightened,
intelligent, creative, benign God; and as every rebellious faction must have its chief, the hemisphere of
winter, (the subterraneous empire of darkness and
woe), together with its stars (a nation of black angels,
giants, or demons), had for leader a malignant Genius,
whose part was assigned, by the different people of
the earth, to that star which appeared to them the
most remarkable. In Egypt it was originally the
Scorpion, the first sign of the Zodiac after the balance, and the hoary chief of the wintry signs: then it
was the bear or the polar ass, called Typhon, that is
to say, deluge (60), on account of the rains which
poured down upon the earth during the dominion of
that star. In Persia, at a subsequent period (61), it

was the serpent, which, under the name of Ahrimanes, formed the basis of the system of Zoroaster;
and it is the same, Christians and Jews, that is become your serpent of Eve (the celestial origin), and
that of the cross; in both cases the emblem of Satan, the great adversary of the Ancient of Days, sung
by Daniel.   In Syria it was the hog or wild boar, enemy of Adonis, because in that country the office of
the Northern bear was made to devolve upon the animal whose fondness for mire and dirt is emblematical
of winter.   And it is for this reason that you, children
of Moses and of Mahomet, hold this animal in abhorrence, in imitation of the priests of Memphis and
Balbec, who detested him as the murderer of their
God the sun.   This is likewise, O Indians! the type
of your Chib-en, which was once the Pluto of your
brethren the Greeks and Roman; your Brama also,
(God the creator,) is only the Persian Ormuzd, and
the Osiris of Egypt, whose very name expresses a
creative power, producer of forms.   And these Gods
were worshipped in a manner analogous to their real
or fictitious attributes, and this worship, on account
of the difference of its objects, was divided into two
distinct branches.   In one, the benign God received
a worship of joy and love; whence are derived all religious acts of a gay nature (62), festivals, dances,
banquets, offerings of flowers, milk, honey, perfumes;
in a word, of every thing that delights the senses
and the soul.   In the other, the maligin God, on the
contrary, received a worship of fear and pain; whence
originated all religious acts of the sombre kind (63),
tears, grief, mourning, self-denial, blood-offerings,
and cruel sacrifices.

    "From the same source flowed the division of ter-
restrial beings into pure and impure, sacred or abominable, according as their species was found among
the respective constellations of the two Gods, and
made part of their domains.   This produced, on

one hand, the superstitions of pollution and purification; and on the other, the pretended efficacious virtues of amulets and talismans.

"You now understand," continued the orator, addressing himself to the Indians, Persians, Jews, Christians and Mussulmans; "you now understand the origin of those ideas of combats and rebellion, which equally prevade your respective mythology. You perceive what is meant by white and black angels; by the cherubs and seraphs with heads of an eagle, a lion or a bull; the Deus, devils or demons with horns of goats and tails of snakes; the thrones and dominions, ranged in seven orders or gradations, like the seven spheres of the planets; all of them beings acting the same parts, partaking of the same attributes in the Vedas, the Bibles, or the Zendavasta: whether their chief be Ormuzd or Brama, Typhon or Chib-en, Michael or Satan; whether their form be that of giants with a hundred arms and feet of serpents, or that of Gods metamorphosed into lions, storks, bulls and cats, as they appear in the sacred tales of the Greeks and Egyptians: you perceive the successive genealogy of these ideas, and how in proportion to their remoteness from their sources, and as the mind of man became refined, their gross forms were purified, and reduced to a state less shocking and repulsive.

"But, just as the system of two opposite principles or deities originated in that of symbols; in the same manner you will find a new system spring out of this, to which it served in its turn as a foundation and support."

SECT. V.   *Mystical or moral worship, or the system*

of a future state.

"IN reality, when the vulgar heard talk of a new heaven and another world, they soon gave a body to these fictions; they erected on it a solid stage and real scenes; and their notions of geography and astronomy served to strengthen, if they did not give rise to the allusion.

"On the one hand, the Phenician navigators, those who pass the pillars of Hercules to fetch the pewter of Thule and the amber of the Baltic, related that at the extremity of the world, the boundaries of the ocean (the Mediterranean), where the sun sets to the countries of Asia, there were fortunate Islands, the abode of an everlasting spring; and at a farther distance, hyperborean regions, placed under the earth (relatively to the tropics), where reigned an eternal night*. From these stories, badly understood, and no doubt confusedly related, the imagination of the people composed the Elysian Fields (64), delightful sports in a world below, having their heaven, their sun, and their stars; and Tartarus, a place of darkness, humidity, mire, and chilling frost. Now, inasmuch as mankind, inquisitive about all that of which they are ignorant, and desirous of a protracted existence, had already everted their faculties respecting what was to become of them after death, inasmuch, as they had early reasoned upon that principle of life which animates the body, and which quits it without changing the form of the body, and had conceived to themselves airy substances, phantoms and shades, they loved to believe that they should resume in the

* Nights of six months duration.

subterranean world that life which it was so painful to lose; and this abode appeared commodious for the reception of those beloved objects which they could not prevail on themselves to renounce.

"On the other hand, the astrological and philosophical priests told such stories of their heavens as perfectly quadrated with these fictions. Having, in their metaphorical language, denominated the equinoxes and solstices the gates of heaven, or the entrance of the seasons, they explained the terrestrial phenomena by saying, that through the gate of horn (first the bull, afterwards the ram,) vivifying fires descended, which, in spring, gave life to vegetation, and aquatic Spirits, which caused, at the solstice, the overflowing of the Nile: that through the gate of ivory, (originally the Bowman, or Sagittarius, then the Balance,) and through that of Capricorn, or the urn, the emanations or influences of the heavens returned to their source and re-ascended to their origin; and the Milky Way which passed through the doors of the solstices, seemed to them to have been placed there on purpose to be their road and vehicle (65). The celestial scene farther presented, according to their Atlas, a river (the Nile, designated by the windings of the Hydra); together with a barge (the vessel Argo), and the dog sirius, both bearing relation to that river, of which they foreboded the overflowing. These circumstances, added to the preceding ones, increased the probability of the fiction; and thus, to arrive at Tartarus or Elysium, souls were obliged to cross the rivers Styx and Acheron, in the boat of Charon the ferryman, and to pass through the doors of horn and ivory, which were guarded by the mastiff Cerberus. At length a civil usage was joined to all these inventions, and gave them consistency.

"The inhabitants of Egypt having remarked that the putrefaction of dead bodies became in their burning climate the source of pestilence and diseases, the custom was introduced in a great number of states, of burying the dead at a distance from the inhabited districts, in the desert which lies at the West. To arrive there it was necessary to cross the canals of the river in a boat, and to pay a toll to the ferryman, otherwise the body, remaining unburied, would have been left a prey to wild beasts. This custom suggested to her civil and religious legislators, a powerful means of affecting the manners of her inhabitants; and addressing savage and uncultivated men with the motives of filial piety and reverence for the dead, they introduced, as a necessary condition, the undergoing that previous trial which should decide whether the deceased deserved to be admitted upon the footing of his family honours into the *black city*. Such an idea too well accorded with the rest of the business not to be incorporated with it: it accordingly entered for an article into religious creeds, and hell had its Minos and its Radamanthus, with the wand, the chair, the guards and the urn, after the exact model of this civil transaction. The Divinity then, for the first time, became a subject of moral and political consideration, a legislator, by so much the more formidable as, while his judgment was final and his decrees without appeal, he was unapproachable to his subjects. This mythological and fabulous creation, composed as it was of scattered and discordant parts, then became a source of future punishments and rewards, in which divine justice was supposed to correct the vices and errors of this transitory state. A spiritual and mystical system, such as I have mentioned, acquired so much the more credit as it applied itself to the mind by every argument suited to it. The oppressed looked thither for an indemnification, and entertained the consoling hope of vengeance; the oppressor expected by the costliness of his offerings to secure to himself impunity, and at the same time employed this principle to inspire the vulgar with timidity; kings and priests, the heads of the people, saw in it a new source of power, as they reserved to themselves the privilege of awarding the favours or the censure of the great Judge of all, according to the opinion they should inculcate of the odiousness of crimes and the meritoriousness of virtue.

"Thus, then, an invisible and imaginary world entered into competition with that which was real. Such, O Persians! was the origin of your renovated earth, your city of resurrection, placed under the equator, and distinguished from all other cities by this singular attribute, that the bodies of its inhabitants cast no shade (66). Such, O Jews and Christians! disciples of the Persians, was the source of your new Jerusalem, your paradise and your heaven, modelled upon the astrological heaven of Hermes. Meanwhile, your hell, O ye Mussulmans! a subterraneous pit surmounted by a bridge, your balance of souls and good works, your judgment pronounced by the angels Monkir and Nekir, derives its attributes from the mysterious ceremonies of the cave of Mithra (67); and your heaven is exactly coincident with that of Osiris, Ormudz, and Brama."

SECT. VI. *Sixth System: The animated world, or worship of the universe under different emblems.*

"WHILE the nations were losing themselves in the dark labyrinth of mythology and fables, the physiological priests, pursuing their studies and enquiries about the order, and disposition of the universe, came to fresh results, and set up fresh systems of powers and moving causes.

" Long confined to simple appearances, they had
only seen in the motion of the stars an unknown play
of luminous bodies, which they supposed to roll
round the earth, the central point of all the spheres;
but from the moment they had discovered the rotundity of our planet, the consequences of the first fact
led them to other considerations, and from inference
to inference they rose to the highest conceptions of
astronomy and physics.

" In truth, having conceived the enlightened and
simple idea, that the celestial globe is a small circle
inscribed in the greater circle of the heavens, the theory of the concentral circles naturally presented itself to their hypothesis, to resolve the unknown circle of the terrestrial globe by known points of the celestial circle; and the measure of one or several degrees of the meridian, gave precisely the total circumference. Then taking for compass the diameter of
the earth, a fortunate genius described with auspici-
ous boldness the immense orbits of the heavens; and,
by an unheard of abstraction, man, who scarcely peoples the grain of sand of which he is the inhabitant,
embraced the infinite distances of the stars, and
launched himself into the abyss of space and duration. There a new order of the universe presented
itself, of which the petty globe that he inhabited no
longer appeared to him to be the centre: this important part was transferred to the enormous mass of the
sun, which became the inflamed pivot of eight cir-
cumjacent spheres, the movements of which were
henceforward submitted to exact calculation.

" The human mind had already done a great deal,
by undertaking to resolve the disposition and order of
the great beings of nature; but not contented with
this first effort, it wished also to resolve its mechanism, and discover its origin and motive principle.
And here it is that, involved in the abstract and metaphysical depths of motion and its first cause, of the

inherent or communicated properties of matter, together with its successive forms and extent, or, in other
words, of boundless space and time, these physiological divines lost themselves in a chaos of subtle argument and scholastic controversy.

"The action of the sun upon terrestrial bodies,
having first led them to consider its substance as
pure and elementary fire, they made it the focus and
reservoir of an ocean of igneous and luminous fluid,
which, under the name of ether, filled the universe,
and nourished the beings contained therein. They
afterwards discovered, by the analysis of a more accurate philosophy, this fire, or a fire similar to it, entering into the composition of all bodies, and perceived
that it was the grand agent in that spontaneous motion, which in animals is denominated life, and in
plants vegetation. From hence they were led to conceive of the mechanism and action of the universe,
as of a homogeneous WHOLE, a single body, whose
parts, however distant in place, had a reciprocal connexion with each other (69); and of the world as a
living substance, animated by the organical circulation of an igneous or rather electrical fluid (70),
which, by an analogy borrowed from men and animals, was supposed to have the sun for its heart
(71).

"Meanwhile, among the theological philosophers,
one sect beginning from those principles, the result
of experiment, said: That nothing was annihilated in
the world; that the elements were unperishable;
that they changed their combinations, but not their
nature; that the life and death of beings were nothing more than the varied modifications of the same
atoms; that matter contained in itself properties,
which were the cause of all its modes of existing;
that the world was eternal (72), having no bounds
either of space or duration. Others said: That the

whole universe was God; and, according to them, God was at once effect and cause, agent and patient, moving principle and thing moved, having for laws the invariable properties which constitute fatality; and they designated their idea sometimes by the emblem of PAN (the GREAT ALL); or of Jupiter, with a starry front, a planetary body, and feet of animals; or by the symbol of the Orphic egg*, whose yolk suspended in the middle of a liquid encompassed by a vault, represented the globe of the sun swimming in ether in the middle of the vault of heaven (73); or by the emblem of a large round serpent, figurative of the heavens, where they placed the first principle of motion, and for that reason of an azure colour, studded with gold spots (the stars), and devouring his tail, that is, re-entering into himself, by winding continually like the revolutions of the spheres; or by the emblem of a man, with his feet pressed and tied together to denote immutable existence, covered with a mantle of all colours, like the appearance of nature, and wearing on his head a sphere of gold (74), figurative of the sphere of the planets; or by that of another man sometimes seated upon the flower of *Lotos*, borne upon the abyss of the waters, at others reclined upon a pile of twelve cushions, signifying the twelve celestial signs. And this, O nations of India, Japan, Siam, Thibet, and China! is the theology, which, invented by the Egyptians, has been transmitted down and preserved among yourselves, in the pictures you gave of Brama, Beddou, Sommanacodom, and Omito. This, O ye Jews and Christians! is the counterpart of an opinion, of which you have retained a certain portion, when you describe God as *the breath of life moving upon the face of the waters*, alluding to the wind (75), which at the origin of the world, that is, at

* Vide Œdip. Ægypt. tom. II. p. 205.

the departure of the spheres from the sign of the
Crab, announced the overflowing of the Nile, and
seemed to be the preliminary of creation."

SECT. VII. *Seventh System: Worship of the* SOUL
of the WORLD; *that is, the element of fire,
the vital principle of the universe.*

"BUT a third set of the theological philosophers,
disgusted with the idea of a being at once effect and
cause, agent and patient, and uniting in one and the
same nature all contrary attributes, distinguished the
moving principle from the thing moved; and laying
it down as a datum that matter was in itself inert,
they pretended that it received its properties from a
distinct agent, of which it was only the envelope or
case. Some made this agent the igneous principle,
the acknowledged author of all motion; others made
it the fluid called ether, because it was thought to be
more active and subtile: now, as they denominated
the vital and motive principle in animals, a soul, a
spirit; and as they always reasoned by comparison,
and particularly by comparison with human existence,
they gave to the motive principle of the whole universe the name of soul, intelligence, spirit; and God
was the vital spirit, which, diffused through all beings, animated the vast body of the world. This idea
was represented sometimes by Jupiter, essence of motion and animation, principle of existence, or rather
existence itself (76); at other times by Vulcan, of
Phtha, elementary principle of fire, or by the altar of
Vesta, placed centrally in her temple, like the sun in
the spheres; and again by *Kneph*, a human being
dressed in deep blue, holding in his hands a sceptre
and a girdle (the Zodiac), wearing on his head a cap

with feathers, to express the fugacity of thought, and producing from his mouth the great egg (77).

"As a consequence from this system, every being containing in itself a portion of the igneous or etherial fluid, the universal and common mover; and that fluid, soul of the world, being the Deity, it followed that the souls of all beings were a part of God himself, partaking of all his attributes, that is, being an indivisible, simple, and immortal substance : and hence is derived the whole system of the immortality of the soul, which at first was eternity (78). Hence also its transmigrations known by the name metempsychosis, that is to say, passage of the vital principle from one body to another; an idea which sprung from the real transmigration of the material elements. Such, O Indians, Budsoists, Christians, Mussulmans, was the origin of all your ideas of the spirituality of the soul! Such was the source of the reveries of Pythagoras and Plato, your institutors, and who were themselves but the echoes of another, the last sect of visionary philosophers that it is necessary to examine.

SECT. VIII.   *Eighth system: The world a machine: worship of the Demi-ourgos, or supreme artificer.*

"HITHERTO the theologians, in exercising their faculties on the detached and subtile substances of ether and the igneous principle, had not however ceased to treat of existences palpable and perceptible to the senses, and their theology had continued to be the theory of physical powers, placed sometimes exclusively in the stars, and sometimes disseminated through the universe. But at the period at which we are arrived, some superficial minds, losing the chain of ideas which had directed these profound enquiries, or ignorant of the facts which served as their basis, rendered abortive all the results that had been obtained from them, by the introduction of a strange and novel chimera. They pretended that the universe, the heavens, the stars, the sun, differed in no respect from an ordinary machine; and applying to this hypothesis a comparison drawn from the works of art, they erected an edifice of the most whimsical sophisms. " A machine," said they, " cannot form itself, there must be a workman to construct it; its very existence implies this. The world is a machine: it has therefore an artificer (79)."

" Hence the *Demi-ourgos*, or supreme artificer, the autocrator and sovereign of the universe. It was in vain that the ancient philosophy objected to the hypothesis, that this artificer did not stand in less need of parents and an author, and that a scheme, which added only one link to the chain, by taking the attribute of eternity from the world and giving it to the creator, was of little value. These innovations, not contented with a first paradox, added a second, and applying to their artificer the theory of human understanding, pretended that the *Demi-ourgos* fashioned his machine upon an archetype or idea extant in his mind. In a word; just as their masters, the natural philosophers, had placed the *primum mobile* in the sphere of the fixed stars, under the appellation of intelligence and reason, so their apes, the spiritualists, adopting the same principle, made it an attribute of the *Demi-ourgos*, representing this being as a distinct substance, necessarily existing, to which they applied the terms of *Mens* or *Logos*; in other words, understanding and speech. Separately from this being, they held the existence of a solar principle, or soul of the world, which, taken with the preceding, made three gradations of divine personages; first, the *De-*

P

mi-ourgos or supreme artificer; secondly, the *Logos,* understanding or speech: and thirdly, the spirit or soul of the world (80). And this, O Christians! is the fiction on which you have founded your doctrine of the Trinity; this is the system, which, born a Heretic in the Egyptian temples, transmitted a Heathen to the schools of Greece and Italy, is now Catholic or Orthodox by the conversion of its partisans, the disciples of Pythagoras and Plato, to Christianity.

" Thus the Deity, after having been originally considered as the sensible and various action of meteors and the elements; then as the combined power of the stars, considered in their relation to terrestrial objects; then as those terrestrial objects themselves, in consequence of confounding symbols with the things they represented; then as the complex power of Nature, in her two principal operations of production and destruction; then as the animated world without distinction of agent and patient, cause and effect; then as the solar principle or element of fire acknowledged as the sole cause of motion—the Deity, I say, considered under all these different views, became at last a chimerical and abstract being; a scholastic subtlety of substance without form, of body without figure; a true delirium of the mind beyond the power of reason at all to comprehend. But in this its last transformation, it seeks in vain to conceal itself from the senses: the seal of its origin is indelibly stamped upon it. All its attributes, borrowed from the physical attributes of the universe, as immensity, eternity, indivisibility, incomprehensibleness; or from the moral qualities of man, as goodness, justice, majesty; and its very names (81), derived from the physical beings which were its types, particularly the sun, the planets, and the world, present to us continually, in spite of those who would corrupt and disguise it, infallible marks of its genuine nature.

" Such is the chain of ideas through which the
human mind had already run at a period anterior to
the positive recitals of history; and since their systematic form proves them to have been the result of
one scene of study and investigation, every thing in-
clines us to place the theatre of investigation, where
its primitive elements were generated, in Egypt.
There their progress was rapid, because the idle curiosity of the theological philosophers had, in the re-
tirement of the temples, no other food than the enigma of the universe, which was ever present to their
minds; and because, in the political dissensions
which long disunited that country, each state had its
college of priests, who, being in turns auxiliaries or
rivals, hastened by their disputes the progress of
science and discovery (82).

" On the borders of the Nile there happened at
that distant period, what has since been repeated all
over the globe. In proportion as each system was
formed, it excited by its novelty quarrels and schisms:
then, gaining credit even by persecution, it either destroyed anterior ideas, or incorporated itself with and
modified them. But political institutions taking
place, all opinions, by the aggregation of states and
mixture of different people, were at length confounded: and the chain of ideas being lost, theology, plunged in a chaos, became a mere logogryph of old traditions no longer understood. Religion, losing its object, was now nothing more than a political expedient
by which to rule the credulous vulgar; and was embraced either by men credulous themselves and the
dupes of their own visions, or by bold and energetic
spirits, who formed vast projects of ambition."

SECT. IX.	*Religion of Moses, or worship of the soul
of the world (You-piter).*

"OF this latter description was the Hebrew legislator, who, desirous of separating his nation from
every other, and of forming a distinct and exclusive
empire, conceived the design of taking for its basis
religious prejudices, and of erecting round it a sacred
rampart of rites and opinions. But in vain did he
proscribe the worship of symbols, the reigning religion at that time in Lower Egypt and Phenicia (83);
his God was not on that account the less an Egyptian
God, of the invention of those priests whose disciple
Moses had been, and *Yahouh* (84), detected by his
very name, which means essence of beings, and by
his symbol, the fiery bush, is nothing more than the
soul of the world, the principle of motion, which
Greece shortly after adopted under the same denomination in her *You-piter*, generative principle, and
under that of *Ei* existence (85); which the Thebans
consecrated by the name of *Kneph*; which Saiis worshipped under the emblem of *Isis veiled*, with this inscription, *I am all that has been, all that is, and all
that will be, and no mortal has drawn aside my veil*;
which Pythagoras honoured under the appellation of
Vesta, and which the Stoic philosophy defined with
precision, by calling it the principle of fire. In vain
did Moses wish to blot from his religion whatever
could bring to remembrance the worship of the stars;
a multiplicity of traits in spite of his exertions still
remained to point it out: the seven lamps of the
great candlestick, the twelve stones or signs of the
Urim of the high priest, the feast of the two equinoxes, each of which at that epocha formed a year,
the ceremony of the lamb or celestial ram, then at its

fifteenth degree; lastly, the name of Osiris, even preserved in his song (86), and the ark or coffer, an imitation of the tomb in which that God was inclosed;
all these remain to bear record to the genealogy of
his ideas, and their derivation from the common
source."

SECT. X.   *Religion of Zoroaster.*

"ZOROASTER was also a man of the same bold and
energetic stamp; who, five centuries after Moses,
and in the time of David, revived and moralized
among the Medes and Bactrians the whole Egyptian
system of Osiris, under the names of Ormuzd and Ahrimanes.   He called the reign of summer, virtue and
good; the reign of winter, sin and evil; the renovation of nature in spring, creation; the revival of the
spheres in the secular periods of the conjunction, resurrection, and his future life; hell, paradise, were
the Tarsarus and Elysium of the ancient astrologers
and geographers; in a word, he only consecrated the
already-existing reveries of the mystic system."

SECT. XI.   *Budoism, or religion of the Samaneans.*

"IN the same rank must be included the promulgators of the sepulchral doctrine of the Samaneans;
who, on the basis of the metempsychosis, raised the
misanthropic system of self-renunciation and denial,
who, laying it down as a principle, that the body is
only a prison, where the soul lives in impure confine-
ment; that life is but a dream, an illusion, and the
world a place of passage to another country, to a life
without end; placed virtue and perfection in absolute insensibility, in the abnegation of physical or-

gans, in the annihilation of all being : whence resulted the fasts, penances, macerations, solitude, con-
templations, and all the deplorable practices of the
mad-headed Anchorets."

SECT. XII.   *Braminism, or the Indian System.*

"FINALLY of the same cast were the founders of
the Indian system; who, refining after Zoroaster upon the two principles of creation and destruction, introduced an immediate one, that of conservation, and
upon their trinity in unity, of Brama, Chiven, and
Bichenou, accumulated a multitude of traditional allegories, and the alembicated subtleties of their meta-
physics.

"These are the materials, which scattered through
Asia, existed there for many ages, when, by a fortuitous course of events and circumstances, new combinations of them were introduced on the banks of the
Euphrates and on the shores of the Mediterranean."

SECT. XIII.   *Christianity, or the allegorical worship
of the Sun, under the cabalistical names of* CHRISEN
or CHRIST, *and* YESUS *or* JESUS.

"IN constituting a separate people, Moses had
vainly imagined that he should guard them from the
influence of every foreign idea: but an invincible inclination, founded on affinity of origin, continually
called back the Hebrews to the worship of the neighbouring nations; and the relations of commerce that
necessarily subsisted between them, tended every day
to strengthen the propensity. While the Mosaic institution maintained its ground, the coercion of go-

vernment and the laws was a considerable obstacle to
the inlet of innovations; yet even then the principal
places were full of idols, and God the sun had his
chariot and horses painted in the palaces of kings,
and in the very temple of Yahouh: but when the
conquest of the kings of Nineveh and Babylon had
dissolved the bands of public power, the people left
to themselves, and solicited by their conquerors, no
longer kept a restraint on their inclinations, and profane opinions were openly professed in Judea. At
first the Assyrian colonies, placed in the situation of
the old tribes, filled the kingdom of Samaria with the
dogmas of the Magi, which soon penetrated into Judea. Afterwards Jerusalem having been subjugated,
the Egyptians, Syrians and Arabs, entering this open
country, introduced their tenets, and the religion of
Moses thus underwent a second alteration. In like
manner the priests and great men, removing to Babylon, and educated in the science of the Chaldeans, imbibed, during a residence of seventy years, every principle of their theology, and from that moment the
dogmas of the evil Genius (Satin), of the archangel
Michael (87), of the Ancient of Days (Ormudz), of
the rebellious angels, the celestial combats, the immortality of the soul, and the resurrection, dogmas
unknown to Moses, or rejected by him, since he observes a perfect silence respecting them, became na-
turalized among the Jews.

"On their return to their country, the emigrants
brought back with them these ideas: and at first the
innovations occasioned disputes between their partisans, the Pharisees, and the adherents to the ancient
national worship, the Sadducees: but the former, seconded by the inclination of the people, and the habits they had already contracted, and supported by
the authority of the Persians, their deliverers, finally
gained the ascendency, and the theology of Zoroaster
was consecrated by the children of Moses (88).

" A fortuitous analogy between two leading ideas, proved particularly favourable to this coalition and formed the basis of a last system, not less surprising in its fortune than in the causes of its formation.

" From the time that the Assyrians had destroyed the kingdom of Samaria, some sagacious spirits foresaw, announced, and predicted the same fate to Jerusalem: and all their predictions were stamped by this particularity, that they always concluded with prayers for a happy re-establishment and regeneration, which were in like manner spoken of in the way of prophecies. The enthusiasm of the Hierophants had figured a royal deliverer, who was to re-establish the nation in its ancient glory: the Hebrews were again to become a powerful and conquering people, and Jerusalem the capital of an empire that was to extend over the whole world.

" Events having realized the first part of those predictions, the ruin of Jerusalem, the people clung to the second with a firmness of belief proportioned to their misfortunes; and the afflicted Jews waited with the impatience of want and of desire for that victorious king and deliverer that was to come, in order to save the nation of Moses, and restore the throne of David.

"The sacred and mythological traditions of precedent times had spread over all Asia a tenet perfectly analogous. A great mediator, a final judge, a future saviour, was spoken of, who, as king, God, and victorious legislator, was to restore the golden age upon earth (89), to deliver the world from evil, and regain for mankind the reign of good, the kingdom of peace and happiness. These ideas and expressions were in every mouth, and they consoled the people under that deplorable state of real suffering into which they had been plunged by successive conquests and conquerors, and the barbarous despotism of their governments. This resemblance between the oracles of different nations and the predictions of the prophets, excited the attention of the Jews; and the prophets had doubtless been careful to infuse into their pictures, the spirit and style of the sacred books employed in the Pagan mysteries. The arrival of a great ambassador, of a final saviour, was therefore the general expectation in Judea, when at length a singular circumstance was made to determine the precise period of his coming.

"It was recorded in the sacred books of the Persians and the Chaldeans, that the world, composed of a total revolution of twelve thousand periods, was divided into two partial revolutions, of which one, the age and reign of good was to terminate at the expiration of six thousand, and the other the age and reign of evil, at the expiration of another six thousand.

"Their first authors had meant by these recitals, the annual revolution of the great celestial orb (a revolution composed of twelve months or signs each divided into a thousand parts), and the two systematic periods of winter and summer, each consisting equally of six thousand. But these equivocal expressions having been erroneously explained, and having received an absolute and moral, instead of their astrological and physical sense, the result was, that the annual was taken for a secular world, the thousand periods for a thousand years; and judging, from the appearance of things, that the present was the age of misfortune, they inferred that it would terminate at the expiration of the six thousand pretended years (90).

"Now, according to the Jewish computation, six thousand years had already nearly elapsed since the supposed creation of the world (91). This coincidence produced considerable fermentation in the minds of the people. Nothing was thought of but the approaching termination. The Hierophants were interrogated, and their sacred books examined. The great Meditator and final Judge was expected, and his advent desired, that an end might be put to so many calamities. This was so much the subject of conversation, that some one was said to have seen him, and a rumour of this kind was all that was wanting to establish a general certainty. The popular report became a demonstrated fact; the imaginary ·being was realized; and all the circumstances of mythological tradition being in some manner connected with this phantom, the result was an authentic and regular history, which from henceforth it was blasphemy to doubt.

" In this mythological history the following traditions were recorded: "That, *in the beginning, a man and a woman had, by their fall, brought sin and evil into the world.*" (Examine plate II.)

" By this was denoted the astronomical fact of the celestial Virgin, and the herdsman (Bootes) who, setting heliacally at the autumnal equinox, resigned the heavens to the wintry constellations, and seemed, in sinking below the horizon, to introduce into the world the genius of evil, Ahrimanes, represented by the constellation of the serpent (92).

" *That the woman had decoyed and seduced the man* (93)."

" And in reality, the Virgin setting first, appears to draw the Herdsman (Bootes) after her.

" *That the woman had tempted him, by offering him fruit pleasant to the sight and good for food, which gave the knowledge of good and evil.*"

" Manifestly alluding to the Virgin, who is depicted holding a bunch of fruit in her hand, which she appears to extend towards the Herdsman: in like manner the branch, emblem of autumn, placed in the picture of Mithra (94) on the front of winter and summer seems to open the door, and to give the knowledge, the key, of good and evil.

"*That this couple had been driven from the celestial garden, and that a cherub with a flaming sword had been placed at the door to guard it.*"

"And when the Virgin and the Herdsman sink below the Western horizon, Perseus rises on the opposite side (95), and sword in hand, this Genius may be said to drive them from the summer heaven, the garden and reign of fruits and flowers.

"*That from this virgin would be born, would spring up a shoot, a child, that should crush the serpent's head, and deliver the world from sin.*"

"By this was denoted the Sun, which, at the period of the summer solstice, at the precise moment that the Persian Magi drew the horoscope of the new year, found itself in the bosom of the Virgin, and which, on this account, was represented in their astrological pictures, in the form of an infant suckled by a chaste virgin (96), and afterwards became, at the vernal equinox the Ram or Lamb, conqueror of the constellation of the Serpent, which disappeared from the heavens.

"*That in his infancy, this restorer of the divine or celestial nature, would lead a mean, humble, obscure, and indigent life.*"

"By which was meant, that the winter sun was humbled, depressed below the horizon, and that this first period of his four ages, or the seasons, was a period of obscurity and indigence, of fasting and privation.

"*That being put to death by the wicked, he would gloriously rise again, ascend from hell into heaven, where he would reign for ever.*"

By these expressions was described the life of the same Sun, who, terminating his career at the winter solstice, when Typhon and the rebellious angels exercised their sway, seemed to be put to death by them; but shortly after revived and rose again (97) in the firmament, where he still remains.

"These traditions went still farther, specifying his astrological and mysterious names, maintaining that he was called sometimes *Chris* or Conservator (98); and hence the Hindoo God, *Chris-en*, or *Christna*; and the Christian *Chris-tos* the son of Mary. That at other times he was called *Yes*, by the union of three letters, which, according to their numerical value, form the number 608, one of the solar periods (99). And behold, O Europeans, the name which, with a Latin termination has become your *Yes-us* or Jesus; the ancient and cabalistical name given to young Bacchus, the clandestine son of the virgin Minerva, who in the whole history of his life, and even in his death, calls to mind the history of the God of the Christians: that this is the star of day, o fwhich they are both of them emblems."

At these words a violent murmur arose on the part of the Christian groupes; but the Mahometans, the Lamas, and the Hindoos, having called them to order, the orator thus concluded his discourse.

"You are not to be told," said he, "in what manner the rest of this system was formed in the chaos and anarchy of the three first centuries: how a multiplicity of opinions divided the people, all of which were embraced with equal zeal and retained with equal obstinacy, because alike founded on ancient tradition, they were alike sacred. You know how, at the end of three centuries, government having espoused one of these sects, made it the orthodox religion; that is to say, the predominated religion, to the exclusion of the rest, which, on account of their inferiority, were denominated heresies; how, and by what means of violence and seduction this religion was propagated and gained strength, and afterwards became divided and weakened; how, six centuries after the innovation of Christianity, another system was formed out' of its materials and those of the Jews, and a political and theological empire was created by Mahomet at the expence of that of Moses and the vicars of Jesus.

" Now if you take a retrospect of the whole history of the spirit of religion, you will find that in its origin it had no other author than the sensations and wants of man : that the idea of God had no other type, no other model, than that of physical powers, material existences, operating good or evil, by impressions of pleasure or pain on sensible beings. You will find that in the formation of every system, this spirit of religion pursued the same track, and was uniform in its proceedings ; that in all, the dogma never failed to represent, under the name of God, the operations of nature, and the passions and prejudices of men ? that in all, morality had for its sole end, desire of happiness and aversion to pain ; but that the people and the majority of legislators, ignorant of the true road that led thereto, invented false, and therefore contrary ideas of virtue and vice, of good and evil, that is, of what renders man happy or miserable. You will find, that in all, the means and causes of propagation and establishment exhibited the same scenes, the same passions, and the same events ; continual disputes about words, false pretexts for inordinate zeal, for revolutions, for wars, lighted up by the ambition of chiefs, by the chicanery of promulgators, by the credulity of proselytes, by the ignorance of the vulgar, and by the grasping cupidity and the intolerant pride of all. In short, you will find that the whole history of the spirit of religion is, merely that of the fallibility and uncertainty of the human mind, which, placed in a world that it does not comprehend, is yet desirous of solving the enigma ; and which, the astonished spectator of this mysterious and visible prodigy, invents, causes, supposes ends, builds systems ; then, finding one defective, abandons it for

O

another not less vicious : hates the error that it has renounced, is ignorant of the new one that it adopts ; rejects the truth of which it is in pursuit, invents chimeras of heterogeneous and contradictory beings, and, ever dreaming of wisdom and happiness, looses itself in·a labyrinth of torments and illusions."

―――

CHAP. XXIII.

END OF ALL RELIGIONS THE SAME.

THUS spoke the orator, in the name of those who had made the origin and genealogy of religious ideas their peculiar study.

The theologians of the different systems now expressed their opinions of this discourse. " It is an impious representation," said some, " which aims at nothing less than the subversion of all belief, the introducing insubordination into the minds of men, and annihilating our power and ministry."—" It is a romance," said others, " a tissue of conjectures, fabricated with art, but destitute of foundation."---The moderate and prudent said, " Supposing all this to be true, where is the use of revealing these mysteries ?. Our opinions are doubtless pervaded with errors, but those errors are a necessary curb on the multitude. The world has gone on thus for two thousand years ; why should we now alter its course ?"

The murmur of disapprobation, which never fails to rise against every kind of innovation, already began to increase, when a numerous groupe of plebians and untaught men of every country and nation, without prophets, without doctors, without religious worship, advancing in the sand, attracted the attention of the whole assembly: and one of them, addressing himself to the legislators, spoke as follows:

" Mediators and umpires of nations! The strange recitals that have been made during the whole of the present debate, we never till this day heard of; and our understanding, astonished and bewildered at such a multitude of doctrines, some of them learned, others absurd, and all unintelligible, remains in doubt and uncertainty. One reflection however has struck us: in reviewing so many prodigious facts, so many contradictory assertions, we could not avoid asking ourselves, Of what importance to us are all these discussions? Where is the necessity of our knowing what happened five or six thousand years ago, in countries of which we are ignorant, among men who will ever be unknown to us? True or false, of what importance is it to us to know whether the world has existed six thousand years or twenty thousand; whether it was made of something or of nothing; of itself, or by an artificer, equally in his turn requiring an author? What! uncertain as we are of what is passing around us, shall we pretend to ascertain what is transacting in the sun, the moon, and imaginary spaces? Having forgotten our own infancy, shall we pretend to know the infancy of the world? Who can attest what he has never seen? Who can certify the truth of what no one comprehends?

" Beside, what will it avail as to our existence, whether we believe or reject these chimeras? Hitherto neither our fathers nor ourselves have had any idea of them, and yet we do not perceive that on that account we have experienced more or less sun, more or less subsistence, more or less good or evil.

" If the knowledge of these things be necessary, how is it that we have lived as happily without it as those whom it has so much disquieted? If it be su-

perfluous, why should we now take upon ourselves
the burthen ?"—Then addressing himself to the doctors and theologians: How can it be required of us,
poor and ignorant as we are, whose every moment is
scarcely adequate to the cares of our subsistence and
the labour- of which you reap the profit; how can
it be required of us to be versed in the numerous histories you have related, to read the variety of books
which you have quoted, and to learn the different
languages in which they are written ? If our lives
were protracted to a thousand years, scarcely would
it be sufficient for this purpose."

" It is not necessary," said the doctors, " that you
should acquire all this science: we possess it in your
stead."

" Meanwhile,' replied these children of simplicity,
" with all your science, do you agree among yourselves ? What then is its utility ? Besides, how can
you answer for us ? If the faith of one man may be
the substitute of the faith of many, what need was
there that you should believe ? Your fathers might
believe for you; and that would have been the more
reasonable, since they were the eye-witnesses upon
whose credit you depend. Lastly, what is this circumstance which you call belief, if it has no practical
tendency ? And what practical tendency can you discover in this question, whether the world be eternal
or no ?"

" To believe wrong respecting it would be offensive
to God," said the doctors.

" How do you know that ?" cried the children of
simplicity.

" From our scriptures," replied the doctors.

" We do not understand them," rejoined the simple men.

" We understand them for you," said the doctors.

"There lies the difficulty," resumed the simple men. "By what right have you appointed yourselves mediators between God and us?"

"By the command of God," said the doctors

"Give us the proof of that command," said the simple men.

"It is in our scriptures,"said the doctors.

"We do not understand them," answered the simple men. "nor can we understand how a just God can place you over our heads. Why does our common Father require us to believe the same propositions with a less degree of evidence? He has spoken to you: be it so; he is infallible, he cannot deceive you. But we are spoken to by you; and who will assure us that you are not deceived, or that you are incapable of deceiving? If we are mistaken, how can it consist with the justice of God, to condemn us for the neglect of a rule with which we were never acquainted?"

"He has given you the law of nature," said the doctors.

"What is the law of nature?" said the simple men. "If this law be sufficient, why does he give us another? If it be insufficient, why did he give us that?"

"The judgments of God," replied the doctors, "are mysterious; his justice is not restrained by the rules of human justice."

"If justice with him and with us," said the simple men, "mean a different thing, what criterion can we have to judge of his justice? And once more, to what purpose all these laws? What end does he purpose by them?"

"To render you more happy," replied a doctor, "by rendering you better and more virtuous. God has manifested himself by so many oracles and prodigies to teach mankind the proper use of his benefits, and to dissuade them from injuring each other."

" If that be the case," said the simple men, " the studies and reasonings you told us of are unnecessary: we want nothing but to have it clearly made out to us, which is the religion that best fulfils the end that all propose to themselves."

Instantly, every groupe boasting of the superior excellence of its morality, there arose among the partisans of the different systems of worship, a new dispute more violent than any preceding one. "Ours," said the Mahometans, "is the purest morality, which teaches every virtue useful to men and acceptable to God. We profess justice, disinterestedness, resignation, charity, alms-giving, and devotion. We torment not the soul with superstitious fears; we live free from alarm, and we die without remorse."

" And have you the presumption," replied the Christian priests, " to talk of morality; you whose chief has practised licentiousness, and preached doctrines that are a scandal to all purity, and the leading principle of whose religion is homicide and war? For the truth of this we appeal to experience. For twelve centuries past your fanaticism has never ceased to spread desolation and carnage through the nations of the earth; and that Asia, once so flourishing, now languishes in insignificance and barbarism, is ascribable to your doctrine; to that doctrine, the friend of ignorance, the enemy of all instruction, which, on the one hand, consecrating the most absolute despotism in him who commands, and on the other, imposing the most blind and passive obedience on those who are governed, has benumbed all the faculties of man, and plunged nations in a state of brutality.

" How different is the case with our sublime and celestial morality! It is she that drew the earth from its primitive barbarity, from the absurd and cruel superstitions of idolatry, from human sacrifices (100), and the orgies of Pagan mystery: it is she that has purified the manners of men, proscribed incest and adultery, polished savage nations, abolished slavery, introduced new and unknown virtues to the world, universal charity, the equality of mankind in the eyes of God, forgiveness and forgetfulness of injuries, extinction of the passions, contempt of worldly greatness, and, in short, taught the necessity of a life perfectly holy and spiritual."

"We admire," said the Mahometans, "the ease with which you can reconcile that evangelical charity and meekness of which you so much boast, with the injuries and outrages that you are continually exercising towards your neighbour. When you criminate with so little ceremony the morals of the great character revered by us, we have a fair opportunity of retorting upon you in the conduct of him whom you adore: but we disdain such advantages, and, confining ourselves to the real object of the question, we maintain, that your gospel morality is by no means characterised by the perfection which you ascribe to it. It is not true, that it has introduced into the world new and unknown virtues: for example, the equality of mankind in the eyes of God, and the fraternity and benevolence which are the consequence of this equality, were tenets formerly professed by the sects of Hermetics and Samaneans, (101), from whom you have your descent. As to forgiveness of injuries it had been taught by the Pagans themselves; but in the latitude you give to it, it ceases to be a virtue, and becomes an immorality and a crime. Your boasted precept, *to him that strikes thee on thy right cheek, turn the other also,* is not only contrary to the feelings of man, but a flagrant violation of every principle of justice; it emboldens the wicked by impunity, degrades the virtuous by the servility to which it subjects them; delivers up the world to disorder and tyranny, and dissolves the bands of society: such is the true spirit of your doctrine. The precepts and parables of your gospel also never represent God other than as a despot, acting by no rule of equity; than as a partial father, treating a debauched and prodigal son with greater favour than his obedient and virtuous children; than as a capricious master, giving the same wages to him who has wrought but one hour, as to those who have borne the burthen and heat of the day, and preferring the last comers to the first. In short, your morality throughout is unfriendly to human intercourse, a code of misanthropy, calculated to give men a disgust for life and society, and attach them to solitude and celibacy.

" With respect to the manner in which you have practised your boasted doctrine, we in our turn appeal to the testimony of fact, and ask; Was it your evangelical meekness and forbearance which excited those endless wars among your sectaries, those atrocious persecutions of what you call heretics, those crusades against the Arians, the Manicheans, and the Protestants; not to mention those which you have committed against us, nor the sacrilegious associations still subsisting among you, formed of men who have sworn to perpetuate them * ? Was it the charity of your gospel that led you to exterminate whole nations in America, and to destroy the empires of Mexico and Peru; that makes you still desolate Africa, the inhabitants of which you sell like cattle, notwithstanding the abolition of slavery that you pretend your religion has effected ; that makes you ravage India whose domains you usurp; in short, is it charity that has prompted you for three centuries past to disturb the peaceable inhabitants of three continents, the most prudent of whom, those of Japan and China, have been constrained to banish you from their country, that they might escape your chains and recover their domestic tranquillity ?"

* The Oath taken by the Knights of the Order of Malta, is to kill, or make the Mahometans prisoners, for the glory of God.

Here the Bramins, the Rabbins, the Bonzes, the Chamans, the Priests of the Molucca Islands, and of the coast of Guinea, overwhelming the Christian doctors with reproaches, cried, " Yes, these men are robbers and hypocrites, preaching simplicity to inveigle confidence; humility the more easy to enslave; poverty, in order to appropriate all riches to themselves; they promise another world the better to invade this; and while they preach toleration and charity, they commit to the flames, in the name of God, those who do not worship him exactly as they do."

" Lying priests," retorted the missionaries. " it is you who abuse the credulity of ignorant nations, that you may bend them to your yoke; your ministry is the art of imposture and deception: you have made religion a system of avarice and cupidity; you feign to have correspondence with spirits, and the oracles they issue are your own wills: you pretend to read the stars, and your desires only are what destiny decrees: you make idols speak, and the Gods are the mere instruments of your passions; you have invented sacrifices and libations for the sake of the profit you would thus derive from the milk of the flocks, and the flesh and fat of victims; and under the cloak of piety you devour the offerings made to Gods, who cannot eat, and the substance of the people, obtained by industry and toil."

" And you," replied the Bramins, the Bonzes, and the Chamans, " sell to the credulous survivor vain prayers for the souls of his dead relatives. With your indulgences and absolutions you have arrogated to yourselves the power and functions of God himself; and making a traffic of his grace, you have put heaven up to auction, and have founded, by your system of expiation, a tariff of crimes that has perverted the consciences of men (102)."

" Add to this," said the Imans, " that with these men has originated the most insidious of all wickedness, the absurd and impious obligation of recounting to them the most impenetrable secrets of actions, of thoughts of *velléites*, (confession): by means of which their insolent curiosity has carried its inquisition even to the sacred sanctuary of the nuptial bed (103), and the inviolable asylum of the heart."

By thus reproaching each other, the chiefs of the different worships revealed all the crimes of their ministry, all the hidden vices of their profession, and it appeared that the spirit, the system of conduct, the actions and manners of priests, were, among all nations, uniformly the same ; that every where they had formed secret associations, corporations of individuals, enemies to the rest of the society [104]:— that they had attributed to themselves certain prerogatives and immunities, in order to be exempt from the burthens which fell upon the other classes :— that they shared neither the toil of the labourer, nor the perils of the soldier, nor the vicissitudes of the merchant :—that they led a life of celibacy, to avoid domestic inconveniences and cares : that, under the garb of poverty, they found the secret of becoming rich, and of procuring every enjoyment : that under the name of mendicants, they collected imposts more considerable than those paid to princes :—that under the appellation of gifts and offerings, they obtained a certain revenue unaccompanied with trouble or expence : that upon the pretext of seclusion and devotion, they lived in indolence, and licentiousness :— that they had made alms a virtue, that they might subsist in comfort upon the labour of other men :— that they had invented the ceremonies of worship to attract the reverence of the people, calling themselves the mediators and interpreters of the Gods, with the sole view of assuming all his power ; and that for this purpose, according to the knowledge or ignorance of those upon whom they had to work, they made themselves, by turns, astrologers, casters of planets, augurers, magicians (106), necromancers, quacks, courtiers, confessors of princes, always aiming at influence for their own exclusive advantages:— that sometimes they had exalted the prerogative of kings, and held their persons to be sacred, to obtain their favour or participate in their power:—that at others they had decried this doctrine and preached the murder of tyrants (reserving it to themselves to specify the tyranny), in order to be revenged of the slights and disobedience they had experienced from them:—that at all times they had called by the name of impiety what proved injurious to their interest;— had opposed public instruction, that they might monopolize science; and in short, had universally found the secret of living in tranquillity amidst the anarchy they occasioned; secure, under the despotism they sanctioned; in indolence, amidst the industry they recommended: and in abundance, in the very bosom of scarcity; and all this, by carrying on the singular commerce of selling words and gestures to the credulous, who paid for them as for commodities of the greatest value (107).

Then the people, seized with fury, were upon the point of tearing to pieces the men who had deceived them; but the legislators, arresting this sally of violence, and addressing the chiefs and doctors, said: "And is it thus, O institutors of the people, that you have misled and abused them?"

And the terrified priests replied, "O legislators, we are men and the people are so superstitious! their weakness excited us to take advantage of it*."

And the kings said: "O legislators, the people are

---

* Consider in this view the Brabanters.

so servile and so ignorant! they have prostrated themselves before the yoke which we scarcely had the boldness to show to them*."

Then the legislators, turning towards the people, said to them: "Remember what you have just heard: it contains two important truths. Yes, it is yourselves that cause the evils of which you complain; it is you that encourage tyrants by a base flattery of their power, by an absurd admiration of their pretended beneficence, by converting obedience into servility, and liberty into licentiousness, and receiving every imposition with credulity. Can you think of punishing upon them the errors of your own ignorance and selfishness?"

And the people, smitten with confusion, remained in a melancholy silence.

━━

CHAP. XXIV.

SOLUTION OF THE PROBLEM OF CONTRADICTIONS.

THE legislators then resumed their address. "O nations!" said they, "we have heard the discussion of your opinions; and the discord that divides you has suggested to us various reflections, which we beg leave to propose to you as questions which it is necessary you should solve.

"Considering, in the first place, the numerous and contradictory creeds you have adopted, we would ask

---

* The inhabitants of Vienna, for example, who harnessed themselves like cattle, and drew the chariot of Leopold.

on what motives your persuasion is founded? Is it from deliberate choice that you have enlisted under the banners of one prophet rather than under those of another? Before you adopted this doctrine in preference to that, did you first compare, did you maturely examine them? Or has not your belief been rather the chance result of birth, and of the empire of education and habit? Are you not born Christians on the banks of the Tiber, Mahometans on those of the Euphrates, Idolaters on the shores of India, in the same manner as you are born fair in cold and temperate regions, and of a sable complexion under the African sun! And if your opinions are the effect of your position on the globe, of parentage, of imitation, are such fortuitous circumstances to be regarded as grounds of conviction and arguments of truth?

"In the second place, when we reflect on the proscriptive spirit and the arbitrary intolerance of your mutual claims, we are terrified at the consequences that flow from your principles. Nations! who reciprocally doom each other to the thunderbolts of celestial wrath, suppose the universal Being whom you revere, were at this moment to descend from heaven among this crowd of people, and, clothed in all his power, were to sit upon this throne to judge you: suppose him to say—" Mortals! I consent to adopt your own principles of justice into my administration. Of all the different religions you profess, a single religion shall now be preferred to the rest; all the others, this vast multitude of standards, of nations, of prophets, shall be condemned to everlasting destruction. Nor is this enough: among the different sects of the chosen religion one only shall experience my favour, and the rest be condemned. I will go farther than this: of this single sect, of this one religion, I will reject all the individuals whose conduct has not corresponded to their speculative precepts. O man! few indeed will then be the number of the

R

elect you assign me! Penurious hereafter will be the stream of beneficence which will succeed to my unbounded mercy! Rare and solitary will be the catalogue of admirers that you henceforth destine to my greatness and my glory."

And the legislators arising said: "It is enough; you have pronounced your will. Ye nations, behold the urn in which your names shall be placed; one single name shall be drawn from the multitude; approach and conclude this terrible lottery."—But the people, seized, with terror cried: "No, no; we are brethren and equals, we cannot consent to condemn each other."—Then the legislators having resumed their seats, continued: "O men! who dispute upon so many subjects, lend an attentive ear to a problem we submit to you, and decide it in the exercise of your own judgments."—The people accordingly lent the strictest attention; and the legislators lifting one hand towards heaven, and pointing to the sun, said: "O nations! is the form of this sun which enlightens you triangular or square?"—And they replied with one voice, "It is neither, it is round."

Then taking the golden balance that was upon the altar, "This metal," asked the legislators, "which you handle every day, is a mass of it heavier than any other mass of equal dimensions of brass?"—"Yes," the people again unanimously replied; "gold is heavier than brass."

The legislators then took the sword. "Is this iron less hard than lead?"—"No," said the nations.

"Is sugar sweet and gall bitter?"—"Yes."

"Do you love pleasure, and hate pain?"—"Yes."

"Respecting these objects, and a multiplicity of others of a similar nature, you have then but one opinion. Now tell us, is there an abyss in the centre of the earth, and are there inhabitants in the moon?"

At this question a general noise was heard, and every nation gave a different answer. Some replied in the affirmative, others in the negative; some said it was probable, others that it was an idle and ridiculous question, and others that it was a subject worthy of inquiry; in short, there prevailed among them a total disagreement.

After a short interval, the legislators having restored silence: "Nations," said they, "how is this to be accounted for? We proposed to you certain questions, and you were all of one opinion without distinction of race or sect: fair or black, disciples of Mahomet or of Moses, worshippers of Bedou or of Jesus, you all gave the same answer. We now propose another question, and you all differ! whence this unanimity in one case, and this discordance in the other?"

And the groupe of simple and untaught men replied: "The reason is obvious. Respecting the first questions, we see and feel the objects; we speak of them from sensation; respecting the second, they are above the reach of our senses, and we have no guide but conjecture."

"You have solved the problem," said the legislators; "and the following truth is thus by your own confession established: Whenever objects are present and can be judged of by your senses, you invariably agree in opinion; and you differ in sentiment only when they are absent and out of your reach.

"From this truth flows another equally clear and deserving of notice. Since you agree respecting what you with certainty know, it follows, that when you disagree, it is because you do not know, do not understand, are not sure of the object in question: or in other words, that you dispute, quarrel and fight among yourselves, for what is uncertain, for that of which you doubt. But is this wise? is this the part of rational and intelligent beings?

"And is it not evident, that it is not truth for which you contend; that it is not her cause you are jealous of maintaining, but the cause of your own passions and prejudices; that it is not the object as it really exists that you wish to verify, but the object as it appears to you; that it is not the evidence of the thing that you are anxious should prevail, but your personal opinion, your mode of seeing and judging? There is a power that you want to exercise, an interest that you want to maintain, a prerogative that you want to assume; in short, the whole is a struggle of vanity. And as every individual, when he compares himself with every other, finds himself to be his equal and fellow, he resists by a similar feeling of right; and from this right, which you all deny to each other, and from the inherent consciousness of your equality, spring your disputes, your combats, and your intolerance.

"Now, the only way of restoring unanimity is by returning to nature, and taking the order of things which she has established for your director and guide; and this farther truth will then appear from your uniformity of sentiment.

"That real objects have in themselves an identical, constant, and invariable mode of existence, and that in your organs exists a similar mode of being affected and impressed by them.

"But at the same time, inasmuch as these organs are liable to the direction of your will, you may receive different impressions, and find yourselves under different relations towards the same objects; so that you are with respect to them, as it were a sort of mirror, capable of reflecting them, such as they are, and capable of disfiguring and misrepresenting them.

"As often as you perceive the objects, such as they are, your feelings are in accord with the objects, and you agree in opinion; and it is this accord that constitutes truth.

"On the contrary, as often as you differ in opinion, your dissensions prove that you do not see the objects such as they are, but vary them.

"Whence it appears, that the cause of your dissensions is not in the objects themselves, but in your minds, in the manner in which you perceive and judge.

"If therefore we would arrive at uniformity of opinion, we must previously establish certainty, and verify the resemblance which our ideas have to their models. Now this cannot be obtained, except so far as the objects of our enquiry can be referred to the testimony and subjected to the examination of our senses. Whatever cannot be brought to this trial is beyond the limits of our understanding; we have neither rule to try it by, nor measure by which to institute a comparison, nor source of demonstration and knowledge concerning it.

"Whence it is obvious, that, in order to live in peace and harmony, we must consent not to pronounce upon such objects, nor annex to them importance; we must draw a line of demarcation between such as can be verified and such as cannot, and separate, by an inviolable barrier, the world of fantastic beings from the world of realities : that is to say, all civil effect must be taken away from theological and religious opinions.

"This, O nations! is the end that a great people, freed from their fetters and prejudices, have proposed to themselves; this is the work in which, by their command, and under their immediate auspices, we were engaged, when your kings and your priests came to interrupt our labours. Kings and priests, you may yet for a while suspend the solemn publication of the laws of nature; but it is no longer in your power to annihilate or to subvert them."

A loud cry was then heard from every quarter of the general assembly of nations ; and the whole of the people, unanimously testifying their adherence to the

sentiments of the legislators, encouraged them to resume their sacred and sublime undersaking. "Investigate," said they, " the laws which nature, for
our direction, has implanted in our breasts, and form
from thence an authentic and immutable code. Nor
let this code be calculated for one family, or one nation only, but for the whole without exception. Be
the legislators of the human race, as ye are the interpreters of their common nature. Shew us the line
that separates the world of chimeras from that of realities; and teach us, after so many religions of error and delusion, the religion of evidence and truth."

Upon this, the legislators resuming their enquiry
into the physical and constituent attributes of man,
and the motives and affections which govern him in
his individual and social capactiy, unfolded in the
following terms the laws on which Nature herself
has founded his felicity.

END OF THE FIRST PART.

NOTES.

PAGE 1. (*) *Eleventh year of Abd-ul Hamid.* That is, 1784 of the Christian æra, and 1198 of the Hegira. The emigration of the Tartars took place in March, immediately on the manifesto of the empress declaring the Crimea to be incorporated with Russia.—*A mussalman prince of the name of Gengis Khan.* It was Chahin Guerai. Gengis Kham was borne and served by the kings whom he conquered: Chahin, on the contrary, after selling his country for a pension of eighty thousand roubles, accepted the commission of captain of guards to Catherine II. He afterwards returned home, and, according to custom, was strangled by the Turks.

Page 4. (a). *The precious thread of Serica.* That is, the silk originally derived from the mountainous country where the *great wall* terminates, and which appears to have been the cradle of the Chinese empire. The *tissues of Cassimere.* The shawls which Ezekiel seems to have described under the appellation of Choud-choud. The *gold of Ophir.* This country, which was one of the twelve Arab cantons, and which has so much and so unsuccessfully been sought for by the antiquaries, has left however some trace of itself in Ofor, in the province of Oman, upon the Persian Gulph, neighbouring on one side to the Sebeans, who are celebrated by Strabo for their plenty of gold, and on the other to Aula or Hevila, where the pearl fishery was carried on. See the 7th chapter of Ezekiel, which gives a very curious and extensive picture of the commerce of Asia at that period.

Page 5. (b). *This Syria contained a hundred flourishing cities.* According to Josephus and Strabo, there were in Syria twelve millions of souls; and the traces that remain of culture and habitation confirm the calculation.

Page 8. (c). *A blind fatality.* This is the universal and rooted prejudice of the East. "It was written," is there the the answer to every thing. Hence result an unconcern and apathy, the most powerful impediments to instruction and civilization.

Page 16. (d). *The too famous peninsula of India.* Of what real good has been the commerce of India to the mass of the people ? On the contrary, how great the evil occasioned by the superstition of this country having been added to the general superstition ?

Page 17. (e). *Ancient kingdom of Ethiopia*. In the next volume of the Encyclopædia will appear a memoir respecting the chronology of the twelve ages anterior to the passing of Xerxes into Greece, in which I conceive myself to have proved, that Upper Egypt formerly composed a distinct kingdom, known to the Hebrews by the name of *Kous*, and to which the appellation of Ethiopia was specially given. This kingdom preserved its independence to the time of Psammeticus, at which period, being united to the Lower Egypt, it lost its name of Ethiopia, which thenceforth was bestowed upon the nations of Nubia, and upon the different hordes of Blacks, including Thebes, their metropolis.

Page ib. (f). *Thebes with its hundred palaces*. The idea of a city with a hundred gates, in the common acceptation of the word, is so absurd, that I am astonished the equivoque has not before been felt.

It has ever been the custom of the East to call palaces and houses of the great by the name of gates, because the principal luxury of these buildings consists in the singular gate leading from the street into the court, at the farthest extremity of which the palace is situated. It is under the vestibule of this gate that conversation is held with passengers, and a sort of audience and hospitality given. All this was doubtless known to Homer; but poets made no commentaries, and readers love the marvellous.

This city of Thebes, now Lougsor, reduced to the condition of a miserable village, has left astonishing monuments of its magnificence. Particulars of this may be seen in the plates of Norden, in Pocock, and in the recent travels of Bruce. These monuments give credibility to all that Homer has related of its splendour, and lead us to infer of its political power and external commerce.

Its geographical position was favourable to this twofold object. For, on one side, the valley of the Nile, singularly fertile, must have early occasioned a numerous population; and, on the other, the Red Sea giving communication with Arabia and India, and the Nile with Abyssinia and the Mediterranean. Thebes was thus naturally allied to the richest countries on the globe; an alliance that procured it an activity so much the greater, as Lower Egypt, at first a swamp, was nearly, if not totally uninhabited. But when at length this country had been drained by the canals and dikes which Sesostris constructed, population was introduced there, and wars arose which proved fatal to the power of Thebes. Commerce then took another route, and descended to the point of the Red Sea, to the canals of Sesostris (see Strabo), and wealth and activity were transferred to Memphis. This is manifestly what Diodorus means, when he tells us (Lib. I. Sect. 2.) that as soon as Memphis was established and made a wholesome and delicious abode, kings abandoned Thebes to fix themselves there. Thus Thebes continued to decline, and Memphis to flourish till the time of Alexander, who, building Alexandria on the border of the sea, caused Memphis to fall in its turn; so that prosperity and power seem to have descended historically step by step along the Nile; whence it results both physically and historically, that the existence of Thebes was prior to that of the other cities. The testimony of writers is very positive in this respect. " The Thebans," says Diodorus, " consider themselves as the most ancient people of the earth, and assert, that with them originated philosophy and the science of the stars. Their situation, it is true, is infinitely favourable to astronomical observation, and they have a more accurate division of time into months and years than other nations, &c."

What Diodorus says of the Thebans, every author and himself elsewhere repeat of the Ethiopians, which tends more firmly to establish the identy of place of which I have spoken. " The Ethiopians conceive themselves (says he, Lib. III.) to be of greater antiquity than any other nation; and it is probable that born under the sun's path, its warmth may have ripened them earlier than other men. They suppose themselves also to be the inventors of divine worship, of festivals, of solemn assemblies, of sacrifices, and every other religious practice. They affirm that the Egyptians are one of their colonies, and that the Delta, which was formerly sea, became land by the conglomeration of the earth of the higher country, which was washed down by the Nile. They have, like the Egyptians, two species of letters, hieroglyphics and the alphabet; but among the Egyptians the first was known only to the priests, and by them transmitted from father to son, whereas both species are common among the Ethiopians."

" The Ethiopians," says Lucian, page 995, " were the first who invented the science of the stars, and gave names to the planets, not at random and without meaning, but descriptive of the qualties which they conceived them to possess; and it was from them that this art passed, still in an imperfect state, to the Egyptians."

It would be easy to multiply citations upon this subject; from all which it follows, that we have the strongest reason to believe that the country neighbouring to the tropic, was the cradle of the sciences, and of consequence that the first learned nation was a nation of Blacks, for it is incontrovertible, that by the term Ethiopians, the ancients meant to represent a people of black complexion, thick lips, and woolly hair. I am therefore inclined to believe, that the inhabitants of Lower Egypt were originally a foreign colony imported from Syria and

Arabia, a medley of different tribes of savages, originally shepherds and fishermen, who by degrees formed themselves into a
nation, and who, by nature and descent, were enemies of the
Thebans, by whom they were no doubt despised and treated as
barbarians.

I have suggested the same ideas in my travels into Syria,
founded upon the black complexion of the Sphinx. I have
since ascertained, that the antique images of Thebais have the
same characteristic; and Mr. Bruce has offered a multitude of
analogous facts; but this traveller, of whom I heard some mention at Cairo, has so interwoven these facts with certain systematic opinions, that we should have recourse to his narratives
with caution.

It is singular that Africa, situated so near us, should be the
country on earth which is the least known. The English are at
this moment making attempts, the success of which ought to
excite our emulation.

Page *ib.* (*g*). *Here were the ports of the Idumeans*, Ailah
(Eloth), and Atsiom-Gaber (Hesion-Geber). The name of the
first of these towns still subsists in its ruins, at the point of the
gulph of the Red Sea, and in the route which the pilgrims take
to Mecca Hesion has at present no trace, any more than Qol-
zoum and Faran: it was, however, the harbour for the fleets of
Solomon. The vessels of this prince, conducted by the Tyrians,
sailed along the coast of Arabia to Ophir in the Persian Gulph,
thus opening a communication with the merchants of India and
Ceylon. That this navigation was entirely of Tyrian invention,
appears both from the pilots and shipbuilders employed by the
Jews; and the names that were given to the trading islands, viz.
Tyrus and Aradus, now Barhain. The voyage was performed
in two different modes, either in canoes of osiers and rushes,
covered on the outside with skins done over with pitch; these
vessels were unable to quit the Red Sea, or so much as to leave
the shore. The second mode of carrying on the trade was by
means of vessels with decks of the size of our long boats, which
were able to pass the strait and to weather the dangers of the
ocean; but for this purpose it was necessary to bring the wood
from Mount Lebanus and Cilicia, where it is very fine and in
great abundance. This wood was first conveyed in floats from
Tarsus to Phenicia, for which reason the vessels were called
ships of Tarsus; from whence it has been ridiculously inferred,
that they went round the promontory of Africa as far as Tor-
tosa in Spain. From Phenicia it was transported on the backs
of camels to the Red Sea, which practice still continues, because the shores of this sea are absolutely unprovided with
wood even for fuel These vessels spent a complete year in
their voyage, that is sailed one year, sojourned another, and
did not return till the third. This tediousness was owing, first
to their cruizing from port to port, as they do at present; se-

condly, to their being detained by the Monsoon currents; and thirdly, because, according to the calculations of Pliny and Strabo, it was the ordinary practice among the ancients to spend three years in a voyage of twelve hundred leagues. Such a commerce must have been very expensive, particularly as they were obliged to carry with them their provisions and even fresh water. For this reason Solomon made himself master of Palmyra, which was at that time inhabited, and was already the magazine and high road of merchants by way of the Euphrates. This conquest brought Solomon much nearer to the country of gold and pearls. This alternative of a route either by the Red Sea or by the River Euphrates was to the ancients, what in latter times has been the alternative in a voyage to the Indies, either by crossing the Isthmus of Suez or doubling the Cape of Good Hope. It appears that till the time of Moses this trade was carried on across the desert of Syria and Theais; that afterwards it fell into the hands of the Phenicians, who fixed its site upon the Red Sea, and that it was mutual jealousy that induced the kings of Nineveh and Babylon to undertake the destruction of Tyre and Jerusalem. I insist the more upon these facts, because I have never seen any thing reasonable upon the subject.

Page 18. (*h.*) *Babylon, the ruins of which are trodden under foot of men.* It appears that Babylon occupied on the eastern bank of the Euphrates a space of ground six leagues in length. Throughout this space bricks are found, by means of which daily additions are made to the town of Helle. Upon many of these are characters written with a nail similar to those of Persepolis. I am indebted for these facts to Mr. de Beauchamp, grand vicar of Babylon, a traveller equally distinguished for his knowledge of astronomy and his veracity.

Page 33. (*i*). *Those wells of Tyre.* See respecting these monuments, my travels into Syria, vol. ii. p. 214.

Those artificial banks of the Euphrates. From the town or village of Samaouat the course of the Euphrates is accompanied with a double bank, which descends as far as its junction with the Tigris, and from thence to the sea, being a length of about a hundred leagues French measure. The height of these artificial banks is not uniform, but increases as you advance from the sea; it may be estimated at from twelve to fifteen feet. But for them, the inundation of the river would bury the country around, which is flat, to an extent of twenty or twenty-five leagues; and even notwithstanding these banks, there has been in modern times an overflow which has covered the whole triangle formed by the junction of this river to the Tigris, being a space of country of 130 square leagues. By the stagnation of these waters an epidemical disease of the most fatal nature was occasioned. It follows from hence, 1. That all the flat country bordering upon these rivers was originally a marsh;

2. That this marsh could not have been inhabited previously to the construction of the banks in question; 3. That these banks could not have been the work but of a population prior as to date : and the elevation of Babylon therefore must have been posterior to that of Nineveh, as I think I have chronologically demonstrated in the memoir above cited. See Encyclopedia, vol. xiii. of Antiquities.

Page ib. (q). *Those conduits of Meden.* The modern Aber-bidjan, which was a part of Medea, the mountains of Kourdes-tan, and those of Diarbekr, abound with subterranean canals, by means of which the ancient inhabitants conveyed water to their parched soil in order to fertilize it. It was regarded as a meritorious act, and a religious duty prescribed by Zoroaster, who, instead of preaching celibacy, mortifications, and other pretended virtues of the monkish sort, repeats continually in the passages that are preserved respecting him in the Sad-der and the Zend-avesta, " That the action most pleasing to God is to plough and cultivate the earth, to water it with running streams, to multiply vegetation and living beings, to have numerous flocks, young and fruitful virgins, a multitude of children, &c. &c.

Page 34. (l). *This inequality, the result of accident, was taken for the law of nature.* Almost all the ancient philosophers and politicians have laid it down as a principle that men are born unequal, that nature has created some to be free, and others to be slaves. Expressions of this kind are to be found in Aristotle, and even in Plato, called the divine, doubtless in the same sense as the mythological reveries which he promulgated. With all the people of antiquity, the Gauls, the Romans, the Athenians, the right of the strongest was the right of nations ; and from the same principle are derived all the political disorders and public national crimes that at present exist.

Page ib. (m). *Paternal tyranny laid the foundation of political despotism.* Upon this single expression it would be easy to write a long and important chapter. We might prove in it, beyond contradiction, that all the abuses of national governments have sprung from those of domestic government, from that government called patriarchal, which superficial minds have extolled without having analyzed it. Numberless facts demonstrate that with every infant people, in every savage and barbarous state, the father, the chief of the family, is a despot, and a cruel and insolent despot. The wife is his slave, the children his servants. This king sleeps or smokes his pipe, while his wife and daughters perform all the drudgery of the house, and even that of tillage and cultivation, as far as occupations of this nature are practised in such societies ; and no sooner have the boys acquired strength, than they are allowed to beat the females and make them serve and wait upon them as they do upon their fathers. Similar to this is the state of our own un-civilized peasants. In proportion as civilization spreads, the manners become milder, and the condition of the women improves, till, by a contrary excess, they arrive at dominion, and then a nation becomes effeminate and corrupt. It is remarkable, that parental authority is great according as the government is despotic. China, India, and Turkey, are striking examples of this. One would suppose that tyrants gave themselves accomplices, and interested subaltern despots to maintain their authority. In opposition to this the Romans will be cited; but it remains to be proved that the Romans were men truly free; and their quick passage from their republican despotism to their abject servility under the emperors, gives room at least for considerable doubts as to that freedom.

Page 37. (n). *Always tending to concenter the power in a single hand.* It is remarkable, that this has in all instances been the constant progress of societies; beginning with a state of anarchy or democracy, that is, with a great division of power they have passed to aristocracy, and from aristocracy to monarchy. Does it not hence follow, that those who constitute states under the democratic form, destine them to undergo all the intervening troubles between that and monarchy; and that the supreme administration by a single chief is the most natural government, as well as that best calculated for peace?

Page 39. (o). *And kings followed the dictates of every depraved taste.* It is equally worthy of remark, that the conduct and manners of princes and kings of every country and every age are found to be precisely the same at similar periods, whether of the formation or dissolution of empires. History every where presents the same pictures of luxury and folly; of parks, gardens, lakes, rocks, palaces, furniture, excess of the table, wine, women, concluding with brutality.

The absurd rock in the garden of Versailles has alone cost three millions. I have sometimes calculated what might have been done with the expence of the three pyramids of Gizah, and I have found that it would easily have constructed, from the Red Sea to Alexandria, a canal 150 feet wide, and 30 deep, completely covered in with cut stones and a parapet, together with a fortified and commercial town, consisting of 400 houses furnished with cisterns. What difference in point of utility between such a canal and these pyramids?

Page 44. (p). *By their led horses, &c.* A Tartar horseman has always two horses, of which he leads one in hand. The *Kalpack* is a bonnet made of the skin of a sheep or other animal. The part of the head covered by this bonnet is shaved, with the exception of a tuft about the size of a crown piece, and which is suffered to grow to the length of seven or eight inches, precisely where our priests place their tonsure. It is by this tuft of hair, worn by the majority of Mussulmans, that the

S

angel of the tomb is to take the elect and carry them into Paradise.

Page 45. *(q)*. *Infidels are in possession of a consecrated land.* It is not in the power of the sultan to cede to a foreign power a province inhabited by TRUE BELIEVERS. The people, instigated by the lawyers, would not fail to revolt. This is one reason which has led those who know the Turks, to regard as chimerical the ceding of Candia, Cyprus, and Egypt, projected by certain European potentates.

Page 48. *(r)*. *Pronouncing mysteriously the word Aum.* This word is in the religion of the Hindoos a sacred emblem of the Divinity. It is only to be pronounced in secret, without being heard by any one. It is formed of three letters, of which the first, *a*, signifies the principle of all, the creator, Brama; the the second, *u*, the conservator Vichenou; and the last, *m*, the destroyer, who puts an end to all, Chiven. It is pronounced like the monosyllable, om, and expresses the unity of those three gods. The idea is precisely that of the Alpha and Omega mentioned in the New Testament.

Page *ib. (s)*. *Whether he ought to begin the ceremony at the elbow,* &c. This is one of the grand points of schism between the partizans of Omar and those of Ali. Suppose two Mahometans to meet on a journey, and to accost each other with brotherly affection: the hour of prayer arrives; one begins his ablution at his fingers, the other at the elbow, and instantly they are mortal enemies. O sublime importance of religious opinions! O profound philosophy of the authors of them!

Page 56. *(t)*. *The horde of Oguzians.* Before the Turks took the name of their chief Othman I. they bore that of Oguzians; and it was under this appellation that they were driven out of Tartary by Gengis, and came from the borders of Gihoun to settle themselves in Anatolia.

Page *ib. (u)*. *A general anarchy take place, as happened in the empire of the Sophis.* In Persia, after the death of Thamas-Koulikan, each province had its chief, and for forty years these chiefs were in a constant state of war. In this view the Turks do not say without reason: "Ten years of a tyrant are less destructive than a single night of anarchy."

Page 61. *(x)*. *From people to people barbarous wars were prevalent.* Read the history of the wars of Rome and Carthage, of Sparta and Messina, of Athens and Syracuse, of the Hebrews and the Phenicians; yet these are the nations of which antiquity boasts as being most polished!

Page 65. *(y)*. *The decision of their disputes.* What is a people? An individual of the society at large. What a war? A duel between two individual people. In what manner ought a society to act when two of its members fight? Interfere and reconcile, or repress them. In the days of the Abbe de Saint

Pierre this was treated as a dream, but happily for the human race it begins to be realized.

Page 67. *(z)*. *The Chinese subjected to an insolent despotism.* The emperor of China calls himself the son of heaven, that is, of God; for in the opinion of the Chinese, the material heaven, the arbiter of fatality, is the Deity himself. "The emperor only shows himself once in ten months, lest the people, accustomed to see him might lose their respect; for he holds it as a maxim, that power can only be supported by force, that the people have no idea of justice, and are not to be governed but by coercion." *Narrative of two Mahometan Travellers in* 851 *and* 877, translated by the Abbe Renaudot in 1718.

Notwithstanding what is asserted by the missionaries, this situation has undergone no change. The bamboo still reigns in China, and the son of heaven bastinades, for the most trivial fault, the Mandarin, who, in his turn, bastinades the people. The Jesuits may tell us that this is the best governed country in the world, and its inhabitants the happiest of men; but a single letter from Amyot has convinced me, that China is a truly Turkish government, and the account of Sonnerat confirms it. See Vol. II. of *Voyage aux Indes*, in 4to.

The irremediable vice of their language. As long as the Chinese shall in writing make use of their present characters, they can be expected to make no progress in civilization. The necessary introductory step must be the giving them an alphabet like our own, or the substituting in the room of their language that of the Tartars; the improvement made in the latter by M. de Langles is calculated to introduce this change. See the *Mantchou alphabet*, the production of a mind truly learned in the formation of language.

Page 68. (1). *In the north I see nothing but cerfs reduced to the level of cattle.* When this was written the revolution in Poland had not taken place. I beg leave to apologize to the virtuous nobles and the enlightened prince by whom it was effected.

Page 72. (2). *And govern yourselves.* This dialogue between the people and the indolent classes, is applicable to every society; it contains the seeds of all the political vices and disorders that prevail, and which may thus be defined; men who do nothing, and who devour the substance of others; and men who arrogate to themselves particular rights and exclusive privileges of wealth and indolence. Compare the Mamlouks of Egypt, the Nobility of Europe, the Nairs of India, the Emirs of Arabia, the Patricians of Rome, the Christian clergy, the Imans, the Bramins, the Bonzes, the Lamas, &c. &c. and you will find in all, the same characteristic feature,—"Men living in idleness at the expence or those who labour."

Page 78. (3). *Equality and Liberty constitute the physical*

basis. In the declaration of rights there is an inversion of ideas
in the first article, liberty being placed before equality, from
which it in reality springs. This defect is not to be wondered
at ; the science of the rights of man is a new science ; it was
invented yesterday by the Americans, to-day the French are
perfecting it, but there yet remains a great deal to be done. In
the ideas that constitute it there is a genealogical order, which
from its basis, physical equality, to the minutest and most remote branches of government, ought to proceed in an uninterrupted series of inferences. This will be demonstrated in the
second part of this work.

Page 83. (4). *A vast hat of the leaves of the palm-tree.*
This species of the palm-tree is called *Latanier.* Its leaf, similar to a fan-mount, grows upon a stalk issuing directly from the
earth. A specimen may be seen in the botanic garden.

Page *ib.* (5). *The contemplation of one species thus infinitely
varied.* A hall of costumes in one of the galleries of the Lou-
vre, would in every point of view be an interesting establishment ; it would furnish an admirable treat to the curiosity of a
great number of men, excellent models to the artist, and useful
subjects of meditation to the physician, the philosopher, and
the legislator. Picture to yourself a collection of the various
faces and figures of every country and nation, exhibiting accurately, colour, features and form ; what a field for investigation
and enquiry as to the influence of climate, manners, aliment,
&c.! It might truly be styled the science of man! Buffon has
attempted a chapter of this nature, but it only serves to exhibit
more strikingly our actual ignorance. Such a collection it is
said is begun at Petersburgh, but it is said at the same time, to
be as imperfect as the vocabulary of the 300 languages. The
enterprize would be worthy of the French nation.

Page 89. (6). *Thus are there sects to the number of seventy-
two.* The Mussulmans enumerate in common seventy-two
sects ; but I read, while I resided among them, a work which
gave an account of more than eighty, all equally wise and important.

Page *ib.* (7). *Has never ceased for twelve hundred years.*
Read the history of Islamism by its own writers, and you will
be convinced that one of the principal causes of the wars which
have desolated Asia and Africa since the days of Mahomet,
has been the apostolical fanaticism of its doctrine. Cæsar has
been supposed to have destroyed three millions of men : it would
be interesting to make a similar calculation respecting every
founder of a religious system.

Page 91. (8). *The Nestorians, the Eutycheans, and a hundred
others.* Consult upon this subject *Dictionnaire des Heresies, par
l'Abbe Pluquet,* in two volumes 8vo. ; a work admirably calculated to inspire the mind with philosophy, in the sense that the

Lacedemonians taught their children temperance, by shewing to them the drunken Heliotes.

Page 92. (9). *Disciples of Zoroaster.* They are the Parses, better known by the opprobious name of Gaures or Guebres, another word for infidels. They are in Asia, what the Jews are in Europe. The name of their pope or high priest is Mobed.

Page 93. (10). *Their Destours,* that is to say, their priests. See, respecting the rites of this religion, *Henry Lord, Hyde,* and the *Zendavesta.* Their costuma is a robe with a belt of four knots, and a veil over the mouth for fear of polluting the fire with their breath.

Page ib. (11). *The resurrection of the body, or the soul, or both.* The Zoroastrians are divided between two opinions, one party believing that both soul and body will rise, the other that it will be the soul only. The Christians and Mahometans have embraced the most solid of the two.

Page ib. (12). *They wear a net over their mouths, &c.* According to the system of the Metempsychosis, a soul, to undergo purification, passes into the body of some insect or animal. It is of importance not to disturb this penance, as the work must in that case begin afresh.—*Paria.* This is the name of a cast or tribe reputed unclean, because they eat of what has enjoyed life.

Page 94. (13). *Brama,—reduced to serve as a pedestal to the Lingham.* See *Sonnerat, Voyage aux Indes,* Vol. I.

Page ib. (14). *Hideous forms of a boar, a lion, &c.* These are the incarnations of Vichenou, or metamorphoses of the sun. He is to come at the end of the world, that is, at the expiration of the great period, in the form of a horse, like the four horses of the apocalypse.

Page ib. (15). *In their devotion, &c.* When a sectary of Chiven hears the name of Vichenou pronounced, he stops his ears, flies, and purifies himself.

Page 95. (16.) *The Chinese worship him under the name of Fot.* The original name of this God is *Baits,* which in Hebrew signifies an egg. The Arabs pronounce it *Baidh,* giving to the *dh* an emphatic sound, which makes it approach to *dz.* Kempfer, an accurate traveller, writes it *Budso,* which must be pronounced *Boudso,* whence is derived the name of *Budsoist,* and of Bonze, applied to the priests. Clement of Alexandria, in his Stromata, writes it *Bedou,* as it is pronounced also by the Chingulais; and St Jerome, *Boudda* and *Boutta.* At Thibet they call it Budd , and hence the name of the country called *Boudtan* and *Tibudd*: it was in this province that this system of religion was first inculcated in Upper Asia: *La* is a corruption of *Allah,* the name of God in the Syriac language, from which many of the Eastern dialects appear to be derived. The chinese having neither *b* nor *d,* have supplied their place by *f* and *t,* and have therefore said *Fout.*

Page 95. (17). *That the soul can exist independently of the senses.* See in Kempfer the doctrine of the Siutoists, which is a mixture of that of Epicurus and of the Stoics.

Page *ib.* (18.) *Talipat screen.* It is a leaf of the *Latanier*, species of the palm tree. Hence the Bonzes of Siam take the appellation of *Talapoin*. The use of this screen is an exclusive privilege.

Page *ib.* (19). *Conjunction of the stars.* The sectaries of Confucius are no less addicted to astrology then the Bonzes. It is indeed the malady of every eastern nation.

Page 96. (20). *The Grand Lama. The Delia-La-Ma*, or immense high priests of *La*, is the same person whom we find mentioned in our old books of travels, by the name of Prester John, from a corruption of the Persian word *Djehan*, which signifies the world, to which has been prefixed the French word prestre or pretre, priest. Thus the *priest world* and the *God world* are in the Persian idiom the same.

Page *ib.* (21). *The excrements of their pontiff.* In a recent expedition the English have found certain idols of the Lamas filled in the inside with sacred pastils from the close stool of the high priest. Mr. Hastings and Colonel Pollier, who is now at Lausanne, are living witnesses of this fact, and undoubtedly worthy of credit. It will be very extraordinary to observe, that this disgusting ceremony is connected with a profound philisophical system, to wit, that of the metempsychosis, admitted by the Lamas. When the Tartars swallow these sacred relics, which they are accustomed to do, they imitate the laws of the universe, the parts of which are incessantly absorbed and pass into the substance of each other. It is upon the model of the serpent who devours his tail, and this serpent is Budd and the world.

Page *ib.* (22). *The inhabitants of Juida, &c.* It frequently happens that the swine devour the very species of serpents which the negroes adore, which is a source of great desolation in the country. President de Brosses, has given us in his history of the *Fetiche*, a curious collection of absurdities of this nature. *The Teleutean dresses, &c.* The Teleuteans, a Tartar nation, paint God as wearing a vesture of all colours, particularly red and green ; and as these constitute the uniform of the Russian dragoons, they compare him to this description of soldiers. The Egyptians also dress the God World in a garment of every colour. *Eusebius Præp. Evang. p. 115. l. 3.* The Teleuteans call God *Bou*, which is only an alteration of Boudd, the God egg and World.

Page 97. (23). *The Kamchadule represents God under the figure of an ill-natured and arbitrary old man.* Consult upon this subject a work entitled, *Description des Peuples soumis a la Russe*, and it will be found that the picture is not overcharged.

Page 101. (24). *His son-in-law Ali, or his Vicars Omar and Aboubekre.* These are the two grand parties into which the Mussulmans are divided. The Turks have embraced the second, the Persians the first.

Page 103. (25). *To make war upon Infidels.* Whatever the advocates for the philosophy and civilization of the Turks may assert, to make war upon infidels is considered by them as an obligatory precept and an act of religion. See *Reland de Relig. Moham.*

Page 105. (28). *Your system rests entirely on mystical interpretations.* When we read the fathers of the church, and see upon what arguments they have built the edifice of religion, we are inexpressibly astonished with their credulity, or their knavery; but allegory was the rage of that period: the Pagans employed it to explain the actions of their Gods, and the christians acted in the same spirit when they employed it after their fashion.

Page 110. (27). *It was not till four hundred years after.* See the Chronology of the twelve ages, in which I conceive myself to have clearly proved that Moses lived about 1400 years before Jesus Christ, and Zoroaster about a thousand.

Page 111. (28.) *In the corrected publication of their sacred books.* In the first periods of the Christian church, not only the most learned of those who have since been denominated heretics, but many of the orthodox, conceived Moses to have written neither the law nor the Pentateuch, but that the work was a compilation made by the elders of the people and the Seventy, who, after the death of Moses, collected his scattered ordinances, and mixed with them things that were extraneous; similar to what happened as to the Koran of Mahomet. See *Les Clementines,* Homel. 2. sect. 51. and Homel. 3. sect. 42.

Modern critics, more enlightened or more attentive than the ancients, have found in Genesis in particular, marks of its having been composed on the return from the captivity; but the principal proofs have escaped them. These I mean to exhibit in an analysis of the book of Genesis, in which I shall demonstrate that the tenth chapter, among others, which treats of the pretended generations of the man called Noah is a real geographical picture of the world, as it was known to the Hebrews at the epoch of the captivity, which was bounded by Greece or Hellas at the West, mount Caucasus at the North, Persia at the East, and Arabia and Upper Egypt at the South. All the pretended personages from Adam to Abraham or his father Terah, are mythological beings, stars, constellations, countries. Adam is Bootes; Noah is Osyris, Xisuthrus Janus, Saturn; that is to say, Capricorn, or the celestial Genius that opened the year. The Alexandrian Chronicle says expressly, page 85, that Nimrod was supposed by the Persians to be their first king, as having invented the art of hunting, and that he was translated into heaven, where he appears under the name of Orion.

Page 111. (29). *Creation of the world in six gehans*, or periods, or into six *gahan bars*, that is, six periods of time. These periods are what Zoroaster calls the *thousands of God* or of *light*, meaning the six summer months. In the first, say the Persians, God created (arranged in order) the heavens; in the second the waters; in the third the earth; in the fourth trees; in the fifth animals; and in the sixth man; corresponding with the account in Genesis. For particulars, see *Hyde*, ch. 9. and *Henry Lord*, ch. 2. *On the religion of the ancient Persians.* It is remarkable, that the same tradition is found in the sacred books of the Etrurians, which relate, "that the Fabricator of all things had comprised the duration of his work in a period of twelve thousand years, which period was distributed to the twelve houses of the sun." In the first thousand God made heaven and earth; in the second, the firmament; in the third, the sea and the waters; in the fourth, the sun, moon, and stars; in the fifth, the soul of animals, birds, and reptiles; in the sixth, man. See, *Suidas*, at the *Tyrrhena*; which shows first, the identity of their theological and astrological opinions; and, secondly, the identity, or rather confusion of ideas, between absolute and systematical creation; that is, the periods assigned for renewing the face of nature, which were at first the period of the year, and afterwards periods of 60, of 600, of 25,000, of 36,000, and of 432,000 years.

Page 112 (30.) *Auricular Confession*, &c. The modern Parses and the ancient Mithriacs, who are the same sect, observe all the Christian sacraments, even the laying on of hands, in confirmation. "The priest of Mithra," says Tertullian, (de Proescriptione, c. 40.) " promises absolution from sin on confession and baptism; and, if I rightly remember, Mithra marks the soldiers in the forehead (with the chrism, called in Egyptian *Kouphi*): he celebrates the sacrifice of bread, which is the resurrection, and presents the crown to his followers, menacing them at the same time with the sword.

In these mysteries they tried the courage of the initiated with a thousand terrors, presenting fire to his face, a sword to his breast, &c.; they also offered him a crown which he refused, saying, God is my crown: and this crown is to be seen in the celestial sphere by the side of Bootes. The personages in these mysteries were distinguished by the names of the animal constellations. The ceremony of mass is nothing more than an imitation of these mysteries and those of Eleusis. The benediction *the Lord be with you*, is a literal translation of the formular of admission *chon-k. am, p-ak*. See *Beausob. Hist. du Manicheisme*, vol. ii.

Page 113 (31.) *The Vedes, the Chastres, and the Pourans.*
These are the sacred volumes of the Hindoos; they are sometimes written *Vadams, Pouranams, Chastrans,* because the
Hindoos, like the Persians, are accustomed to give a nasal
sound to the terminations of their words, which we represent
by the affixes *on* and *an,* and the Portuguese by the affixes *om*
and *am.* Many of these books have been translated, thanks to
the liberal spirit of Mr. Hastings, who has founded at Cal-
cutta a literary society and a printing press. At the same time,
however, that we express our gratitude to this society, we must
be permitted to complain of its exclusive spirit, the number of
copies printed of each book being such as it is impossible to
purchase them even in England; they are wholly in the hands
of the East India proprietors. Scarcely even is the Asiatic Mis-
cellany known in Europe, and a man must be very learned in
oriental antiquity before he so much as hears of the Jones's,
the Wilkins's, and the Halhed's, &c. As to the sacred books
of the Hindoos, all that are yet in our hands are the Bhagvat
Geeta, the Ezour-Vedam, the Bagavadam, and certain fragments of the Chastres printed at the end of the Bhagvat Geeta.
These books are in Indostan what the Old and New Testament
are in Christendom, the Koran in Turkey, the Sadder and the
Zendavesta among the Parses, &c. When I have taken an
extensive survey of their contents, I have sometimes asked myself, what would be the loss to the human race if a new Omar
condemned them to the flames? and unable to discover any
mischief that would ensue, I call the imaginary chest that contains them, the box of Pandora.

Page ib. (32). *Brama, Bichen,* or *Vichenou, Chib,* or *Chiben.*
These names are differently pronounced according to the
different dialects: thus they say *Birmah, Bremma, Brouma.*
Bichen has been turned into *Vichen* by the easy exchange of a
B for a *V,* and into *Vichenou* by means of a grammatical affix.
In the same manner *Chib,* which is synonimous with Satan,
and signifies adversary, is frequently written *Chib-a* add *Chiv-en;*
he is called also *Rouder* and *Routr-en,* that is, the destroyer.

Page 114. (33.) *In the shape of a tortoise.* This is the constellation *testudo,* or the *lyre,* which was at first a tortoise, on
account of its slow motion round the Pole; then a lyre, because it is the shell of this reptile on which the strings of the
lyre are mounted. See an excellent memoir of *M. Dupuis, sur*
l'Origine des Constellations, in 4to.

Page 116. (34.) *That you have borrowed the ancient Paganism*
of the Western World. All the ancient opinions of the Egyptian and Grecian theologians are to be found in India, and they
appear to have been introduced, by means of the commerce of
Arabia and the vicinity of Persia, time immemorial.

Page 116. (35). *Breathed upon the face of the waters* This cos-
mogony of the Lamas, the Bonzes, and even the Bramins, as

Henry Lord asserts, is literally that of the ancient Egyptians. "The Egyptians," says Porphyry, "call *Kneph*, intelligence, or efficient cause of the universe. They relate that this God vomited an egg, from which was produced another God named *Phtha* or Vulcan, (igneous principle, or the sun,) and they add, that this egg is the world." *Euseb. Præp. Evang.* p. 115.

"They represent," says the same author in another place, the God *Kneph*, or efficient cause, under the form of a man in deep blue (the colour of the sky), having in his hand a sceptre, a belt round his body, and a small bonnet royal of light feathers on his head, to denote how very subtile and fugacious the idea of that being is." Upon which I shall observe, that *Kneph* in Hebrew signifies a wing, a feather, and that this colour of sky-blue is to be found in the majority of the Indian Gods, and is, under the name of Narayan, one of their most distinguishing epithets.

Page 118. (36). *That the Lamas were a degenerate sect of the Nestorians.* This is asserted by our missionaries, and among others by Georgi in his unfinished work of the Thibetan alphabet ; but if it can be proved that the Manicheans were but plagiarists, and the ignorant echo of a doctrine that existed fifteen hundred years before them, what becomes of the declarations of Georgi? See upon this subject *Beausob. Hist. du Manicheisme.*

But the Lama demonstrated, &c. The eastern writers in general agree in placing the birth of *Bedou* 1027 years before Jesus Christ, which makes him the cotemporary of Zoroaster, with whom, in my opinion, they confound him. It is certain that his doctrine notoriously existed at that epoch: it is found entire in that of Orpheus, Pythagoras, and the Indian gymnosophists. But the gymnosophists are cited at the time of Alexander as an ancient sect already divided into Brachmans and Samaneans. See *Bardesanes en Saint Jerome, Epitre a Joviem.* Pythagoras lived in the ninth century before Jesus Christ. See *Chronology of the Twelve Ages* ; and Orpheus is of still greater antiquity. If, as is the case, the doctrine of Pythagoras and that of Orpheus are of Egyptian origin, that of Bedou goes back to the common source; and in reality the Egyptian priests recite that Hermes, as he was dying said : " I have hitherto lived an exile from my country, to which I now return. Weep not for me, I ascend to the celestial abode, where each of you will follow in his turn : there God is : this life is only death." *Chalcidius in Thimœam.* Such was the profession of faith of the Samaneans, the sectaries of Orpheus, and the Pythagoreans. Farther, Hermes is no other than Bedou himself; for among the Indians, Chinese, Lamas, &c. the planet Mercury, and the corresponding day of the week (Wednesday,) bear the name of Bedou: and this accounts for his

being placed in the rank of mythological beings and discovers
the illusion of his pretended existence as a man, since it is evident that Mercury was not a human being, but the Genius or
Decan, who, placed at the summer solstice, opened the Egyptian year : hence his attributes taken from the constellation
Syrius, and his name of Anubis, as well as that of Esculapius,
having the figure of a man and the head of a dog : hence his
serpent, which is the Hydra, emblem of the Nile (Hydor, humidity); and from this serpent he seems to have derived his
name of Hermes, as *Remes* (with a *schin*), in the oriental languages, signifies serpent.   Now Bedou and Hermes being the
same names, it is manifest of what antiquity is the system ascribed to the former.   As to the name of Samanean, it is precisely that of Chaman preserved in Tartary, China, and India.
The interpretation given to it is, *man of the woods*, a hermit mor-
tifying the flesh, such being the characteristic of this sect ; but
its literal meaning is *celestial* (Samaoui), and explains the system of those who are called by it.   This system is the same
as that of the sectaries of Orpheus, of the Essenians, of the
ancient Anchorets of Persia, and the whole Eastern country.
See *Porphyry, de Abstin. Animal.*   These celestial and penitent
men, carried in India their insanity to such an extreme, as to
wish not to touch the earth, and they accordingly lived in
cages suspended to trees, where the people, whose admiration
was not less absurd, brought them provisions.   During the
night there were frequent robberies, rapes, and murders, and
it was at length discovered that they were committed by those
men, who, descending from their cages, thus indemnified themselves for their restraint during the day.   The Bramins, their
rivals, embraced the opportunity of exterminating them ; and
from that time their name in India has been synonymous with
hypocrite.   See *Hist. de la Chine*, in 5 vols. 4th at the note
page 50 ; *Hist. de Huns*, 2 vols. ; and preface to the *Ezour-
Vedam.*

Page 118. (*37.) Demonstrate his existence, &c.* They are absolutely no other monuments of the existence of Jesus Christ as a
human being, than a passage in Josephus, (*Antiq. Jub. lib.
18. c. 3.)* a single phrase in Tacitus, (*Annal. lib.* 15. c. 44.)
and the Gospels. But the passage in Josephus is unanimously
acknowledged to be apocryphal, and to have been interpolated
towards the close of the third century. (*See Trad. de Josephe,
par M. Gillet*); and that of Tacitus is so vague, and so evidently taken from the deposition of the Christians before the
tribunals, that it may be ranked in the class of evangelical re-
cords.   It remains to enquire of what authority are these re-
cords.   "All the world knows," says Faustus, who, though a
Manichean, was one of the most learned men of the third century ; "All the world knows, that the Gospels were neither
written by Jesus Christ, nor his apostles, but by certain un-

known persons, who, rightly judging that they should not obtain belief respecting things which they had not seen, placed at the head of their recitals the names of contemporary apostles." See *Beausob.* vol. i. and *Hist. des Apologists de la Relig. Chret. par Burigni,* a sagacious writer, who has demonstrated the absolute uncertainty of those foundations of the Christian religion; so that the existence of Jesus is no better proved than that of Osiris and Hercules, or that of Fot or Bedou, with whom, says M. de Guignes, the Chinese continually confound him, for they never call Jesus by any other name than Fot. *Hist. de Huns.*

Page 118. (38.) *Your Gospels are taken from the books of the Mithriacs.* That is to say, from the pious romances formed out of the sacred legends of the Mysteries of Mithra, Ceres, Isis, &c.; from whence are equally derived the books of the Hindoos and the Bonzes. Our missionaries have long remarked a striking resemblance between those books and the Gospels. M. Wilkins expressly mentions it in a note in the Bhagvat Geeta. All agree that Krisna, Fot, and Jesus, have the same characteristic features; but religious prejudice has stood in the way of drawing from this circumstance the proper and natural inference. To time and reason must it be left to display the truth.

Page 119. (39.) *The interior and secret doctrine.* The Budsoists have two doctrines, the one public and ostensible, the other interior and secret, precisely like the Egyptian priests. It may be asked, why this distinction? It is, that as the public doctrine recommends offerings, expiations, endowments, &c. the priests find their profit in teaching it to the people; whereas the other, teaching the vanity of worldly things, and attended with no lucre, it is thought proper to make it known only to adepts. Can the teachers and followers of this religion be better classed than under the heads of knavery and credulity.

Page 120. (40.) *That happiness and misfortune, &c.* These are the expressions of La Loubere, in his description of the kingdom of Siam and the theology of the Bonzes. Their dogmas, compared with those of the ancient philosophers of Greece and Italy, give a complete representation of the whole system of the Stoics and Epicureans, mixed with astrological superstitions, and some traits of Pythagorism.

Page 126. (41.) *The original barbarous state of mankind.* It is the unanimous testimony of history, and even of legends, that the first human beings were every where savages, and that it was to civilize them, and teach them *to make bread,* that the Gods manifested themselves.

Page 127. (42.) *Man receives no ideas but through the medium of his senses.* The rock on which all the ancients have split, and which has occasioned all their errors, has been their supposing the idea of God to be innate and coeternal with the soul; and hence all the reveries developed in Plato and Jamblicus. See *Timæus*, the *Phedon*, and *De Myst. Ægyptiorum*, sect. 13. c. 2.

Page 131. (43.) *Record of all the monuments of antiquity.* It clearly results, says Plutarch, from the verses of Orpheus and the sacred books of the Egyptians and Phrygians, that the ancient theology, not only of the Greeks, but of all nations, was nothing more than a system of physics, a picture of the operations of nature, wrapped up in mysterious allegories and enigmatical symbols, in a manner that the ignorant multitude attended rather to their apparent than to their hidden meaning, and even in what they understood of the latter, supposed there to be something more deep than what they perceived. *Fragment of a work of Plutarch now lost, quoted by Eusebius, Præpar. Evan. lib. 3. ch. 1. p. 83.*

The majority of philosophers, says Porphyry, and among others Chæremon (who lived in Egypt in the first age of Christianity), imagine there never to have been any other world than the one we see, and acknowledge no other Gods of all those recognized by the Egyptians, than such as are commonly called planets, signs of the Zodiac, and constellations; whose aspects, that is, rising and setting, are supposed to influence the fortunes of men; to which they add, their divisions of the signs into decans and dispensers of time, whom they style lords of the ascendant, whose names, virtues, in the relieving distempers, rising, setting, and presages of future events, are the subjects of almanacks; (for be it observed, that the Egyptian priests had almanacks the exact counterpart of Matthew Lansberg's;) for when the priests affirmed that the sun was the architect of the universe, Chæremon presently concludes that all their narratives respecting Isis and Osiris, together with their other sacred fables, referred in part to the planets, the phases of the moon, and the revolution of the sun, and in part to the stars of the daily and nightly hemispheres and the river Nile; in a word, in all cases to physical and natural existences, and never to such as might be immaterial and incorporeal. All these philosophers believe, that the acts of our will, and the motion of our bodies, depend upon those of the stars to which they are subjected, and they refer every thing to the laws of physical necessity, which they call destiny or *Fatum*, supposing a chain of causes and effects which binds, by I know not what connection, all beings together, from the meanest atom to the supreme power and primary influence of the Gods; so that, whether in their temples or in their idols, the only subject of worship is the power of destiny. *Porphyr. Epist. ad Junebonem.*

Page ib (44). *The practice of agriculture required the observation and knowledge of the heavens.* It continues to be repeated every day, on the indirect authority of the book of Genesis, that astronomy was the invention of the children of Noah. It has been gravely said, that while wandering shepherds in the plains of Shinar, they employed their leisure in composing a planetary system: as if shepherds had occasion to know more than the Polar star, and if necessity was not the sole motive of every invention! If the ancient shepherds were so studious and sagacious, how does it happen that the modern ones are so stupid, ignorant, and inattentive ? And it is a fact, that the Arabs of the desert know not so many as six constellations, and understand not a word of astronomy.

Page 132. (45.) *Genii, Gods, authors of good and evil.* It appears that by the word genius, the ancients denoted a quality, a generative power ; for the following words, which are all of one family, convey this meaning: *generary, genos, genesis, genus, gens.*

The Sabeans, ancient and modern, says Maimonides, acknowledge a principal God, the maker and inhabitant of heaven ; but on account of his great distance they conceive him to be inaccessible ; and in imitation of the conduct of people towards their kings, they employ as mediators with him, the planets and their angels, whom they call princes and potentates, and whom they say suppose to reside in those luminous bodies as in palaces or tabernacles, &c. *More-Nebuchin, pars* 3. *c.* 29.

Page ib (46.) *And even a sex derived from the gender of its appellation.* According as the gender of the object was in the language of the nation masculine or feminine, the Divinity who bore its name was male or female. Thus the Cappadocians called the moon God, and the sun Goddess ; a circumstance which gives to the same beings a perpetual variety in ancient mythology.

Page 133. (47) *Morality was a judicious practice of all that is conducive to the preservation of existence.* We may add, says Plutarch, that these Egyptian priests always regarded the preservation of health as a point of the first importance, and as indispensably necessary to the practice of piety and the service of the Gods. See his account of *Isis and Osiris,* towards the end.

Page ib. (48.) *That its principles* (those of astronomy,) *can be traced back to a period of* 17,000 *years.* The historical orator follows here the opinion of Mr. Dupuis, who, in his learned memoir concerning the origin of the constellations, has assigned many plausible reasons to prove that *Libra* was formerly the sign of the vernal, and *Aries* of the nocturnal equinox; that is, that since the origin of the actual astronomical system, the procession of the equinoxes has carried forward by seven signs the primitive order of the Zodiac. Now estimating the procession at about seventy years and a half to a degree, that is, 2,115 years to each sign; and observing that *Aries* was in its fifteenth degree, 1,447 years before Christ; it follows, that the first degree of *Libra* could not have coincided with the vernal equinox more lately than 15,194 years before Christ; to which if you add 1790 since Christ, it appears that 16,984 have elapsed since the origin of the Zodiac. The vernal equinox coincided with the first degree of *Aries* 2,504 years before Christ, and with the first degree of *Taurus*, 4619 years before Christ. Now it is to be observed, that the worship of the Bull is the principal article in the theological creed of the Egyptians, Persians, Japanese, &c.; from whence it clearly follows, that some general revolution took place among those nations at that time. The chronology of five or six thousand years in Genesis is little agreeable to this hypothesis; but as the book of Genesis cannot claim to be considered farther back than Abraham, we are at liberty to make what arrangements we please in the eternity that preceded.

Page 133. (49.) *When reason finds there a zone of heaven equally free from the rains of the equator and the fogs of the North.* Mr. Bailli, in placing the first astronomers at Seliungenskoy, near the lake Baikal, paid no attention to this twofold circumstance: it equally argues against their being placed at Axoum on account of the rains, and the *Zimb fly* of which Mr. Bruce speaks.

Page 135. (50.) *Men gave to the stars, &c.* "The ancients," says Maimonides, directing all their attention to agriculture, gave names to the stars derived from their occupation during the year." *More-Neb. pars 3.*

Page. 136. (51.) *They call by the name of serpents the figured traces of the orbits.* The ancients had verbs from the substantives *crab, goat, tortoise,* as the French have at present the verbs *serpenter, coqueter.* The history of all languages is nearly the same.

Page 138. (52.) *If they had not seen in them talismans partaking of the nature of the stars.* The ancient astrologers, says the most learned of the jews (Maimonides), having sacredly assigned to each planet a colour, an animal, a tree, a metal, a fruit, a plant, formed from them all a figure or representation of the star, taking care to select for the purpose a proper moment, a fortunate day, such as the conjunction of the star, or some other favourable aspect. They conceived that by their magic ceremonies they could introduce into those figures or idols the influences of the superior beings after which they were modelled. These were the idols that the Chaldean Sabeans adored; and in the performance of their worship they were obliged to be dressed in the proper colour. The astrologers, by their practices, thus introduced idolatry, desirous of being regarded as the dispensers of the favours of heaven; and as agriculture was the sole employment of the ancients, they succeeded in persuading them, that the rain and other blessings of the seasons were at their disposal. Thus the whole art of agriculture was exercised by rules of astrology, and the priests made talismans or charms which were to drive away locusts, flies, &c. See *Maimonides, More-Nebuchim, pars* 3. c. 29.

The priests of Egypt, Persia, India, &c. pretended to bind the Gods to their idols, and to make them come from heaven at their pleasure. They threatened the sun and moon if they were disobedient, to reveal the secret mysteries, to shake the skies, &c. &c. *Euseb. Præcep. Evang. p.* 198, *and Iamblicus de Mysteriis Ægypt.*

Page 138. (53.) *The sun was supposed to assume their forms* (the forms of the twelve animals). These are the very words of Iamblicus de Symbolus Ægyptiorum. c. 2. sect. 7. The sun was the grand Proteus, the universal metamorphist.

Page. 139. (54.) *Your tonsure is the disk of the sun.* The Arabs, says Herodotus, shave their heads in a circle and about the temples, in imitation of Bacchus (that is the sun,) who shaves himself, they say, in this manner. Jeremiah speaks also of this custom. The tuft of hair which the Mahometans preserve, is taken also from the sun, who was painted by the Egyptians at the winter solstice, as having but a single hair on his head. *Your stole its Zodiac.* The robes of the goddess of Syria and of Diana of Euhesus, from whence are borrowed the dress of priests, have the twelve animals of the Zodiac painted on them. *Rosaries* are found upon all the Indian idols, constructed more than four thousand years ago : and their use in the East has been universal for time immemorial. The *crosier* is precisely the staff of Bootes or Osiris (See Plate II.) All the Lamas wear the *mitre* or cap in the shape of a cone, which was an emblem of the sun.

Page 140. (55.) *Having said that a planet entered into a sign, their conjunction was denominated a marriage, &c.* These are the very words of Plutarch in his account of Isis and Osiris. The Hebrews say, in speaking of the generations of the Patriarchs, *et ingressus est in eam.* From this continual equivoque of ancient language, proceeds every mistake.

Page ib. (56.) *The combination of these figures had also a meaning.* The reader will doubtless see, with pleasure, some examples of ancient hieroglyphics.

" The Egyptians (says Hor-appolo) represent eternity by the figure of the sun and moon. They designate the world by a blue serpent with yellow scales (stars, it is the Chinese Dragon.) If they were desirous of expressing the year, they drew a picture of Isis, who is also in their language called *Sothis*, or dog star, one of the first constellations, by the rising of which the year commences; its inscription at Sais was, *It is I that rise in the constellation of the Dog.*

" They also represent the year by a palm tree, and the mouth by one of its branches; because it is the nature of this tree to produce a branch every month. They farther represent it by the fourth part of an acre of land." (The whole acre divided into four denotes the bissextile period of four years. The abbreviation of this figure of a field in four divisions, is manifestly the letter *ha* or *het*, the seventh in the Samaritan alphabet; and in general all the letters of the alphabet are merely astronomical hieroglyphics; and it is for this reason that the mode of writing is from right to left, like the march of the stars) — " They denote a prophet by the image of a dog. because the dog-star (*Anoubis*) by its rising gives notice of the inundation. *Noubi* in Hebrew signifies prophet —They represent inundation by a lion, because it takes place under that sign; and hence, says Plutarch, the custom of placing at the gates of temples figures of lions with water issuing from their mouths.— They express the idea of God and Destiny by a star. They also represent God, says Porphyry, by a black stone, because his nature is dark and obscure. All white things express the celestial and luminous Gods: all circular ones the world, the moon, the sun, the destinies: all semicircular ones, as bows and crescents, are also descriptive of the moon. Fire and the Gods of Glympus, they represent by pyramids and obelisks: (the name of the son *Baal* is found in this latter word): the sun, by a cone (the mitre of Osiris): the earth, by a cylinder (which revolves): the generative power of the air, by the *phalus*, and that of the earth, by a triangle, emblem of the female organ. *Euseb. Præcep. Evang. p.* 98.

" Clay, (says Iamblicus de Symbolis, sect. 7. c. 2.) denotes matter, the generative and nutrimental power, every thing which receives the warmth and fermentation of life.

" A man sitting upon the *Lotos* or *Nenuphar*, represents the moving spirit (the sun), which, in like manner as the plant lives in the water without any communication with clay, exists equally distinct from matter, swimming in empty space, resting on itself: it is round also in all its parts like the leaves, the flowers and the fruit of the Lotos. (Brama has the eyes of the Lotos, says Chaster Neadirsen, to denote his intelligence: his eye swims over every thing, like the flowers of the Lotos on the waters). A man at the helm of a ship, adds Iamblicus, is descriptive of the sun which governs all. And Porphyry tells us, that the sun is also represented by the man in a ship resting upon an amphibious crocodile (emblem of air and water).

" At Elephantine they worshipped the figure of a man in a sitting posture painted blue, having the head of a ram, and the horns of a goat which encompassed a disk: all which represented the sun and moon's conjunction at the sign of the ram; the blue colour denoting the power of the moon at the period of junction, to raise water into clouds. *Euseb. Præcep. Evang. p.* 116.   **T 3**

" The hawk is an emblem of the sun and of light, on account
of his rapid flight and his soaring into the highest regions of
the air where light abounds.

" A fish is the emblem of aversion, and the *Hippopotamus* of
violence, because it it is said to kill its father and ravish its mother. Hence, says Plutarch, the emblematical inscription of
the temple of Sais, where we see painted on the vestibule, 1.
A child. 2. An old man. 3. A hawk. 4. A fish. 5. A hippopotamus; which signify, 1. Entrance (into life). 2. Departure. 3. God. 4. Hatred. 5. Injustice. (See *Isis and Osiris.*)

" The Egyptians, adds he, represent the world by a Scara-
bens, because this insect pushes, in a direction contrary to that
in which it proceeds, a ball containing its eggs, just as the
heaven of the fixed stars causes the revolution of the sun (the
yolk of an egg) in an opposite direction to its own.

" They represent the world also by the number *five*, being
that of the elements, which, says Diodorous, are earth, water,
air, fire, and ether or *spiritus*. The Indians have the same
number of elements, and according to Macrobius's Mystics they
are the supreme God, or *primum mobile*, the intelligence, or
mens, born of him, the soul of the world which proceeds from
him, the celestial spheres and all things terrestrial. Hence,
adds Plutarch, the analogy between the Greek *pente*, five, and
pan, all.

" The ass," says he again, " is the emblem of Typhon, because like that animal he is of a reddish colour. Now Typhon
signifies whatever is of a miry or clayey nature; and in Hebrew I find the three words, *clay, red*, and *ass*, to be formed
from the same root, *hamr*. Iamblicus has farther told us, that
clay was the emblem of matter; and he elsewhere adds, that
all evil and corruption proceeded from matter; which, compared with the phrase of Macrobius, *all is perishable*, liable to
change in the celestial sphere, gives us the theory, first physical
then moral, of the system of good and evil of the ancients.

Page 143. (57). *The senseless cause of superstition.* These are
properly the words of Plutarch, who relates that those various worships were given by a king of Egypt to the different
towns to disunite and enslave them (and these kings had been
taken from the cast of priests). See *Isis and Osiris*.

Page 145. (58). *In the projection of the celestial sphere.*
The ancient priests had three kinds of spheres, which it may be
useful to make known to the reader.

" We read in Eusebius," says Porphyry, " that Zoroaster
was the first who, having fixed upon a cavern pleasantly situated in the mountains adjacent to Persia, formed the idea of
consecrating it to Mithra (the sun), creator and father of all
things : that is to say, having made in this cavern several
geometrical divisions, representing the seasons and the elements, he imitated on a small scale the order and disposition

of the universe by Mithra. After Zoroaster it became a custom to consecrate caverns for the celebration of mysteries; so that in like manner as temples were dedicated to the Gods, rural altars to heroes and terrestrial deities, &c. subterraneous abodes to infernal deities, so caverns and grottoes were consecrated to the world, to the universe, and to the nymphs; and from hence Pythagoras and Plato borrowed the idea of calling the earth a cavern, a cave, *de Antro Nympharum.*

Such was the first projection of the sphere in relief; though the Persians give the honour of the invention to Zoroaster, it is doubtless due to the Egyptians; for we may suppose, from this projection being the most simple, that it was the most ancient; the caverns of Thebes, full of similar pictures, tend to strengthen this opinion.

The following was the second projection, " The prophets or hierophants," says Bishop Synnesius, " who had been initiated in the mysteries, do not permit the common workmen to form idols or images of the Gods; but they descend themselves into the sacred caves, where they have concealed coffers, containing certain spheres, upon which they construct those images secretly and without the knowledge of the people, who despise simple and natural things, and wish for prodigies and fables." *(Syn. in Calvit.)* That is, the ancient priests had armillary spheres like ours; and this passage, which so well agrees with that of Chæremon, gives us the key to all their theological astrology.

Lastly, they had *flat models* of the nature of Plate II. with this difference, that they were of a very complicated nature, having every fictitious division of decan and subdecan, with the hieroglyphic signs of their influence. Kircher has given us a copy of one of them in his Egyptian Œdipus, and Gybelin a figured fragment in his book of the calendar (under the name of the Egyptian Zodiac). The ancient Egyptians, says the astrologer Julius Firmicus (*Astron. lib.* ii. and *lib.* iv. *c.* 16.) divide each sign of the Zodiac into three sections; and each section was under the direction of an imaginary being, whom they called *Decan,* or *chief of ten;* so that there were three Decans a month, and thirty-three a year. Now these Decans, who were also called Gods (*Thoi*), regulate the destinies of mankind —and they were placed particularly in certain stars. They afterwards imagined in every ten three other Gods, whom they called *arbiters;* so that there were nine for every month, and these were farther divided into an infinite number of powers. (The Persians and the Indians made their spheres on similar plans; and if a picture thereof were to be drawn from the description given by Scaliger at the end of Manilius, we should find in it a complete explanation of their hieroglyphics, for every article forms one).

Page 145. (59). *The adverse Genii.* It was for this reason

the Persians always wrote the name of Ahrimanes inverted thus ;
ᗺ⅄ɹɯɐuǝs.

Page *ib.* (60). *Typhon, that is to say, deluge.* Typhon, pronounced Touphon by the Greeks, is precisely the *touphan* of
the Arabs, which signifies deluge ; and these deluges in mythology are nothing more than winter and the rains, or the overflowing of the Nile : as their pretended fires which are to
destroy the world are simply the summer season. And it is for
this reason that Aristotle (*De Meteor, lib.* i. c. xiv.) says, that
the winter of the great cyclic year is a deluge ; and its summer
a conflagration. " The Egyptians," says Porphyry, " employ
every year a talisman in remembrance of the world : at the
summer solstice they mark their houses, flocks, and trees with
red, supposing that on that day the whole world had been set
on fire It was also at the same period that they celebrated
the pyrhic or fire dance." (And this illustrates the origin of
purifications by fire and by water : for having denominated the
tropic of cancer the gate of heaven, and of genial heat or celestial fire, and that of Capricorn the gate of deluge or of water, it
was imagined that the spirits or souls who passed through
these gates in their way to and from heaven, were *roasted* or
bathed ; hence the baptism of Mithra, and the passage through
flames, observed throughout the East long before Moses).

Page 145. (61.) *In Persia in a subsequent period.* That is,
when the ram became the equinoxial sign, or rather when the
alteration of the skies shewed that it was no longer the Bull.
See Note 48.

Page 146. (62). *Whence are derived all religious acts of a gay
nature.* All the ancient festivals respecting the return and
exaltation of the sun were of this description; hence the *hilaria*
of the Roman calendar at the period of the passage (Pascha) of
the vernal equinox. The dances were imitations of the march of
the planets. Those of the Dervises still represent it to this day.

Page *ib.* (63). *All religious acts of the sombre kind.* " Sacrifices of blood," says Porphyry, " were only offered to Demons and evil Genii to avert their wrath. Demons are fond of
blood, humidity, steuch," *Apud Euseb. Præp. Ev. p.* 173.

" The Egyptians," says Plutarch, " only offer bloody victims
to Typhon. They sacrifice to him a red ox, and the animal
immolated is held in execration, and loaded with all the sins of
the people." (The Goat of Moses.) See *Isis and Osiris.*

*Division of terrestrial beings into pure and impure, sacred and
abominable.* Strabo says, speaking of Moses and the Jews,
" Circumcision and the prohibition of certain kinds of meat
sprung from superstition."—And I observe, respecting the
ceremony of circumcision, that its object was to take from the
symbol of Osiris, *(Phallus)* the pretended obstacle to fecundity ;
an obstacle which bore the seal of Typhon, " whose nature,"
says Plutarch, " is made up of all that *hinders, opposes, causes
obstruction.*"

Page 143. (64). *Elysian Fields. Aliz,* in the Phenician or Hebrew language signifies dancing and joyous.

Page 149. (65). *The Milky-way.* See *Macrob. Som. Scip.* c. 12. and Note (78).

Page 151. (66). *The bodies of its inhabitants cast no shade.* There is on this subject a passage in Plutarch, so interesting and explanatory of the whole of this system, that we shall cite it entire. Having observed that the theory of good and evil had at all times occupied the attention of philosophers and theologians, he adds, "Many suppose there to be two Gods of opposite inclinations, one delighting in good, the other in evil ; the first of these is called particularly by the name of God, the second by that of Genius or Demon. Zoroaster has denominated them Oromaze and Ahrimanes, and has said that, of whatever falls under the cognizance of our senses, light is the best representation of the one, and darkness and ignorance of the other. He adds, that Mithra is an intermediate being, and it is for this reason the Persians call Mithra, the *mediator* or *intermediator.* Each of these Gods has distinct planets, and animals, consecrated to him ; for example, dogs, birds, and hedge-hogs, belonging to the good Genius, and all aquatic animals to the evil one.

" The Persians also say, that Oromaze was born or formed out of the purest light ; Ahrimanes, on the contrary, out of the thickest darkness ; that Oromaze made six Gods as good as himself, and Ahrimanes opposed to them six wicked ones : that Oromaze afterwards multiplied himself threefold (Hermes trismegistus), and removed to a distance as remote from the sun as the sun is remote from the earth ; that he there formed stars, and, among others, *Syrius,* which he placed in the heavens as a guard and centinel. He made also twenty four other Gods, which he inclosed in an egg ; but Ahrimanes created an equal number on his part, who broke the egg, and from that moment good and evil were mixed (in the universe). But Ahrimanes is one day to be conquered, and the earth to be made *equal* and *smooth,* that all men may live happy.

Theopompus adds, from the books of the Magi, that one of these Gods reigns in turn every three thousand years, during which the other is kept in subjection ; that they afterwards contend with equal weapons during a similar portion of time, but that in the end the evil Genius will fall (never to rise again.) Then men will become happy, and their bodies cast no shade. The God who meditates all these things reclines at present in repose, waiting till he shall be pleased to execute them." See *Isis and Osiris.*

There is an apparent allegory through the whole of this passage. The egg is the fixed sphere, the world ; the six Gods of Oromaze are the six signs of summer, those of Ahrimanes the six signs of winter. The forty-eight other Gods are the forty-

eight constellations of the ancient sphere, divided equally between Ahrimanes and Oromaze. The office of *Syrius*, as guard
and centinel, tells us that the origin of these ideas was Egyptian;
finally, the expression that the earth is to become *equal* and
smooth, and that the bodies of happy beings are to cast no
shade, proves that the equator was considered as their true
paradise.

Page 151, (67.) *The cave of Mithra.* See Note (58). In the
caves which priests every where constructed, they celebrated
mysteries which consisted (says Origen against Celsus) in imitating the motion of the stars, the planets, and the heavens.
The initiated took the name of constellations and assumed the
figures of animals. One was a lion, another a raven, and a
third a ram. Hence the use of masks in the first representation of the drama. See *Ant. Devoile*, vol. ii. p. 244. " In the
mysteries of Ceres the chief in the procession called himself the
creator; the bearer of the torch was denominated the sun;
the person nearest to the altar, the moon; the herald or dea-
con, Mercury. In Egypt there was a festival in which the men
and women represented the year, the age, the seasons, the
different parts of the day, and they walked in procession after
Bacchus. *Athen. lib.* v. *c.* 7. In the cave of Mithra was a ladder with seven steps, representing the seven spheres of the
planets, by means of which souls ascended and descended. This
is precisely the ladder in Jacob's vision, which shows that at
that epocha the whole system was formed. There is in the
French king's library, a superb volume of pictures of the Indian Gods, in which the ladder is represented with the souls of
men mounting it."

Page 152. (68.) *Exact calculation.* Consult the ancient
astronomy of M. Bailli, and you will find our assertions respecting the knowledge of the priests amply proved.

Page 153. (69). *A reciprocal connection.* These are the very
words of Iamblicus. *De Myst. Ægypt.*

Page *ib.* (70). *Or rather electrical fluid.* The more I consider what the ancients understood by *ether*, and *spirit*, and
what the Indians call *akache*, the stronger do I find the analogy between it and electrical fluid. A luminous fluid, principle of warmth and motion, pervading the universe, forming the
matter of the stars, having small round particles, which insin-
uate themselves into bodies, and fill them by dilating itself, be
their extent what it will, what can more strongly resemble
electricity?

Page *ib.* (71). *Was supposed to have the sun for his heart.*
Natural philosophers, says Macrobius, call the sun the heart of
the world. *Som. Scip.* c. 20. The Egyptians, says Plutarch,
call the East the *face*, the North the *right-side*, and the South
the *left side* of the world, because there the heart is placed.
They continually compare the universe to a man; and hence

the celebrated *microcosm* of the Alchymists. We observe by the bye, that the Alchymists, Cabalists, Freemasons, Magnetisers, Martinists, and every other such sort of visionaries, are but the mistaken disciples of this ancient school ; we say mistaken, because, in spite of their pretensions the thread of the ocult science is broken.

Page 153. (72.) *That the world was eternal.* See the Pythagorean *Ocellus Lucanus.*

Page 154. (73.) *The Orphic egg.* This comparison of the sun with the yolk of an egg, refers, 1. To its round and yellow figure ; 2. To its central situation ; 3. To the germ or principle of life contained in the yolk. May not the oval form of the egg allude to the ellipsis of the orbs ; I am inclined to this opinion. The word Orphic offers a farther observation. Macrobius says, *(Som. Scip. c.* 11. and c. 20), that the sun is the brain of the universe, and that it is from analogy that the skull of a human being is round like the planet, the seat of intelligence. Now the word Orph (with *ain)* signifies in Hebrew the brain and its seat *(cervix)*: Orpheus, then, is the same as Bedou or Baits ; and the Bonzes are those very Orphics which Plutarch represents as quacks, who ate no meat, vended talismans and little stones, and deceived individuals, and even governments themselves. See a learned Memoir of *Freret sur les Orphiques, Acad. des Inscrip.* vol 23. *in* 4to.

Page ib. (74). *Wearing on his head a sphere of gold.* See *Porphyry in Eusebius. Præp. Evang. lib.* 5. p. 115.

Page ib. (75). *Alluding to the wind.* The Northern or *Elesian* wind, which commences regularly at the solstice with the inundation.

Page 155. (76). *You-piter.* This is the true pronunciation of the Jupiter of the Latins. *Existence itself.* This is the signification of the word *You.* See Note (84).

Page 156. (77). *Producing the great egg.* See Note (35). ,

Page ib. (78). *The immortality of the soul, which at first was eternity.* In the system of the first spiritualists, the soul was not created with, or at the same time as the body, in order to be inserted in it : its existence was supposed to be anterior and from all eternity. Such, in a few words, is the doctrine of Macrobius on this head. *Som. Scip. passim.*

" There exists a luminous, igneous, subtle fluid, which, under the name of ether and spiritus, fills the universe. It is the essential principle and agent of motion and life, it is the Deity. When an earthly body is to be animated, a small round particle of this fluid gravitates through the milky way towards the lunar sphere, where, when it arrives, it unites with a grosser air, and becomes fit to associate with matter : it then enters, and entirely fills the body, animates it, suffers, grows, increases, and diminishes with it : lastly, when the body dies, and its gross elements dissolve, this incorruptible particle takes its leave of it, and returns to the grand ocean of ether, if not retained by its union with the lunar air: it is this air or gas, which, retaining the shape of the body, becomes a phantom or ghost, the perfect representation of the deceased. The Greeks called this phantom the image or idol of the soul; the Pythagoreans, its chariot, its frame; and the Rabbinical school, its vessel or boat. When a man had conducted himself well in this world, his whole soul, that is its chariot and ether, ascended to the moon, where a separation took place : the chariot lived in the lunar Elysium, and the ether returned to the fixed sphere, that is, to God : for the fixed heaven says Macrobius, was by many called by the name of God (c. 14). If a man had not lived virtuously, the soul remained on earth to undergo purification, and was to wander to and fro like the ghosts of Homer, to whom this doctrine must have been known since he wrote after the time of Pherecydes and Pythagoras, who were his promulgators in Greece. Herodotus upon this occasion, says, that the whole romance of the soul and its transmigrations, was invented by the Egyptians, and propagated in Greece by men, who pretended to be its authors. I know their names, adds he, but shall not mention them (lib. 2). Cicero, however, has positively informed us, that it was Pherecydes, master of Pythagoras. Tescul. lib. 1. sect. 16. Now admitting that this system was at that period a novelty, it accounts for Solomon's treating it as a fable, who lived 130 years before Pherecydes. " who knoweth," says he, " the spirit of a man that it goeth upwards ? I said in my heart, concerning the estate of the sons of men, that God, might manifest them, and that they might see that they themselves are beasts. For that which befalleth the sons of men, befalleth beasts ; even one thing befalleth them ; as the one dieth so dieth the other ; yea, they have all one breath, so that a man hath no pre-eminence above a beast, for all is vanity." Eccles. c. iii. v. 19.

And such had been the opinion of Moses as a translator of Herodotus, (M. Archer of the Academy of Inscriptions,) justly observes in note 389 of the second book, where he says also, that the immortality of the soul was not introduced among the Hebrews, till their intercourse with the Assyrians. In other respects, the whole Pythagorean system, properly analysed, appears to be merely a system of physics badly understood.

Page 157. (79.) The world is a machine; it has therefore an artificer. All the arguments of the spiritualists are founded on this. See Macrobius, at the end of the second book, and Plato with the comments of Marcilius Ficinus.

Page 158. (80.) The demi-ourgos, the logos, and the spirit. These are the real types of the Christian Trinity. See Note (99).

Page ib. (81.) Its very names. In our last analysis we found all the names of the Deity to be derived from some material object in which it was supposed to reside. We have given a considerable number of instances ; let us add one more rela-

tive to our word *God.* This is known to be the *Deus* of the
Latins, and the *Theos* of the Greeks. Now by the confession of
Plato *(in Cratylo,)* of Macrobius *((Saturn, lib.* 1. *c.* 24.*),* and of
Plutarch *(Isis and Osiris)*, its root is *thein,* which signifies to
wander, like *planein,* that is to say, it is synonimous with planets ; because all our authors, both the ancient Greeks and
barbarians particularly worshipped the planets.   I know that
such inquiries into etymologies have been much decried : but
if, as is the case, words are the representative signs of ideas,
the genealogy of the one becomes that of the other, and a good
etymological dictionary would be the most perfect history of
the human understanding. It would only be necessary, in
this inquiry, to observe certain precautions, which have hitherto been neglected, and particularly to make an exact comparison of the value of the letters of the different alphabets.   But
to continue our subject, we shall add, that in the Phenician
language, the word *thah* (with *ain*) signifies also to wander, and
appears to be the derivation of *thein.* If we suppose *Deus* to be
derived from the Greek *Zeus,* a proper name of *You-piter* having *zaw,* I live, for its root, its sense will be precisely that of *you,*
and will mean *soul* of the world, *igneous* principle. See Note
(84) *Div-us,* which only signifies Genius, God of the second order,
appears to me to come from the oriental word *div* substituted
for *dib,* wolf and chacal, one of the emblems of the sun.   At
Thebes, says Macrobius, the sun was painted under the form of
a wolf or chacal, for there are no wolves in Egypt.   The reason of this emblem, doubtless is that the chacal, like the cock, an-
nounces by its cries, the sun's rising ; and this reason is confirmed by the analogy of the words *likos,* wolf, and *lyke,* light of
the morning, whence comes *lux.*

Dius, which is to be understood also of the sun, must be derived from *dih,* a hawk. " The Egyptians," says Porphyry
(Euseb. Præcep. Evang. p. 92.) " represent the sun under the
emblem of a hawk, because this bird soars to the highest regions of air where light abounds."   And in reality we continually see at Cairo large flights of these birds, hovering in the air,
from whence they descend not but to stun us with their
shrieks, which are like the monosyllable *dih* : and here, as in
the preceding example, we find an analogy between the word
dies, day, light, and *Dius,* God, Sun.

Page 159 (82.) *The progress of science and discovery.* One of
the proofs that all these systems were invented in Egypt, is,
that this is the only country where we see a complete body of
doctrine formed from the remotest antiquity.

Clements Alexandrinus has transmitted to us *(Stromat. lib.*
6.*)* a curious detail of the 42 volumes which were borne in the
procession of Isis. " The priest," says he, " or chanter, carries one of the symbolic instruments of music, and two of the
books of Mercury ; one containing hymns of the Gods, the

U

other the list of kings.   Next to him the *horoscope* (the regulator of time), carries a palm and a dial, symbols of astrology; he must know by heart the four books of Mercury which treat of astrology: the first on the order of the planets; the second on the risings of the sun and moon, and the two last on the rising and aspect of the stars.   Then comes the sacred author, with feathers on his head (like *Kneph*) and a book in his hand, together with ink, and a reed to write with (as is still the practice among the Arabs.)   He must be versed in hieroglyphics, must understand the description of the universe, the course of the sun, moon, stars, and planets; be acquainted with the division of Egypt into 36 *nomes*, with the course of the Nile, with instruments, measures, sacred ornaments, and sacred places.   Next comes the stole bearer, who carries the cubit of justice, or measure of the Nile, and a cup for the libations; he bears also in the procession ten volumes on the subject of sacrifices, hymns, prayers, offerings, ceremonies, festivals.   Lastly arrives the prophet, bearing in his bosom a pitcher, so as to be exposed to view: he is followed by persons carrying bread (as at the marriage of Cana).   This prophet, as president of the mysteries, learns ten other sacred volumes, which treat of the laws, the Gods, and the discipline of the priests.   Now there are in all forty-two volumes, thirty-six of which are studied, and got by heart by these personages, and the remaining six are set apart to be consulted by the *pastophores*: they treat of medicine, the construction of the human body (anatomy) diseases, remedies, instruments," &c.

We leave the reader to deduce all the consequences of such an Encyclopedia.   It is ascribed to Mercury; but Jamblicus tells us that each book, composed by priests, was dedicated to that God, who, on account of his title of Genius, or *decan*, opening the zodiac, presided over every enterprise. He is the *Janus* of the Romans, and the *Guianesa* of the Indians, and it is remarkable that *Yanus* and *Guianes* are homonymous.   In short, it appears that these books are the source of all that has been transmitted to us by the Greeks and Latins in every science, even in alchymy, necromancy, &c.   What is most to be regretted in their loss, is that part which related to the principles of medicine and diet, in which the Egyptians appear to have made a considerable progress, and to have delivered many useful observations.

Page 160 (83.) *The reigning religion in Lower Egypt.* " At a certain period," says Plutarch (*de Iside*), " all the Egyptians have their animal Gods painted.   The Thebans are the only people who do not employ painters, because they worship a God whose form comes not under the senses, and cannot be represented.   And this is the God whom Moses, educated at Heliopolis, adopted; but the idea was not of his invention.

Page ib. (84). *AndYahouh.* Such is the true pronunciation of the Jehovah of the moderns, who violate in this respect every rule of criticism ; since it is evident, that the ancients, particularly the Eastern Syrians and Phenicians, were acquainted neither with the *Je* nor the *V*, which are of Tartar origin. The subsisting usage of the Arabs, which we have re-established here, is confirmed by Diodorus, who calls the God of Moses *Iaw*, (*lib. 1.*) and *Iaw* and *Iahouh* are manifestly the same word : the identity continues in that of *Ioupiter*; but in order to render it more complete, we shall demonstrate the signification to be the same.

In Hebrew, that is to say, in one of the dialects of the common language of Lower Asia, *Yahouh* is the participle of the verb *hih*, to exist, to be, and signifies existing ; in other words, the principle of life, the mover or even motion (the universal soul of beings.) Now what is Jupiter? Let us hear the Greeks and Latins explain their theology. " The Egyptians," says Diodorus, after Manatho, priest of Memphis, in giving names to the five elements, called *spirit*, or ether, *Youpiter*, on account of the true meaning of that word: for *spirit* is the source of life, author of the vital principle in animals ; and for this reason they considered him as the father, the generator of beings." For the same reason Homer says, father, and king of men and gods : (*Diod. lib. 1. sect. 1.*)

" Theologians," says Macrobius, " consider You-piter ; as the soul of the world." Hence the words of Virgil : " Muses, let us begin with You-piter ; the world is full of You-piter," (*Somn. Scip. ch. 17.*) And in the Saturnalia he says, " Jupiter is the sun himself." It was this also which made Virgil say : " The spirit nourishes the life (of beings), and the soul diffused through the vast members (of the universe), agitates the whole mass, and forms but one immense body."

" Ioupiter," says the ancient verses of the Orphic sect, which originated in Egypt ; verses collected by Onomacritus in the days of Pisistratus, " Ioupiter represented with the thunder in his hand, is the beginning, origin, end, and middle of all things : a single and universal power, he governs every thing : heaven, earth, fire, water, the elements, day, and night. These are what constitute his immense body : his eyes are the sun and moon ; he is space and eternity ; in fine," adds Porphyry, " Jupiter is the world, the universe, that which constitutes the essence and life of all beings. Now," continues the same author, " as philosophers differed in opinion respecting the nature and constituent parts of this God, and as they could invent no figure that should represent all his attributes, they painted him in the form of man. He is in a sitting posture, in allusion to his immutable essence : the upper part of his body is uncovered, because it is in the upper regions of the universe (the stars), that he most conspicuously displays himself. He is covered from the waist downwards, because respecting terrestrial things he is more secret and concealed. He holds a sceptre in his left hand, because on the left side is the heart, and the heart is the seat of the understanding, which (in human beings) regulates every action." *Euseb. Præper. Evang. p.* 100.

The following passage of the geographer and philosopher Strabo, removes every doubt as to the identity of the ideas of Moses, and those of the heathen theologians.

" Moses, who was one of the Egyptian priests, taught his followers, that it was an eggregious error to represent the Deity under the form of animals, as the Egyptians did, or in the shape of man, as was the practice of the Greeks and Africans. That alone is the Deity, said he, which constitutes heaven, earth, and every living thing; that which we call the *world,* the *sum of all things, nature* ; and no reasonable person will think of representing such a being by the image of any one of the objects around us. It is for this reason, that, rejecting every species of images or idols, Moses wished the Deity to be worshipped without emblems, and according to his proper nature ; and he accordingly ordered a temple worthy of him to be erected," &c. *Geograph. lib.* 16. *p.* 1104, edition of 1707.

The theology of Moses has, then, differed in no respect from that of his followers, that is to say, from that of the Stoics and Epicureans, who consider the Deity as the soul of the world. This philosophy appears to have taken birth, or to have been desseminated when Abraham came into Egypt (200 years before Moses), since he quitted his system of idols for that of the God *Yahouh* ; so that we may place its promulgation about the seventeenth or eighteenth century before Christ; which corresponds with what we have said, Note (78).

As to the history of Moses, Diodorus properly represents it when he says, *lib* 34 and 40, " That the Jews were driven out of Egypt at a time of dearth, when the country was full of foreigners, and that Moses, a man of extraordinary prudence and courage, seized this opportunity of establishing his religion in the mountains of Judea." It will seem paradoxical to assert, that the 600,000 armed men whom he conducted thither ought to be reduced to 6,000; but I can confirm the assertion by so many proofs drawn from the books themselves, that it will be necessary to correct an error which appears to have arisen from the mistake of the transcribers.

Page 160. (85). *Ei existence.* This was the monosyllable written on the gate of the temple of Delphos. Plutarch has made it the subject of a dissertation.

Page 161. (86.) *The name of Osiris preserved in his song.* These are the literal expressions of the book of Deuteronomy, ch. 32. " The works of *Tsour* are perfect." Now *Tsour* has been translated by the word creator; its proper signification is to give *forms*, and this is one of the definitions of Osiris in Plutarch.

Page 163. (87). *Of the Archangel Michael.* "The names of the angels and of the months, such as Gabriel, Michael, Yar, Nisau, &c came from Babylon with the Jews;" says expressly the Talmud of Jerusalem. See *Beausob. Hist. du Manich.* Vol. II. p. 624. where he proves that the saints of the Almanac are in imitation of the 365 angels of the Persians, and Jamblicus in his Egyptian Mysteries, *sect.* 2.,c. 3. speaks of angels, archangels, seraphims, &c. like a true christian.

Page *ib.* (88). *Theology of Zoroaster.* The whole philosophy of the gymnosophists," says Diogenes Laertius, on the authority of an ancient writer, " is derived from that of the Magi, and many assert that of the Jews to have the same origin." *Lib.* 1. *c.* 9. Magasthenes, an historian of repute in the days of Seleucus Nicanor, and who wrote particularly upon India, speaking of the philosophy of the ancients respecting natural things, puts the Brachmans and the Jews precisely on the same footing.

Page 164. (89.) *To restore the golden age upon earth.* This is the reason of the application of the many Pagan oracles to Jesus, and particularly the fourth eclogue of Virgil, and the Sybilline verses so celebrated among the ancients.

Page 165. (90.) *At the expiration of the six thousand pretended years.* We have already seen, note 29, this tradition current among the Tuscans: it was disseminated through most nations, and shows us what we ought to think of all the pretended creations and terminations of the world, which are merely the beginnings and endings of astronomical periods invented by astrologers. That of the year or solar revolution being the most simple and perceptible, served as a model to the rest, and its comparison gave rise to the most whimsical ideas. Of this description is the idea of the four ages of the world among the Indians. Originally these four ages were merely the four seasons; and as each season was under the supposed influence of a planet, it bore the name of the metal appropriated to that planet: thus spring was the age of the sun, or of gold: summer the age of the moon, or of silver; autumn the age of Venus, or of brass; and winter the age of Mars, or of iron. Afterwards, when astronomers invented the great year of 25 and 36 thousand common years, which had for its object the bringing back all the stars to one point of departure and a general conjunction, the ambiguity of the terms introduced a similar ambiguity of ideas; and the myriads of celestial signs and periods of duration which were thus measured, were easily converted into so many revolutions of the sun. Thus the different periods of creation which have been so great a source of difficulty and misapprehension to curious inquirers, were in

reality nothing more than hypothetical calculations of astronomical periods. In the same manner the creation of the world
has been attributed to different seasons of the year, just as these
different seasons have served for the fictitious period of these
conjunctions, and of consequence has been adopted by different nations for the commencement of an ordinary year. Among
the Egyptians this period fell upon the summer solstice, which
was the commencement of their year; and the departure of the
spheres, according to their conjectures, fell, in like manner,
upon the period when the sun enters Cancer. Among the Persians the year commenced at first in the spring, or when the
sun enters Aries; and from thence the first Christians were
led to suppose that God created the world in the spring : this
opinion is also favoured by the book of Genesis; and it is farther remarkable, that the world is not there said to be created by the
God of Moses (Yahouh), but by the Elohim or gods in the
plural, that is, by the angels or genii, for so the word constantly
means in the Hebrew books. If we farther observe that the
root of the word Elohim signifies strong or powerful, and that
the Egyptians called their decans strong and powerful leaders,
attributing to them the creation of the world, we shall presently
perceive that the book of Genesis affirms neither more nor less
than that the world was created by the decans, by those very
genii whom, according to Sanchoniathon, Mercury existed
against Saturn and who were called Elohim. It may be further asked, why the plural substantive Elohim is made to agree
with the singular verb bara (the Elohim creates)? The reason
is, that after the Babylonish captivity the unity of the Supreme Being was the prevailing opinion of the Jews; it was
therefore thought proper to introduce a pious solecism in
language, which it is evident had no existence before Moses:
thus in the names of the children of Jacob many of them are
compounded of a plural verb, to which Elohim is the nomina-
tive case understood, as Raouben (Reuben), they have looked
upon me, and Samaonni (Simeon), they have granted me my prayer,
to wit, the Elohim. The reason of this etymology is to be
found in the religious creeds of the wives of Jacob, whose gods
were the tarraphim of Laban, that is, the angels of the Persians, and the Egyptian decans.

   Page 165. (91.) Six thousand years had already nearly elapsed
since the supposed creation of the world. According to the computation of the Seventy, the period elapsed consisted of about
5,600 years, and this computation was principally followed.
It is well known how much, in the first ages of the church,
this opinion of the end of the world agitated the minds of men.
In the sequel, the general councils, encouraged by finding
that the general conflagration did not come, pronounced the
expectation that prevailed heretical, and its believers were called Millenarians; a circumstance curious enough, since it is evident from the history of the Gospels that Jesus Christ was a
Millenarian, and of consequence a heretic.

Page 166. (92.) *Constellation of the serpent.* " The Persians,"
says Chardin, " call the constellation of the serpent *Ophiucus*
serpent of Eve; and this serpent *Ophiucus* or *Ophioneus*, plays a
similar part in the theology of the Phenicians;" for Pherecydes, their disciple, and the master of Pythagoras, said
" that *Orphioneous serpentinus* had been chief of the rebels
against Jupiter." See Mars, Ficin. Apol. Socrat. p. m. 797.
col. 2. I shall add, that *œphah* (with ain) signifies in Hebrew
serpent.

Page ib. (93.) *Seduced the man.* In a physical sense to se-
duce, *seducere*, means only to attract, to draw after us.

Page ib. (94.) *Picture of Mithra.* See this picture in Hyde,
page 111, edition of 1760.

Page 167. (95.) *Perseus rises on the opposite side.* Rather the
head of Medusa; that head of a woman once so beautiful,
which Perseus cut off, and which he holds in his hand, is only
that of the virgin, whose head sinks below the horizon at the
very moment that Perseus rises; and the serpents which surround it are Ophiucus and the Polar Dragon, who then occupy the Zenith. This shews us in what manner the ancients
composed all their figures and fables. They took such constellations as they found at the same time on the circle of the horizon, and collecting the different parts, they formed groupes
which served them as an almanac in hierglyphic characters.
Such is the secret of all their pictures, and the solution of all
their mythological monsters. The Virgin is also Andromeda,
delivered by Perseus from the whale that *pursues her (prose-
quitor.)*

Page ib. (96.) *By a chaste virgin.* Such was the picture of the
Persian sphere, cited by Aben Ezra in the *Cœlum Poeticum* of
Blacu, p. 71. " The picture of the first decan of the Virgin,"
says that writer, "represents a beautiful virgin with flowing
hair, sitting in a chair, with two ears of corn in her hand, and
suckling an infant, called Jesus by some nations, and Christ in
Greek."

In the library of the king of France is a manuscript in Arabic
marked 1165, in which is a picture of the twelve signs; and
that of the Virgin represents a young woman with an infant by
her side: the whole scene, indeed, of the birth of Jesus, is to
be found in the adjacent part of the heavens. The stable is
the constellation of the charioteer and the goat, formerly Capricorn; a constellation called *præsepe Jovis Heniochi*, *stable of
Iou*; and the word *Iou* is found in the name of Iouseph (Joseph).
At no great distance is the ass of Typhon (the great she-bear)
and the ox or bull, the ancient attendants of the manger. Peter
the porter, is Janus with his keys and bald forehead: the twelve
apostles are the genii of the twelve months, &c. This Virgin
has acted very different parts in the various systems of mythology: she has been the Isis of the Egyptians, who said of her
in one of their inscriptions cited by Julian, *the fruit I have brought*

forth is the sun. The majority of traits drawn by Plutarch apply to her, in the same manner us those of Osiris apply to Bootes : also the seven principal stars of the she-bear, called David's chariot, were called the chariot of Osiris (See *Kirker*,) and the crown that is situated behind, formed of ivy, was called *Chen Osiris*, the tree of Osiris. The Virgin has likewise been Ceres, whose mysteries were the same with those of Isis and Mithra : she has been the Diana of the Ephesians ; the great goddess of Syria, Cybele, drawn by lions ; Minerva, the mother of Bacchus ; Astrea, a chaste virgin taken up into heaven at the end of the golden age; Thems, at whose feet is the balance that was put in her hands ; the Sybil of Virgil, who descends into hell, or sinks below the hemisphere with a branch in her hand, &c.

Page 108 (97). *Rose again in the firmament.* *Resurgere* to rise a second time, cannot signify to return to life, but in a metaphorical sense ; but we see continually mistakes of this kind result from the ambiguous meaning of the words made use of in ancient tradition.

Page ib. (98). *Chris, or conservator.* The Greeks used to express by X. or Spanish iota, the aspirated *ha* of the orientals, who said *haris.* In Hebrew *heres* signifies the sun, but in Arabic the meaning of the radical word is, to guard, to preserve, and of *haris*, guardian, preserver. It is the proper epithet of Vichenou, which demonstrates at once the identity of the Indian and Christian Trinities, and their common origin. It is manifestly but one system, which divided into two branches, one extending to the east, and the other to the west, assumed two different forms; its principal trunk is the Pythagorean system of the soul of the world, or *Ioupiter.* The epithet *piter* or father, having been applied to the demi-ourgos of Plato, gave rise to an ambiguity which caused an inquiry to be made respecting the son of this father. In the opinion of the philosophers the son was understanding, *Nous* and *Logos*, from which the *Latins* made their *Verbum.* And thus we clearly perceive the origin of the *eternal father* and of the *Verbum* his son, proceeding from him (*Mens ex Deo nata.* says Macrobius); the *anima* or *spiritus mundi* was the Holy Ghost : and it is for this reason that Manes, Basiledes, Valentinius, and other pretended heretics of the first ages who traced things to their source, said that God the Father was the supreme inaccessible light (that of the heaven, the *primum mobile*, or the aplanes) ; the Son the secondary light resident in the sun, and the Holy Ghost the atmosphere of the earth, (See *Beausob.* Vol. II. p. 580); hence, among the Syrians, the representation of the Holy Ghost by a dove, the bird of Venus Urania, that is, of the air. The Syrians (says *Nigidius de Cermanico*) assert that a dove sat for a certain number of days on the egg of a fish, and that from this incubation Venus was born : Sextus Empiricus also observes *(Inst. Pyrrh. lib. 3. c. 23.)* that the Syrians abstain from eating doves; which intimates to us a period commencing in the sign Pisces, in the winter solstice. We may farther observe, that if *Chris* comes from *Harisch* by a *chin*, it will signify *artificer*, an epithet belonging to the sun. These variations, which must have embarrassed the ancients, prove it to be the real type of Jesus, as had been already remarked in the time of Tertullian. "Many," says this writer, "suppose with greater probability that the sun is our God, and they refer us to the religion of the Persians." *Apologet. c. 16.*

Page *ib.* (99). *One of the solar periods.* See a curious ode to the Sun, by Martinus Capella, translated by Gebelin.

Page 174. (100). *Human sacrifices.* Read the cold declaration of Eusebius *(Præp. Evang. lib. 1. p. 11.)* who pretends that since the coming of Christ, there have neither been wars, nor tyrants, nor cannibals, nor sodomites, nor persons committing incest, nor savages devouring their parents, &c. When we read these fathers of the church, we are astonished at their insincerity or infatuation.

Page 175. (101). *Sect of Samaneans.* The equality of mankind in a state of nature, and in the eyes of God, was one of the principal tenets of the Samaneans, and they appear to be the only ancients that entertained this opinion.

Page 177. (102). *Perverted the consciences of men.* As long as it shall be possible to obtain purification from crimes, and exemption from punishment by means of money or other frivolous practices; as long as kings and great men shall suppose that building temples or instituting foundations, will absolve them from the guilt of oppression and homicide: as long as individuals shall imagine that they may rob and cheat, provided they observe fast during Lent, go to confession, and receive extreme unction, it is impossible there should exist in society any morality or virtue; and is from a deep conviction of truth, that a modern philosopher has called the doctrine of expiations *la verole des societies.*

Page 178. (103). *Has carried its inquisition even to the sacred sanctuary of the nuptial bed.* The Mussulmans, who suppose women to have no souls, are shocked at the idea of confession, and say, How can an honest man think of listening to the recital of the actions or the secret thoughts of a woman? May we also not ask, on the other hand, how can an honest woman consent to reveal them?

Page *ib.* (104). *That every where they had formed secret associations, enemies to the rest of the society.* That we may understand the general feelings of priests respecting the rest of mankind, whom they always call by the name of the people, let us hear one of the doctors of the church. "The people," says Bishop Synnesius, *in Calvit. page* 315, "are desirous of being deceived, we cannot act otherwise respecting them. The case

was similar with the ancient priests of Egypt, and for this
reason they shut themselves up in their temples, and there
composed their mysteries out of the reach of the eye of the
people." And forgetting what he has just before said, he adds
—" For had the people been in the secret, they might have
been offended at the deception played upon them. In the
mean time how is it possible to conduct one's self otherwise
with the people so long as they are the people ? For my own
part, to myself I shall always be a philosopher, but in dealing
with the mass of mankind I shall be a priest."

" A little jargon," says Gregory Nazianzen to St. Jerome
(Hieron. ad. Nep.) " is all that is necessary to impose on the
people. The less they comprehend, the more they admire.
Our forefathers and doctors of the church have often said, not
what they thought, but what circumstances and necessity dictated to them."

" We endeavour," says Sanchoniathon, " to excite admiration by means of the marvellous." *(Præp. Evang. lib. 3.)*

Such was the conduct of all the priests of antiquity, and is
still that of the Bramins and Lamas, who are the exact counterpart of the Egyptian priests. Such was the practice of the
Jesuits, who marched with hasty strides in the same career. It
is useless to point out the whole depravity of such a doctrine.
In general every association which has mystery for its basis, or
an oath of secrecy, is a league of robbers against society, a league
divided in its very bosom into knaves and dupes ; or, in other
words, agents and instruments. It is thus we ought to judge
of those modern clubs, which, under the name of Illuminatists,
Martinists, Cagliostronists, Freemasons, and Mesmerites, infest
Europe. These societies ape the follies and deceptions of the
ancient Cabalists, Magicians, Orphics, &c. who, says Plutarch,
led into errors of considerable magnitude not only individuals,
but kings and nations.

Page 179. (106). *They made themselves in turns astrologers,
casters of planets, magicians, &c.* What is a magician, in the
sense in which the people understand the word ? A man who
by words and gestures pretends to act on supernatural beings,
and compel them to descend at his call and obey his orders.
Such was the conduct of the ancient priests, and such is still
that of all priests in idolatrous nations, for which reason we
have given them the denomination of magicians.

And when a Christian priest pretends to make God descend
from heaven, to fix him to a morsel of leaven, and to render, by
means of this talisman, souls pure and in a state of grace, what
is all this but a trick of magic ? And where is the difference
between a Chaman of Tartary, who invokes the genii, or an Indian Bramin, who makes his Vichenou descend in a vessel of
water to drive away evil spirits ? Yes, the identity of the spirit

of priests in every age and country is fully established ! Every where it is the assumption of an exclusive privilege, the pretended faculty of moving at will the powers of nature ; and this assumption is so direct a violation of the right of equality, that whenever the people shall regain their importance, they will for ever abolish this sacrilegious kind of nobility, which has been the type and parent stock of the other species of nobility.

Page 179. (107). *Who paid for them as for commodities of the greatest value.* A curious work would be the comparative history of the *agnuses* of the pope and the *pastils* of the grand Lama. It would be worth while to extend this idea to religious ceremonies in general, and to confront, column by column, the analogous or contrasting points of faith and superstitious practices in all nations. There is one more species of superstition which it would be equally salutary to cure, blind veneration for the great; and for this purpose it would be alone sufficient to write a minute detail of the private life of kings and princes. No work could be so philosophical as this : and accordingly we have seen what a general outcry was excited among kings and the panders of kings, when the Anecdotes of the Court of Berlin first appeared. What would be the alarm were the public put in possession of the sequel of this work ! Were the people fairly acquainted with all the crimes and all the absurdities of this species of idol, they would no longer be exposed to covet their specious pleasures, of which the plausible and hollow appearance disturbs their peace, and hinders them from enjoying the much more solid happiness of their own condition.

FINIS.

INDEX.

===

I. J.

K.

L.

M.

O.

P.

Plummer & Brewis, Printers,
Love Lane, Little Eastcheap.

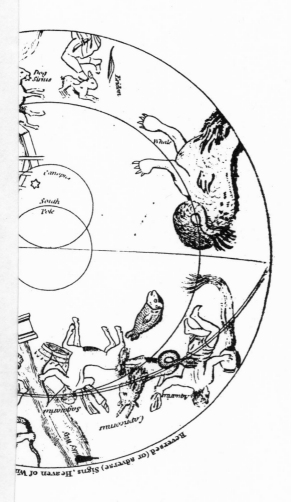

Dog
& Sirius

Eridan

Whale

Canopus

South
Pole

Sagittarius

Capricorn

Aquarius

Milky Way

Reversed (or adverse) Signs, Heaven of Wi

THE

LAW OF NATURE,

OR

PRINCIPLES OF MORALITY,

DEDUCED FROM THE

PHYSICAL CONSTITUTION

OF

Mankind and the Universe.

=

TRANSLATED FROM THE FRENCH OF

C. F. VOLNEY.

=

" For modes of faith, let graceless zealots fight ;
" His can't be wrong, whose life is in the right."

Pope.

THE

LAW OF NATURE.

CHAP. I.

ON THE LAW OF NATURE.

Q. *What is the Law of Nature;*

A. It is the regular and constant order of events, according to which God rules the universe; the order which his wisdom presents to the senses and reason of mankind, to serve them as an equal and general rule of action, and to conduct them, without distinction of country or sect, towards happiness and perfection.

Q. *Give me a clear definition of the word Law.*

A. The word *law*, taken in its literal sense, signifies *reading*; because, in early times, ordinances and regulations principally composed the readings delivered to the people; which were made in order that they might observe them, and not incur the penalties attached to their infraction; whence it follows, that the original usage explaining the true idea, a law may be defined to be, " A command or a prohibition of an action, with the expressed clause of a penalty attached to the infraction, or a reward annexed to the observation of the order."

Q. *Are there such orders in nature?*

A. Yes.

Q. *What means the word Nature?*

A. The word *nature* comprehends three different significations.

1. It means the *universe*, or material world; we say, according to this signification, the *beauties of nature, the riches of nature*: that is, of the objects in heaven and on earth presented to our contemplation.

2. It means the *power* which animates and moves the universe, considering this power as a distinct being, such as the soul is supposed to be with respect to the body. In this second sense we say, the intentions of *nature*, the incomprehensible secrets of *nature*.

3. It means the partial operation of this power, as exerted in each individual being, or in any class of beings; and we say, in this third sense, the *nature* of man is an enigma; every being acts according to its *nature*.

Now, since the actions of each individual, or of each class of beings, are subjected to constant and general rules, which cannot be departed from without changing and disturbing some general or particular order of things, to these rules of action and motion, is given the name of natural laws, or *laws of nature*.

Q. *Give me examples of these laws?*

A. It is a law of nature that the sun enlightens in succession every part of the surface of the terrestrial globe: that his presence excites light and heat: that heat acting on the waters, produces vapours: that these vapours, raised in clouds into the higher regions of the atmosphere, form themselves into rain or snow, and supply, without ceasing the water of springs and rivers.

It is a law of nature that water flows from an upper to a lower situation; that it seeks its level: that it is heavier than air; that all bodies tend towards the earth; that flame rises towards the sky; that it destroys the organization of vegetables and animals; that air is essential to the life of certain animals; that in certain cases water suffocates and kills them: that certain juices of plants and certain minerals attack their organs, and destroy their life; and the same of a variety of facts.

Now, since these facts, and many similar ones, are constant, regular. and immutable, they become so many real and positive commands to which man is bound to conform, under the express penalty of punishment attached to their infraction, or well-being connected with their observance. So that, if a man were to pretend to see clearly in the dark, or is regardless of the progress of the seasons, or the action of the elements; if he pretends to exist under water without drowning; to handle fire without burning himself; to deprive himself of air without suffocating; or to drink poison without destroying himself; he receives from each infraction of the law of nature a corporal punishment proportioned to his trangression. If, on the contrary he observes these laws, and founds his practice on the precise and regular relation which they bear to him, he preserves his existence, and renders it as happy as it is capable of being rendered; and since all these laws, considered in relation to the human species, have in view only one common end, that of their preservation and their happiness; whence it has been agreed to assemble together the different ideas, and express them by a single word, and call them collectively by the name of the *law of nature.*

CHAP. II.

CHARACTERS OF THE LAW OF NATURE.

Q. *WHAT are the characters of the law of nature?*
A. We may reckon ten principal ones.

Q. *What is the first?*
A. To be inherent in, and essential to, the existence of things; consequently to be primitive and anterior to every other law, so that all those which men have adopted from time to time, are only imitations of this; the perfection of which laws is to be measured by their resemblance with this primordial model.

Q. *What is the second?*
A. It is to emanate immediately from God, and to be by him offered to the contemplation of every man, while others are presented to us by men only, who may happen to be either deceivers or deceived.

Q. *What is the third?*
A. It is to be common to every time and country; that is, to be one and universal.

Q. *Is there no other law which is universal?*
A. No; for no other is suited and applicable to every people upon earth; all are local and accidental, sprung from the differing circumstances of places and persons; so that if a given man, or a given event, had not existed, a given law would not have taken place.

Q. *What is the fourth character?*
A. That of being uniform and invariable.

Q. *Is there no other law which is uniform and invariable?*
A. No; for that which according to one is good and virtuous, is evil and vicious according to another; and what is at one time approved, is often condemned at another by the same law.

Q. *What is the fifth character?*

A. To be evident and palpable, since it consists wholly of facts ever present to our senses, and capable of demonstration.

Q. *Are there not other laws evident?*

A. No, for they are founded on past and doubtful facts; on equivocal and suspicious testimony; and on proofs which cannot be presented to the senses.

Q. *What is the sixth character?*

A. To be reasonable; because its precepts, and its whole doctrine, are conformable to reason, and agreeable to the human understanding.

Q. *Is no other law reasonable?*

A. No; for they all contradict the reason and understanding of man, and impose upon him tyrannically, a blind and impracticable belief.

Q. *What is the seventh character?*

A. To be just; because in this law the punishment is proportioned to the transgression.

Q, *Are there no other laws just?*

A. No; for they frequently attach to merit, or to criminality, disproportionate punishment or reward, and impute merit and criminality, to actions which are null or indifferent.

Q. *What is the eighth character?*

A. To be pacific and tolerant; because, according to the law of nature, all men being brethren, and equal in rights, it advises all to peace and toleration, even for their errors.

Q. *Are not other laws pacific?*

A. No; for they all breathe dissension, discord, and war, and divide men among each other by means of exclusive pretensions to truth and power.

Q. *What is the ninth character of this law?*

A. To be equally beneficent to all men, and to teach them all the true method of being better and happier.

Q. Are not the rest likewise beneficent?

A. No; for none teaches the true road to happiness; they all really amount to nothing but pernicious or futile performances; and this is proved by facts, since, after so many laws, religions, legislators, and prophets, men remain still as unhappy and as ignorant as they were five thousand years ago.

Q. What is the last character of the law of nature?

A. It is its being of itself sufficient to render men happier and better, because it includes whatever is good and useful in every other law, civil or religious: that is, it is in its essence the moral part of them all; so that, were they divested of it, they would be reduced to the state of chimerical and imaginary opinions, and be of no practical utility.

Q. Recapitulate all these characters.

A. I have said that the law of nature is,

Primitive;

Immediate, or of original emanation;

Universal;

Invariable;

Evident;

Reasonable;

Just;

Pacific;

Beneficent;

And of itself sufficient:

And it is because it unites in itself all these attributes of perfection and of truth, that there has always existed in the human heart an involuntary and secret inclination to regard it as, in a peculiar sense, the true religion; the only one adapted to the nature of man, and the only one worthy of God, from whom it emanates.

Q. If as you assert, it emanates immediately from God, does it teach us his existence?

A. Yes; very positively; for every man, who observes with attention the astonishing scene of the universe, the more he meditates on the properties and attributes of each existence, and on the admirable order and harmony of their motions, the more will he be convinced that there is a supreme agent, a universal and identical mover, designed by the name God: and it is so true, that the law of nature is sufficient to raise us to the knowledge of God, that whatever men have pretended to know of him by other means has been constantly found to be ridiculous and absurd; and they have been obliged to return to the unchangeable notions of natural reason.

Q. *It is not true then, that the followers of the law of nations are atheists?*

A. No; it is not true. On the contrary, they have stronger and more noble ideas of the divinity than the greater part of mankind; for they do not defile it by the addition of the weaknesses and passions of human nature.

Q. *What is the worship which they render him?*

A. A worship which consists entirely in action; in the observation and practice of all the rules which the supreme wisdom has imposed upon the motions of each being; eternal and unalterable rules, which maintain the order and harmony of the universe, and which considered in relation to man, compose the law of nature.

Q. *Was the law of nature ever known before the present day?*

A. It has been spoken of in every age. The greater part of lawgivers have pretended to make it the basis of their laws; but they have brought forward only a few of its precepts, and have had but vague ideas of it as a whole.

Q. *Why has this happened?*

A. Because, though it is simple in its basis, it forms, in its developement and its consequences, a complicated aggregate, which requires the knowledge of a number of facts, and the whole sagacity of reason, in order to be understood.

Q. *Does not instinct alone instruct us in the law of nature?*

A. No; for instinct signifies only that blind sentiment which leads us, without discrimination, towards whatever pleases our senses.

Q. *Why then is it said that the law of nature is engraven on the hearts of all men?*

A. It is said, for two reasons: 1st. Because it has been remarked that there are actions and sentiments common to all mankind, arising from their similar organization. 2d. Because it was an opinion of the ancient philosophers, that men were born into the world with innate or ready-formed ideas; an opinion which is now demonstrated to be an error.

Q. *Do philosophers then deceive themselves?*

A. Yes; they do.

Q. *How happens this?*

A. 1st. From their nature as men. 2d. Because ignorant persons call every man who reasons a philosopher, whether he reason well or ill. 3d. Because those who reason on a variety of subjects, and are the first to reason on them, are liable to deceive themselves.

Q. *Since the law of nature is not written, may it not be considered as arbitrary and ideal?*

A. No; because it consists altogether in facts, whose demonstration may be at any time recalled before the senses, and form a science as precise and exact as those of geometry and mathematics: and this very circumstance, that the law of nature forms an exact science, is the reason why men, who are born in ignorance, and live in carelessness, have, till this day, known it only superficially.

CHAP. III.

THE PRINCIPLES OF THE LAW OF NATURE AS THEY RELATE TO MAN.

Q. UNFOLD the principles of the law of nature as they relate to man.

A. They are simple, and reducible to a single fundamental principal precept.

Q. What is this precept?

A. Self-preservation.

Q. Is not happiness likewise a precept of the law of nature?

A. Yes; but as happiness is an accidental circumstance, which takes place only in consequence of the unfolding of the faculties of man, and the developement of the social system, it is not the primary and direct end proposed by nature. It is an object of luxury superadded to the necessary and fundamental object of self-preservation.

Q. In what manner does nature command self-preservation?

A. By two powerful and involuntary sensations which she has attached as two guides or guardian genii to all our actions : one, the sensation of pain, by which she informs us of, and turns us from, whatever tends to our destruction.

The other, the sensation of pleasure, by which she attracts and leads us towards every thing that tends to our preservation, and the unfolding of our faculties.

Q. Pleasure then is not an evil or a sin, as the cauists have pretended?

A. No; it is of that class only when it tends to the destruction of life and health, which, as the causists themselves confess, are derived to us from God.

Q. *Is pleasure the principal object of our existence, as some philosophers have asserted?*

A. No; no more than pain is: by pleasure, nature encourages us to live; by pain, it makes us shrink from death.

Q. *How do you prove this assertion?*

A. By two palpable facts; the one, that pleasure, carried too far, conducts into destruction: for instance, a man who abuses the pleasure of eating and drinking, attacks his health, and injures his existence. The other, that pain sometimes tends to our preservation; for instance, a man who orders his mortified limb to be amputated, suffers pain, but it is in order that he may not perish altogether.

Q. *But does not this prove that our senses may deceive us with respect to this end of self-preservation?*

A. Yes; they may for a time.

Q. *How do our sensations deceive us?*

A. In two ways; through our ignorance and our passions.

Q. *When do they deceive us through our ignorance?*

A. When we act without knowing the action and effect of objects on our senses: for instance, when a man handles nettles without knowing their quality of stinging; or when he chews opium in ignorance of its soporific properties.

Q. *When do they deceive us through our passions?*

A. When, though we are acquainted with the hurtful action of objects, we, notwithstanding, give way to the violence of our desires and our appetites: for instance, when a man, who knows that wine inebriates, drinks, notwithstanding, to excess.

Q. *What results from these facts?*

A. The result is, that the ignorance in which we enter the world, and the inordinate appetites to which we give ourselves up, are opposed to our self-preservation; that, in consequence, the instruction of our minds, and the moderation of our passions, are two obligations, or two laws, immediately derived from the first law of preservation.

Q. *But if we are born ignorant, is not ignorance a part of the law of nature?*

A. No more than it is for us to remain in the naked and feeble state of infancy: far from its being a law of nature, ignorance is an obstacle in the way of all her laws. It is the true original sin.

Q. *Whence then has it happened that moralists have existed who considered it as a virtue and a perfection?*

A. Because, through caprice, or misanthrophy, they have confounded the abuse of our knowledge itself; as though, because men misemploy the faculty of speaking, it were necessary to cut out their tongue; as though perfection and virtue consisted in the annihilation, and not in the unfolding and proper employment of our faculties.

Q. *Is instruction then necessarily indispensable for man's existence?*

A. Yes; so indispensable, that, without it, he must be every instant struck and wounded by all the beings which surround him; for, if he did not know the effects of fire, he would burn himself; of water, he would be drowned; of opium, he would be poisoned. If, in the savage state, he is unacquainted with the cunning and subterfuges of animals, and the art of procuring game, he perishes with hunger: if, in a state of society, he does not know the progress of the seasons, he can neither cultivate the earth, nor provide himself with food: and the like may be said of all his actions arising from all his wants.

Q. *But can man, in a a state of solitude, acquire all*

c

these ideas necessary to his existence and the unfolding of his faculties !

A. No; he cannot do it but by the assistance of his fellows living with him in a state of *society.*

Q. *But is not a state of society a state unnatural to man?*

A. No; it is, on the contrary, a necessity, a law imposed upon him by his very organization; for, 1st. Nature has so constituted the human being, that he does not behold his likeness of another sex without experiencing emotions, and an attraction inducing him to live in a domestic state, which is a already a state of society: 2d, In rendering him sensible, she has so organized him, that the sensations of others are reflected into himself, and excite in him co-sentiments of pleasure or pain, which become the attractive force and indissoluble bond of social life: 3d. In fine, the state of society, established on the wants of man, is nothing more than an additional means of fulfilling the law of preservation: and to say, that such a state is unnatural, because it is more advanced towards perfection, is to say that a fruit, which in the woods is bitter and wild, is no longer a production of nature, after having become sweet and delicious in the garden in which it has been culti-vated.

Q. *Why then have philosophers denominated the savage state of life a state of perfection?*

A. Because, as I have before observed, the vulgar have often given the appellation of philosophers, to capricious persons, who, through moroseness, wounded vanity, or disgust with the vices of social life, have formed a chimerical idea of the savage state, contradictory to their own system of the perfectability of man.

Q. *What is the true meaning of the word philoso-pher.*

A. The word philosopher signifies *lover of wisdom:* now, since wisdom consists in the practice of the laws of nature, that man is a true philosopher who understands these laws in their full extent, and, with precision, renders his conduct conformable to them.

Q. What is man in a savage state?

A. A brute and ignorant animal: a mischievous and ferocious beast, like a bear or an ourang-outang.

Q. Is he happy in such a state?

A. No; for he has but the sensations of the moment; and these sensations are habitually sentiments of violent and pressing wants which he cannot gratify; seeing that he is ignorant by nature, and feeble by his state of insulation from society.

Q. Is he free?

A. No; he is the most slavish of beings; his life depends on all that surrounds him; he has not the power to eat when he is hungry, to rest himself when he is weary, or to warm himself when he is cold: he is in danger of perishing every instant. Nature, it is true, has exhibited such beings only, as it were, by chance; and, it is evident, that the efforts of the human race have, from the beginning, been employed to extricate it from this state of violence; so strong is the desire of preservation.

Q. But does not this desire of self-preservation produce in individuals egoism, that is, the love of self; and is not egoism abhorrent to the social state?

A. No; for, if by egoism is understood an inclination to injure others, it is no longer the love of self, but the hatred of our neighbour. The love of self, taken in its true sense, is not only consistent with a state of society, but is likewise its firmest support; since we are under a necessity of not doing injury to others, lest they should, in return, do injury to ourselves.

C 2

Thus the preservation of man, and the unfolding of his faculties, which have in view the same end, are the true law which nature has followed in the production of the human species: and from this simple and fruitful principle, are derived, must be referred, and ultimately measured, all our ideas of good and evil, vice and virtue, justice and injustice, truth and error, of what is permitted and what is forbidden; the foundation of all moral conduct, whether in the individual man, or the man of social life.

———

CHAP. IV.

OF THE BASIS OF MORALITY—OF GOOD—OF EVIL —OF SIN—OF CRIMES—OF VICE AND VIRTUE.

Q. WHAT is good, according to the law of nature!

A. Whatever tends to preserve and ameliorate mankind.

Q. What is evil!

A. Whatever tends to the destruction and deterioration of the human race.

Q. What is understood by PHYSICAL *good or evil, and* MORAL *good and evil?*

A. By the word *physical,* is meant whatever acts immediately upon the body: health is a physical good; sickness is a physical evil. By *moral,* is understood whatever is effected by consequences more or less remote: calumny is a moral evil; a fair reputation is a moral good; because both of them are the occasion of certain dispositions and habits in other men, with respect to ourselves which are useful or prejudicial to our well-being, and which attack or contribute to the means of existence.

Q. *Whatever then tends to preservation or production is good?*

A. Yes; and this is the reason why some legislators have ranked in the class of things pleasing to God, the cultivation of a field, and the fruitfulness of a woman.

Q. *Every thing which tends to bring on death is of consequence evil?*

A. Yes; and for this season, some legislators have extended the idea of evil and sin to the killing of any animals.

Q. *The murder of a man, is it then a crime according to the law of nature?*

A. Yes; and the greatest that can be committed; for all other evils may be repaired, but murder can never be done away.

Q. *What is a sin according to the law of nature?*

A. Whatever tends to disturb the order established by nature, for the preservation and perfectability of man and of society.

Q. *Can intention be a merit or a crime?*

A. No; for it is only an idea without reality; but it is a beginning of sin and evil, by the inclination to act, of which it is the cause.

Q. *What is virtue according to the law of nature?*

A. The practice of actions which are useful to the individual and to society.

Q. *What signifies the word individual?*

A. It signifies a person considered as insulated from every other.

Q. *What is vice according to the law of nature?*

A. It is the practice of actions prejudicial to the individual and to society.

C 3

Q. Have not virtue and vice an object purely spiritual and abstracted from sense ?

A. No; they are always ultimately referable to a physical end ; and this end is invariably the destruction or preservation of the body.

Q. Have vice and virtue degrees of strength and intensity ?

A. Yes : according to the importance of the faculties which they attack or favour; and according to the number of individuals in whom these faculties are thus assisted or injured.

Q. Give me an example ?

A. The action of saving a man's life is more virtuous than that of saving his wealth : the act of saving the lives of ten men is more so than that of saving the life of a single person : and an action, which is useful to the whole human race, is more virtuous than an action useful only to a single nation.

Q. In what manner does the law of nature prescribe the practice of good and virtue, and forbid that of evil and of vice ?

A. By the advantages resulting from the practice of good and virtue in the preservation of our bodies, and the injuries which our very existence receives from the practice of evil and vice.

Q. Its precepts, then are found in and founded upon action ?

A. Yes; they are action itself, considered in its present effect and its future consequences.

Q. What division do you make of the virtues ?

A. We divide them into three classes: 1st, Private virtues, or those which refer to single and insulated persons : 2d. Domestic virtues, or those which relate to families : 3d. Social virtues, or those which respect society at large.

CHAP. V.

OF INDIVIDUAL OR PRIVATE VIRTUES—OF KNOWLEDGE.

Q. *WHICH are the private virtues?*

A. There are five principal ones: namely, knowledge; which comprehend prudence and wisdom.

2d. Temperance; which includes sobriety and chastity.

3d. Courage; or strength of body and mind.

4th. Activity; that is, the love of labour, and a proper employment of our time.

5th. Lastly; cleanliness, or purity of body, as well in our clothing as in our dwellings.

Q. *How does the law of nature prescribe to us the possession of knowledge?*

A. In this way: The man who is acquainted with the causes and effects of things, provides in a very extensive and certain manner for his own preservation and the developement of his faculties. Knowledge is for him, as it were, light acting upon its appropriate organ, making him discern all the objects which surround him, and in the midst of which he moves with precision and clearness. And for this reason, we used to say an *enlightened* man, to designate a wise and well-informed man. By the help of knowledge and information, we are never left without resources and means of subsistence: and whence a philosopher, who had suffered shipwreck, observed justly to his companions, who were lamenting the loss of their fortunes, " As for me, I carry all my fortune in myself."

Q. What is the vice opposed to knowledge?

A. Ignorance.

Q. How does the law of nature forbid ignorance?

A. By the great injury which our existence sustains from it: for the ignorant, who are unacquainted with either causes or effects, commit every instant mistakes, the most pernicious to themselves or others : like a blind man who walks groping his way, and who at every step stumbles against or is jostled by his companions.

Q. What difference is there between an ignorant man and a fool?

A. The same that there is between a blind man who ingenuously acknowledges his want of sight, and a blind man who pretends to see distinctly. Folly is ignorance, with a superadded pretension to knowledge.

Q. Are ignorance and folly common?

A. Yes; very common : they are the habitual and general diseases of mankind.   Above three thousand years since, the wisest of men observed, that the number of fools is infinite ; and the world has not changed.

Q. How happens this?

A. Because to become informed is the work of much time and labour; and because men, born ignorant, but fearful of trouble, find it more convenient to remain blind, and pretend to see clearly.

Q. What difference is there between the man of learning and the man of wisdom.

A. The man of learning possesses the theory, and the man of wisdom the practice.

Q. What is prudence?

A. An anticipated view, a foresight of effects, and the consequences of every event : a foresight by which a man avoids the dangers which threaten him, and seizes and raises up opportunities which are favourable: whence it appears, that he provides, on a large and sure scale, for his present and future conservation ; while the imprudent man, who neither calculates his progress nor his conduct, the efforts required, nor the resistances to overcome, falls every moment into a thousand difficulties and dangers, which, more or less, slowly destroy his faculties and his being.

Q. *When the gospel declares, Happy are the poor in spirit, Does it mean the ignorant and imprudent ?*

A. No; for at the same time that it advises the simplicity of doves, it connects with it the prudent cunning of the serpent. By simpleness of spirit is meant rectitude ; and the precept of the gospel is no other than that of nature.

———

CHAP. VI

OF TEMPERANCE.

Q. *WHAT is temperance?*

A. A well-regulated employment of our faculties ; which prevents our ever exceeding in our sensible pleasures the end of nature, self-conservation. It is the moderation of our passions.

Q. *What is the vice opposed to temperance ?*

A. The want of government over our passions: an over-great eagerness to possess enjoyment: in a word, cupidity.

Q. What are the principal branches of temperance?

A. Sobriety, and continence or chastity.

Q. In what manner does the law of nature enjoin sobriety?

A. By its powerful influence over our health. The man of sobriety digests his food with comfort; he is not opposed by the weight of his aliment: his ideas are clear and easily impressed; he performs every function well; he attends with diligence to his business; he grows old, free from sickness; he does not throw his money away in remedies for disorders; he enjoys with gay good-humour the goods which fortune or prudence have procured for him. Thus does generous nature make a thousand rewards flow from a single virtue.

Q. By what means does she prohibit gluttony?

A. By the numerous evils attached to it. The glutton, oppressed by his aliment, digests with pain and difficulty; his head, disturbed by the fumes arising during bad digestion, is incapable of receiving neat and clear ideas; he gives himself up with fury to the inordinate movements of luxury and anger, which destroy his health; his body becomes fat, heavy, and unfit for labour; he passes through painful and expensive fits of sickness; he rarely lives to old age, and his latter part of life is marked by infirmity and disgust.

Q. Ought we to look upon abstinence and fasting as virtuous actions?

A. Yes; after we have eaten too much; for, in that case, abstinence and fasting are efficacious and simple remedies; but when the body has need of nourishment, to refuse it, and let it suffer through thirst or hunger, is madness, and a real sin against the law of nature.

Q, In what light does this law consider drunkenness?

A. As the vilest and most pernicious of vices. The drunkard, deprived of the sense and reason given us by God, profanes the gifts of the Divinity; he lowers himself to the condition of the brutes: incapable of directing his steps, he totters and falls as in a fit of epilepsy: he wounds himself, and endangers his own life: his weakness in this state renders him the play-thing and the scorn of all around him: he contracts, during his drunkenness, ruinous engagements, and loses the management of his affairs: he suffers violent and outrageous observations to escape him, which raise him up enemies, and bring him to repentance: he fills his house with trouble and chagrin; and he concludes by a premature death, or an old age, comfortless and diseased.

Q. Does the law of nature absolutely forbid the use of wine?

A. No; it only forbids the abuses of it; but as the passage, from the proper to the improper use of it, is, for the vulgar, very short and easy, perhaps those legislators, who have forbidden the use of wine, have, in so doing, rendered a service to mankind.

Q. Does the law of nature forbid the use of certain meats and vegetables, on certain days, or during certain seasons?

A. No; it forbids only what is absolutely prejudicial to health: its precepts on this score vary as men do, and compose a very delicate and important science; for the quality, the quantity and the combination, of our aliments, have a very great influence, not only on the momentary affections of the mind, but likewise on its habits and dispositions. A man fasting is not the same as after repast, though of the most sober kind. A glass of wine, a dish of coffee, produce various degrees of vivacity, activity, disposition to anger, sadness, or gaiety: one species of food, because it lies heavy on the stomach, renders a person morose and peevish; another, which is easily digested, disposes to cheerfulness and love, and produces in us an inclination to be obliging. The use of vegetables, as they afford little nourishment, render the body weak, and induce repose, inactivity, and mildness of character: the use of flesh-meats, as they nourish much, and of spirituous liquors, as they stimulate the nerves, induce liveliness, restlessness, audacity. Now, from these habits of taking different kinds of food, result constitutional habits, which form in the end various temperaments, each distinguished by a peculiar character; and hence it appears, why in hot countries legislators have promulgated, as laws, rules of diet. Long experience had taught the ancients, that the dietetic science composed a considerable portion of that of morals; among the Egyptians, among the ancient Persians, and even among the Greeks, in their Areopagus, affairs of consequence were never debated on, except the members of the council were fasting; and it has been remarked, that among every people who deliberate during the warmth of a repast, or during the fumes of digestion, the debates are invariably furious and turbulent, and their results frequently unreasonable and destructive of the public peace.

———

CHAP. VII.

OF CONTINENCE.

Q. DOES the law of nature prescribe continence?
A. Yes; because moderation, in the enjoyment of

the most violent of our sensations, is not only serviceable, but indispensible for the maintenance of our strength and health; and because it may be demonstrated by a simple calculation, that, in return for a few minutes of privation, we are repaid by long days of vigour of mind and body.

Q. *How does it forbid libertinism?*

A. By the innumerable evils which it entails upon our existence, physical and moral. The man who abandons himself to it, becomes enervated and languid; he is no longer able to attend to his studies or his business; he contracts idle and expensive habits, which diminish his means of livelihood, his reputation and his credit; his intrigues occasion him embarrassments, cares, quarrels, and law-suits, not to take into the account heavy and grievous diseases; the decrease of his strength by an internal and slow poison; the stupefaction of his intellect by the exhaustion of the nervous influence; and, lastly, a premature and infirm old age.

Q. *Is that consummate chastity, which is so much inculcated in monastic institutions, regarded as a virtue by the natural law?*

A. No; for such chastity is neither of utility to the society at large where it is prevalent, nor even to the individuals who are rigorously observant of it; nay, it is demonstrably prejudicial to both. In the first place it is detrimental to society at large, because it checks the progress of its population, which is one of its great sources of wealth and power: and because the persons who devote themselves to a life of celibacy, by confining their views and affections within the narrow sphere of their own existence, for the most part contract a selfish partiality for themselves, which alienates their minds from the general interests of the community.

In the second place it is injurious to individuals,

D

because it excludes them from a multiplicity of affections and relations, which have a considerable share in the formation of the domestic and social virtues. Again, it frequently happens, from the circumstances of age, temperament, and diet, that absolute continence impairs the health, and lays the foundation of serious diseases, by counteracting those laws by which nature maintains and perpetuates the species. Not to mention, that those who are such rigid and enthusiastic advocates for unlimited abstinence in this respect, even where their sincerity cannot be called in question, totally militate against their own doctrine, which consecrates the law of nature by the well-known command, *Be fruitful and multiply.*

Q. *Why is chastity considered as a virtue of greater importance to women than to men?*

A. Because the breach of chastity in women is attended with far more alarming and injurious consequences to themselves and to society; for, exclusively of the afflictions and diseases of every denomination to which they are liable in common with the other sex, they incur all the various inconveniences that precede, accompany, and follow a state of motherhood, of which they run the hazard; and, if this should chance out of the pale of the law, they became exposed to the scorn and derision of the world, which unavoidably embitters the remaining portion of their existence. Again they are surcharged with the expences arising from the maintenance and education of children that are unprotected and without relations; by which means they become impoverished and distressed both in mind and fortune. In this state, deprived of that freshness and that health in which their charms chiefly consist, carrying about with them an unusual and painful burden, they are less sought after by the men; they find no solid establishment, they fall into poverty, misery, abasement, and drag on, in wretchedness, a life of abject unhappiness.

Q. Does the law of nature descend to scruple our desires or thoughts!

A. Yes; because according to the physical laws of the human body, thoughts and desires awaken the senses, and soon stimulate to action. Moreover, by another law of nature, in the organization of our body, these actions become a species of mechanical want, repeated according to periods of days or weeks; so that, at any given epoch, the want or desire to perform a given action, or produce a given secretion, always arises: and if this action or secretion are prejudicial to health, the habit becomes destructive of life itself. Thus desires and thoughts become of real importance in nature.

Q. Ought modesty to be considered as a virtue!

A. Yes: because modesty, considered as a bashful timidity with regard to certain actions, maintains the mind and body in all the habits tending to the good order and self-preservation of the individual. A modest women is esteemed, sought after, established in all the advantages of fortune, which assure her existence, and render it agreeable, while the immodest woman and the prostitute are despised, rejected, and abandoned to misery and disgrace.

———

CHAP. VIII.

OF COURAGE AND ACTIVITY.

Q. ARE courage and strength of body and mind virtues according to the law of nature?

A. Yes; and very important virtues; for they are

D 2

efficacious and indispensible means of effecting our
preservation and well being. The courageous and
strong man repels oppression; defends his life, his
liberty, his property; by his labour he procures for
himself subsistence in abundance, and enjoys it with
tranquillity and peace of mind. If any misfortune
happens to him from which his prudence could not
guard him, he supports it with firmness and resignation; and, for this reason, the ancient moralists accounted strength and courage among their four principal virtues.

Q. *Ought weakness and cowardice to be considered
as vices?*

A. Yes; since it is true that they are connected
with a thousand calamities. The weak and cowardly live in the midst of care, and in perpetual agony;
their health is undermined by the terror they are
under, often an ill-founded one, of danger and attack:
and this terror, which is itself an evil, is not the remedy of any other evil; on the contrary, it renders
man a slave to whoever is desirous of oppressing
him; and by the subjection and abasement of all
his faculties, degrades and corrupts his means of existence, and makes his life depend, as it were, on
the will and caprice of other men.

Q. *But, after what you have said of the influence
of aliments, are not courage and strength, as well as
many other virtues, in a great measure the effect of
our temperament, or physical constitution?*

A. Yes; this is true, to such a degree, that these
qualities are transmitted to us in our birth, and by
our blood, with the elements on which these depend.
Repeated and unvarying facts prove, that, in every
race of animals, certain physical and moral qualities,
attached to the various individuals of each race, are
augmented or diminished according to the combinations and admixture which take place between the
several races.

Q. But if our wills and exertions are not sufficient to procure us these qualities, is it a crime in us to be destitute of them?

A. No; it is not a crime, but a misfortune; it is what the ancients called a melancholy fatality; but even in this case, it still is in some measure in our power to acquire them; for, from the moment that we have learnt on what physical elements depends such and such qualities, we are enabled to prepare for their production, and to excite them to unfold themselves by an able management of the elements; and in this consists the science of education, which, according as it is directed perfects or renders worse both individuals and entire races, so as to change altogether their nature and inclinations; and this it is which renders so important the knowledge of the laws of nature, by which these operations and changes are effected with certainty and of necessity.

Q. Why do you say that activity is a virtue according to the law of nature?

A. Because the man who labours and employs his time usefully, derives, from so doing, innumerable advantages with respect to his existence. Is he poor? his labour furnishes him with subsistence: and if, in addition, he is sober, continent, and prudent, he soon acquires many conveniences, and enjoys the sweets of life: his very labour produces in him those virtues; for as long as he continues to employ his mind and his body, he is not affected by inordinate desires, he is free from dullness; he contracts mild and pleasant habits; he augments his strength and his health; and arrives to an old age of felicity and peace.

Q. Are idleness and sloth, then, vices in the order of nature?

A. Yes; and the most pernicious of all vices; for they lead to every other. In idleness and sloth man

D 3

remains ignorant, and even loses the knowledge which he had before acquired, falling into all the evils which accompany ignorance and folly. In idleness and sloth, man, devoured by listless dullness, gives himself up to all the lusts of sense, whose empire, as it encreases and extends from day to day, renders him intemperate, gluttonous, luxurious, enervate, cowardly, base, and despicable. The certain effects of all which vices are, the ruin of his fortune, the wasting of his health, and the termination of his life in the anguish of disease and poverty.

Q. *If I understand you, it would appear that poverty is a vice?*

A. No; it is not a vice, but still less is it a virtue: for it is much more frequently injurious than useful; it is even commonly the result of vice, or its first occasion; for every individual vice conducts towards indigence, even to the privation of the necessaries of life; and when a man is in want of the necessaries, he is on the point of endeavouring to procure them by vicious methods; that is, methods hurtful to society. All the private virtues, on the contrary, tend to procure for man an abundance of subsistence; and when he has more than he can consume, it becomes more easy for him to give it to others, and to perform actions useful to society.

Q. *Do you look upon riches as a virtue?*

A. No; but still less are they a vice. It is their employment only which can be denominated virtuous or vicious, according as it is useful or hurtful to man and to society. Wealth is an instrument, whose use and employment only determine its viciousness or virtue.

CHAP. IX.

OF CLEANLINESS.

Q. *WHY do you rank cleanliness in the class of virtues?*

A. Because it is really one of the most important, as it has a powerful influence on the health and preservation of the body. Cleanliness, as well in our garments as in our dwellings, prevents the pernicious effects of dampness, of bad smells, and of contagious vapours arising from substances abandoned to putrify: cleanliness keeps up a free perspiration, renews the air, refreshes the blood, and even animates and enlivens the mind. Whence we see that persons, attentive to the cleanliness of their persons and their habitations, are in general more healthy, and less exposed to diseases, than those who live in filth and nastiness; and it may moreover be remarked, that cleanliness brings with it, throughout every part of domestic discipline, habits of order and arrangement, which are among the first and best methods and elements of happiness.

Q. *Is uncleanliness, then, or filthiness, a real vice?*

A. Yes; as real as drunkenness or as sloth, from which, for the most part, it derives its origin. Uncleanliness is a secondary, and often a first, cause of a multitude of slight disorders, and even of dangerous sicknesses. It is well known in medicine, that it generates the itch, the scald-head, the leprosy, no less certainly than the same disorders are produced by

corrupted or acrid elements: that it contributes to
the contagious power of the plague and of malignant
fevers ; that it even gives birth to them in hospitals
and prisons ; that it occasions rheumatism, by incrus-
ting the skin with dirt, and checking perspiration ;
not to mention the disgraceful inconvenience of being
devoured by insects, the unclean appendage of abject
misery.

For this cause, the greater part of the ancient legislators have constituted cleanliness, under the title
of *purity*, one of the essential dogmas of their several
religions ; hence the reason of their driving from society, and subjecting even to corporal punishment
those who suffered themselves to be attacked by the
diseases which are engendered by uncleanliness ; why
they instituted and consecrated the ceremonies of ablution, bathing, baptism, and of purification even by
fire, and by the aromatic effluvia of incenses, myrrhs,
benzoin, &c. So that the whole system of impure
taints, all those rites referring to things clean and
unclean, which in after times degenerated into prejudices and abuses, were, in their origin, derived from
the judicious observations, made by wise and well-
informed men, on the great influence which the cleanliness of the body, both with respect to its clothing
and its habitation, possesses over the health, and, by
an immediate consequence, over the mind and the
moral faculties.

Thus all the individual or private virtues have, for
their more or less direct and more or less proximate
end, the preservation of the man who practises them ;
while, by the preservation of each individual, they
tend to insure that of the family and of society at
large, which is nothing more than the united sum of
those individuals.

CHAP. X.

OF DOMESTIC VIRTUES.

Q. *WHAT do you mean by domestic virtues?*

A. I mean the practice of those actions which are useful to a family, that is, to a number of persons living under one roof.

Q. *What are those virtues?*

A. Economy, parental affection, conjugal love, filial love, brotherly love, and the fulfilment of the reciprocal duties of master and servamt.

Q. *What is economy?*

A. Taken in its most extensive signification, it is the proper administration of whatever concerns the existence of the family or household; but, as subsistence holds the first rank among these circumstances, the word economy has been restricted to the employment of our money in procuring for us the primary wants of life.

Q. *Why is economy a virtue?*

A. Because the man who enters into no useless expence always possesses a superabundance, which constitutes real wealth, and by means of which he procures for himself and his family all that is truly useful and convenient; without taking into the account, that by this means he ensures to himself resources against accidental and unforeseen losses: so that himself and his family live in a tranquil and pleasant state of ease, which is the basis of all human happiness.

Q. *Are dissipation and prodigality, then vices?*

A. Yes; for they bring a man at last to the want of the necessaries of life; he falls into poverty, misery, and abject disgrace; so that even his acquaintance, fearful of being obliged to restore to him what he has squandered with them or upon them, fly from him as a debtor from his creditors, and he is left abandoned by all the world.

Q. *What is parental affection?*

A. The assiduous care which a parent takes to bring up his children in the habit of every action useful to themselves and to society.

Q. *In what respect is parental tenderness a virtue, with respect to parents!*

A. In as much as the parents, who bring up their children in good habits, lay up for the whole course of their lives those enjoyments and aids which are grateful to us at all times, and ensure against old age those supports and consolations which are required by the wants and calamities of that period of life.

Q. *Is parental affection a common virtue?*

A. No; notwithstanding all parents make a parade of it, it is a rare virtue; they do not *love* their children; they *caress* them, and they spoil them: what they love in them, is the agency of their wills, the instruments of their power, the trophies of their vanity, the play-thing of their leisure hours. It is not so much the good of their children that they propose as their submission and obedience: and if amongst children we find so many examples of filial ingratitude, it is because amongst parents there are so many examples of ignorant and despotic kindness.

Q. *Why do you say that conjugal love is a virtue?*

A. Because the concord and union which are the consequence of the affection subsisting between married persons establish in the bosom of their family a multitude of habits which contribute to its prosperity and conservation: united by the bonds of marriage, they love their household and quit it rarely; they superintend every part of its administration; they attend to the education of their children; they keep up the respectfulness and fidelity of their domestics; they prevent all disorder and dissipation; and, by the whole of their good conduct, live in ease and reputation? while those married persons, who have no affection for each other, fill their dwelling with quarrels and distress, excite war among their children and among their domestics, and lead them both into every kind of vicious habit; so that each wastes, pillages, and robs, in their several ways: their revenues are absorbed without return; debts follow debts; the discontented parties fly each other and recur to lawsuits; and the whole family falls into disorder, ruin, disgrace, and the want of the necessaries of life.

Q. *Is adultery a crime according to the law of nature?*

A. Yes; for it is followed by a numerous train of habits hurtful to the married persons, and to their family. The wife or the husband, given up to the love of strangers, neglect their own dwelling, desert it, and divert as much as possible its revenues from their right use, spending them on the object of their affections: hence quarrels, scandal, law-suits, the contempt of children and servants, the pillage and final ruin of the whole house: not to mention that the adulterous woman commits the most heinous of all robberies, giving heirs to her husband of foreign blood, who deprive of their lawful portion his true offspring.

Q. *What is filial love?*

A. It is, on the part of children, the practice of

THE LAW OF NATURE.

such actions as are useful to themselves and to their parents.

Q. What motives does the law of nature present to enforce filial love?

A. Three chief motive: 1st, Sentiment; for from our earliest infancy, the affectionate solicitudes of our parents produce in us the mild habits of attachment. 2d, The sense of justice; for, children owe their parents a return, and, as it were, a reparation, for the troubles, and even for the expences, which they have occasioned them. 3d, Personal interest; for, if we act ill towards our progenitors, we offer our own children examples of rebellion and ingratitude, which authorize them to render us the like at any future day.

Q. Ought we to understand by filial love a passive and blind submision?

A. No; but a reasonable submission, founded on an acquaintance with the mutual rights and duties of parents and of children: rights and duties, without whose observance, their conduct towards each other can amount to nothing better than disorder.

Q. Why is brotherly love a virtue?

A. Because the concord and union which result from the mutual affection of brethren, establish the power, safety, and preservation, of families. Brethren in union mutually defend each other from all oppression, assist each other in their mutual wants, support each other under misfortune, and thus secure their common existence; while brethren in a state of disunion, each being abandoned to his personal strength, fall into all the inconveniences of insulation from society and of individual feebleness. This truth was ingeniously expressed by that of king of Scythia, who, on his death-bed, having called his children round him, ordered them to break a bundle of arrows;

when the young men, though in full vigour, were not able to accomplish this, he took the bundle in his turn, and, having untied it, broke each separate arrow with his fingers. Behold, said he, the effect of union: united in a body you will be invincible; taken separately you will be broken like reeds.

Q. What are the reciprocal duties of masters and servants?

A. The practice of such actions as are respectively and equitably useful to each; and here begin the relations of society; for, the rule and measure of these respective actions is the equilibrium or equality between the service and the reward; between what the one performs and the other gives, which is the fundamental basis of all society.

Thus all the domestic and individual virtues refer more or less immediately, but always without varying, to the physical object of the amelioration and conservation of man; and are, in this view, precepts resulting from the fundamental law proposed by nature in his formation.

━━━

CHAP. XI.

OF THE SOCIAL VIRTUES, AND OF JUSTICE.

Q. WHAT is society?

A. Every aggregate re-union of men living together under the regulations of a contract tacit or expressed for their common preservation.

Q. Are the social virtues many in number?

A. Yes; we may count as many as there are actions useful to society; but they may be all reduced to one principle.

Q. What is this fundamental principle?

A. Justice, which itself alone comprehends all the social virtues.

E

Q. Why do you say that justice is the fundamental and almost only virtue of social life?

A. Because it alone embraces the practice of all those actions which are useful to society; and that every virtue, under the name of charity, humanity, probity, love of country, sincerity, generosity, simplicity of manners, and modesty, are but varied forms, and diversified applications of this axiom, " Do unto another only that which thou would he should do unto thee;" which is the definition of justice.

Q. How does the law of nature ordain justice?

A. By means of three physical attributes which are inherent in the organization of man.

Q. What are these attributes?

A. Equality, liberty, property.

Q. In what sense is equality a physical attribute of man?

A. Because all men, having equally eyes, hands, a mouth, ears, and being alike under the necessity of making use of them for their life's sake, are by this very fact equally entitled to life, and to the use of the elements which contribute to its support. They are all equal before God.

Q. Do you pretend that all men hear, see, and feel equally well; that they have equal wants, and equal and like passions?

A. No; for it is a matter of certainty and daily experience, that one man is short and another long-sighted; that one eats much and another little; that one has moderate and another violent passions; in a word, that a grown person is weak both in body and mind, while another is strong in both.

Q. They are in fact, then, really unequal?

A. Yes; in the unfolding of their faculties and powers, but not in the nature and essence of these powers; it is a stuff of the same kind, but whose dimensions are not equal, nor its weight and value the same, with those of some other pieces: our language has no word calculated to express at the same time sameness of nature and diversity of form and employment. It is a relative equality, and for this reason I said, equal before God, and in the order of nature.

Q. *Why is liberty called a physical attribute of man?*

A. Because all men possessing senses fitted and sufficient for their preservation, no one having need of the eye of another man in order to see, of his ear to hear, of his mouth to eat, or of his foot to walk, they are all made, by this means, naturally independent and free. No one is of necessity subjected to another's rule, nor has right of dominion over him.

Q. *But if a man is born strong, has he not a natural right to master and rule over him who is born weak?*

A. No; for it is neither with respect to himself a matter of necessity, nor a convention between the two; and in this instance we make improper use of the word right, which in its true sense signifies nothing more than justice or reciprocal faculties and power.

Q. *How is property a physical attribute of man?*

A. Since every man is formed equal and similar to his fellows, and consequently free and independent, every one is the absolute master, the entire proprietor of his body, and the products of his labour.

Q. *How is justice derived from these three attributes?*

A. From this circumstance; that men, being equal, free, and owing nothing to each other, have no right to demand any thing of their fellows, but in proportion as they return for it something equivalent; in proportion as the balance of what is given to what is paid remains in equilibrium; and it is this equality this equilibrium, which is called justice and equity;*

---

* Æquitas, æquilibrium, æqualitas, are all of the same family.

E 2

—that is to say, equality and justice are synonymous words; are the same natural law, of which all the social virtues are but applications and derivatives.

———

CHAP, XII.

DEVELOPEMENT OF THE SOCIAL VIRTUES.

Q. *UNFOLD to me how the social virtues are derived from the law of nature. How is charity, or the love of our neighbour, a precept or application of this law.*

A. By reason of the laws of equality and reciprocity; for when we do injury to another, we give him the right of doing us injury in his turn. Thus, by attacking the existence of another, we make an attack upon our own, in consequence of the law of reciprocity. On the contrary, when we do good to our neighbour, we have ground and reason to expect an exchange of good, an equivalent; and such is the character of all the social virtues, to be useful to the man who practices them, by the right of reciprocity which they communicate to him over those to whom his good offices have been of service.

Q. *Charity then is nothing more than justice?*

A. Yes: it is nothing more than than justice, with this single difference, that strict justice confines itself to the assertion, " Do not to others the evil which thou wouldst not they should do unto thee:" and that charity, or the love of our neighbour, goes farther, even to say, " Do unto others the good which you wish to receive from them." Thus the Gospel, when it said that this precept contained all the Law and the Prophets, did no more than announce a precept of the law of nature.

Q. *Does it command us to forgive injuries?*

A. Yes; in as much as such forgiveness consists with the preservation of ourselves.

Q. *Does it contain the precept of turning the one check after being smitten on the other?*

A. No; for, in the first place, it is not consistent with the precept which orders us to love our neighbours *as ourselves*; since, in that case, we should have more love for him who attacks our well-being than for ourselves: 2d. Such a command, taken literally, encourages the wicked to oppression and injustice; and the law of nature has been more wise, in prescribing a given measure of courage and moderation, which makes us forget a first injury, if occasioned by momentary warmth, but which punishes every act tending to oppression.

Q. *Does the law of nature command us to do good to others, without measure or limitation?*

A. No; for it is a certain means of occasioning ingratitude. Such is the power of the sentiment of justice implanted in the hearts of men, that they do not give us credit even for acts of kindness, if accompanied with indiscretion. They have but one measure—that of Justice.

Q. *Is alms giving a virtuous action?*

A. Yes; when conducted according to the same rule; otherwise it degenerates into imprudence and vice, in as much as it encourages indolence, which is hurtful both to the beggar and to the society. No one has a right to enjoy the good or labour of another without rendering an equivalent by his own labour.

Q. *Does the law of nature consider as virtues, hope, and faith, which are usually conjoined with charity?*

A. No; for they are ideas not founded on realities; and, if any good effects result from them, these are rather to the profit of those who have not imbibed such ideas than to those who have; so that it might be, perhaps, allowable to say, that faith and hope are the virtues of dupes, which turn to the advantage of rogues and cheats.

E 3

Q. *Does the law of nature prescribe probity* ?

A. Yes; for probity is nothing more than a respect paid to our own rights, through the medium of the rights of others; a respect derived from a prudent and well made calculation of our own interests, compared with those of others.

Q. *But does not this calculation, which includes the complicated interests and rights of the social state, demand such light, and such knowledge of things, as to render it a science of difficult acquisition* ?

A. Yes; and a science so much the more delicate as the man of probity pronounces sentence in his own cause.

Q. *Is probity, then, a mark of an enlarged and correct mind* ?

A. Yes; for the man of probity almost always neglects some present interest for the sake of one which is future ; while on the other hand, the knave is willing to lose a great interest to come, for the sake of some trifling one which is present.

Q. *Knavery, then, is a sign of false judgment and narrowness of mind* ?

A. Yes; and rogues may be defined to be ignorant or foolish speculators, for they know not their own interests; and, though they affect wariness and, cunning, their artifices seldom fail to expose them and make them known for what they are : to deprive them of the confidence and esteem of others, and of all the advantages which might thence result to their social and physical existence. They neither live in peace with themselves nor with others; and, incessantly alarmed by their conscience and their enemies, they enjoy no other real happiness than that of escaping from the executioner.

Q. *Does the law of nature forbid theft* ?

A. Yes; for the man who steals from another, grants him the liberty to steal in his turn; hence no security in property, nor even in the means of self-preservation. Thus, the man who does injury to another, by a species of re-action is hurt himself.

Q. *Does it forbid the inclination to theft?*

A. Yes; for this inclination naturally leads to action : hence the reason of considering envy as a sin.

Q. *How does it forbid murder?*

A. By the most powerful motives addressed to the desire of self-preservation : for, 1st, The man who attacks another exposes himself to the risk of being killed, according to the law of self-defence : 2d, If he kills his opponent, he gives an equal right, founded on the same law, to the relations and friends of the deceased, and even to the whole community, of killing him, and his life is no longer in security.

Q. *How can a man, according to the law of nature, repair any injury which he has committed?*

A. By conferring a proportionable benefit upon those whom he has injured.

Q. *Does this law allow him to repair it by prayers, vows, offerings to God, fastings, or mortifications?*

A. No! for none of these things have any relation to the action which is meant to be atoned for: they neither restore to him who has been robbed what he has lost, whether it be property or reputation; nor life to him who has been deprived of it : consequently they fail with regard to justice; they constitute an illegitimate contract, by which one man sells to another a good of which he himself is not possessed : they tend to a depravation of morals, as they embolden men to commit every species of crime, in the hope of expiation : and they have been the real-sources of all those evils which have constantly tormented every nation, whose institutions permitted these expiatory practices.

Q. *Is sincerity enjoined by the law of nature?*

A. Yes; for lying, perfidy, and perjury, excite amongst men distrust, dissention, hatred, revenge and a multitude of evils, which tend to the destruc-

tion of society; whilst sincerity and good faith establish confidence, concord, peace, and the other infinite advantages, which are the necessary result of
such a happy state of things.

Q. *Does it prescribe mildness and modesty?*

A. Yes; for an assuming and rude deportment, while
it alienates from us the hearts of other men, infuses
into them a disposition to do us disservice: ostenta-
tion and vanity, by wounding their self-love and exciting their jealousy, prevent us from attaining the
point of real utility.

Q. *Does it prescribe humility as a virtue?*

A. No; for there is a natural propensity in the
human heart to feel a secret contempt for every thing
which conveys to it the idea of weakness; and, by
abasing ourselves, we encourage in others pride and
oppression: we should hold the balance with an even
hand.

Q. *You have classed amongst the social virtues,* simplicity of manners; *what do you mean by that expression?*

A. I mean the confining our wants and desires to
what is really useful for the existence of the individual and his family: that is to say, the man of *simple manners* has few wants, and is content with little.

Q. *How is this virtue recommended to us?*

A. By the numerous, advantages which it bestows,
both upon the individual and upon society at large;
for the man who has few wants, liberates himself at
once from a crowd of cares, troubles, and toils; avoids
a number of disputes and quarrels, which arise from
the eager desire of gain: is free from the cares of ambition, the inquietudes of possession, and the fears of
loss; meeting every where with more than sufficient
for his wants, he is the truly rich man; always content with what he has, he is happy at a small expence;
and the world at large, fearing no rivalship from him,
suffer him to enjoy tranquility, and are disposed to do
him service.

Again, if this virtue of simplicity were extended to a whole people, it secures abundance to them; every thing which they do not immediately consume becomes to them a source of trade and commerce to a very great extent; they labour, they manufacture, and sell their productions to greater advantage than others, and attain the summit both of external and internal prosperity.

Q. What vice is the direct opposite of this virtue?

A. Cupidity and luxury.

Q. Is luxury a vice both in the individual and in society at large?

A. Yes; and to such an extent, that it may be said to include in it the seeds of all others; for the man who makes many things necessary to his happiness, imposes at the same time upon himself all the cares, and submits to all the means of acquiring them, whether they be just or unjust. He has already one enjoyment, he wishes for another; and, in the midst of superfluities, he is never rich: a commodious habitation will not satisfy him, he must have a superb hotel; he is not content with a plentiful table, he must have rare and costly meats; he must have splendid furniture, expensive apparel, and a long useless train of footmen, horses, carriages, and women; he must be constantly at the gaming table, or at places of public entertainment. Now to support their expences, a great deal of money is requisite, and every mode of procuring this is considered at first as lawful, and afterwards necessary; he begins by borrowing, he then swindles, robs, plunders, becomes bankrupt, is at war with mankind, ruins others, and is himself ruined.

Again, if we consider the effects of luxury upon a nation, it produces the same ravages upon a large scale; in consequence of its consuming within itself all its productions, it is poor in the midst of abundance; it has nothing to sell to the foreigner; it manufactures at a heavy expence; it sells its produce at a dear rate, and becomes a tributary for every thing which it imports: it loses its respectability, its strength, and its means of defence and preservation abroad; whilst at home it is undermined, and the bond of union between its members is dissolved. All its citizens, being greedy after enjoyments, are perpetually struggling with each other for the attainment of them; all are either inflicting injuries, or have the disposition to do so; and hence arise those actions and habits of usurpation, which compose what is called *moral corruption*, or intestine war between the members of the same society. Luxury produces rapacity, rapacity the invasion of others by violence or by breach of public faith: from luxury are derived the corruption of the judge, the venality of the witness, the dishonesty of the husband, the prostitution of the wife, parental cruelty, filial ingratitude, the avarice of the master, the theft of the servant, the robbery of public officers of government, the injustice of the legislator, lying, perfidy, perjury, assassination, and all the disorders which destroy society; so that the ancient moralists had an accurate perception of truth, when they declared that all the social virtues were founded upon a simplicity of manners, a limitation of wants, and contentment with a little; and we may take as a certain scale of the virtues or vices of a man, the proportion which his expences bear to his revenue, and calculate, from his demands for money, the extent of his probity, his integrity in fulfilling his engagements, his devotion to the public cause, and the sincerity of his attachment to his country *(patrie.)*

Q. *What do you mean by the word* country (patrie)?

A. I understand by that word a *ccommunity of citizens*, who, united by fraternal sentiments and reciprocal wants, unite their individual forces for the purposes of general security, the re-action of which upon each of them assumes the beneficial and protecting character of *paternity (paternite.)* In society, the members of it form a bank of interest: in a country *(patrie,)* they constitute a family of tender attachments; by means of which charity and the love of our neighbour are extended to a whole nation. Now, as charity cannot be separated from justice, no member of this family can pretend to the enjoyment of any advantages, except in proportion to his exertions: if he consume more than his proportion, he of course encroaches upon another: and he can only attain the means of being generous or disinterested, in proportion as his expences are confined within the limits of his acquisitions or possessions.

Q. *What is your deduction from these principles?*

A. I conclude, from these principles, that all the social virtues consist in the performance of actions useful both to society and to the individual:

That they may all be traced to the physical object of the preservation of man:

That nature, having implanted in our bosoms the necessity of this preservation, imposes all the consequences arising from it as a law, and prohibits as a crime whatever counteracts the operation of this principle:

That we have within us the germ of all virtue and of all perfection: that we have only to attend to the means of exciting it into action:

That we are happy in exact proportion to the obedience we yield to those laws which nature has established with a view to our preservation:

That all wisdom, all perfection, all law, all virtue, all philosophy, consist in the practice of the following axioms, which are founded upon our natural organization:

Preserve thyself.

Instruct thyself.

Moderate thyself.

Live for thy fellow-creatures, in order that they may live for thee.

FINIS.

CONTENTS.

Plummer & Brewis, Printers,
Love Lane, Little Eastcheap.